Freedom, Opportunity, and Security

Freedom, Opportunity, and Security

Economic Policy and the Political System

Douglas Downing

LEXINGTON BOOKS
Lanham • Boulder • New York • London

Published by Lexington Books
An imprint of The Rowman & Littlefield Publishing Group, Inc.
4501 Forbes Boulevard, Suite 200, Lanham, Maryland 20706
www.rowman.com

Unit A, Whitacre Mews, 26-34 Stannary Street, London SE11 4AB

British Library Cataloguing in Publication Information Available

Library of Congress Control Number: 2015950335
ISBN: 978-1-4985-0871-1 (cloth : alk. paper)
eISBN: 978-1-4985-0872-8

♾™ The paper used in this publication meets the minimum requirements of American National Standard for Information Sciences—Permanence of Paper for Printed Library Materials, ANSI/NISO Z39.48-1992.

Printed in the United States of America

Contents

Acknowledgments

Special thanks are owed to my teachers: Guy Orcutt, a pioneer in economic modeling and my advisor; James Tobin, always gracious and wise; Susan Rose-Ackerman, patient advisor to a senior essay writer with a lot to learn; Ray Powell, my first economics teacher; and Chris Arterton, Don Brown, Christophe Chamley, James Fesler, Laurence Kotlikoff, Paul Krugman, Charles Lindblom, Richard Murnane, Richard Nelson, William Nordhaus, Merton Peck, Bruce Russett, T.N. Srinivasan, and Sid Winter. Jennifer Roback-Morse helped a rookie teaching assistant. John Kenneth Galbraith appeared as our graduation class day speaker for the Yale class of 1979. The Yale Political Union provided the opportunity to meet numerous political leaders.

I've had valuable discussions with SPU colleagues Kathleen Braden, Reed Davis, Jon Deming, Lisa Donegan, Ruth Ediger, Al Erisman, Randy Franz, Caleb Henry, Gary Karns, Herb Kierulff, Ken Leonard, Geri Mason, Jennifer Meredith, Kevin Neuhouser, Joanna Poznanska, Ross Stewart, Lisa Surdyk, and Kenman Wong. Deans Joe Hope, Ken Knight, Alec Hill, Jeff van Duzer, Denise Daniels, and Joseph Williams provided leadership at Seattle Pacific University and created opportunities for discussions with students and colleagues. Cindy Strong and Adrienne Meier helped with library resources. Phil Eaton reviewed the manuscript and provided encouragement.

Thanks to William Bennett, David Brooks Tony Campolo, Ben Carson, Stephen Carter, Marion Wright Edelman, Paul Gigot, Jesse Jackson, Sally Jewell, George Mitchell, Edd Noell, Michael Novak, John Perkins, Jay Richards, Robert Shiller, Ron Sider, Jim Wallis, and George Will for speaking at SPU on the issues in the book.

Thanks to Jeff Clark, Sharon Covington, Tim Howard, Mark Lasky, Bill Trimble, and Mark Yoshimi for advice.

Mel Foreman was a mentor during many stages of my academic career, and Dale Foreman provided guidance on the process of making policy. Linda Roberts helped with some time-consuming tasks. Marlys Chandler provided advice on mortgages.

Michael Covington was always available to make insightful comments and helped with suggesting terminology.

Thanks to Emily Roderick, Joseph Parry, Sarah Craig, and Anita Singh at Lexington books for editing and producing the book. Dick Sleight provided artwork.

My grandmother Hannah and my grandfather Thomas both came to this country as young immigrants and became an inspiration to me. My father Robert Downing showed me the first computer I ever saw (in 1964); he demonstrated a commitment to serving the public in his three decades as a public school district administrator, and he reviewed the manuscript in great detail. My mother Peggy Downing told me stories of growing up during the depression, instilling the curiosity to study economics, and she also modeled what it means to be a writer.

And finally thanks to Lori, for her attitude toward furnishing our home (the more bookcases, the better).

All mistakes, unclear points, and weaknesses that remain are totally my fault.

—Douglas Downing
June 2015

Preface

This book is an academic study of political economy which leads to some policy proposals. Most likely you will agree with some proposals in this book, whichever side of the political divide you find yourself on. However, that also means you are likely to disagree with some of the ideas. At least try to keep an open mind. Economics is complicated, and most viewpoints on economics are at least partly true.

We need to study both political science and economics, since they are intricately tied together. The field traditionally has been known as political economy. It's not much help to develop economic policy prescriptions without considering the political environment needed to approve them.

In order to make policy decisions, you have to start with a moral foundation. Since different people have different views of morality this makes it hard to agree on policy. In this book we'll start with the Judeo-Christian teaching of "love your neighbor" in hopes that this will work as a widely accepted common moral foundation for people with a variety of beliefs.

It is awkward being an economist at a party, because people typically ask you what you think about the economy. Then you have to think, "does this person want the three hour answer? or the condensed 30 minute answer?" Then you realize they are probably just making conversation and they hope the conversation will be over in 30 seconds. So, for any of these party-goers who've asked me that over the years and really are interested, this book will provide the answer.

Some detailed appendices, and some updated information are available on the internet. See the web page at http://myhome.spu.edu/ddowning/fos.html for links to this information.

Chapter 1

Economic Policy Questions

Why are there such vehement disagreements about government economic policy? Here are four possible reasons:

1. Different people make different value judgments—they disagree about what *should* happen.
2. Different people expect different results from a particular policy—they disagree about what *will* happen.
3. Sometimes people advocate policies to benefit themselves at the expense of others.
4. Sometimes people align with a political party or movement and advocate the policies that seem to follow from that alignment, without thinking them through.

Can we achieve wider agreement on what economic policy should be? That may be too much to hope for, but at least we can do our best to understand the consequences of certain policies, clarify what value judgment questions incite disagreement, and expose narrow interest policies that exploit the general public. Often differing value judgments arise because society faces trade-offs involving three fundamental values: freedom, opportunity, and security. Society should provide all three of these for all its people. However, it becomes complicated because the three values are interconnected. Sometimes striving for more of one means less of another. The goal of this book is to provide suggestions for how to improve society's ability to achieve freedom, opportunity, and security.

Here are some steps to move toward these goals:

1. reduce narrow interest influence
2. make benefit programs secure and sustainable
3. make macroeconomic policy predictable
4. make sure everyone is responsible for bearing the costs of their actions
5. increase average productivity (the only way to increase average real wages)
6. provide an environment where innovators and entrepreneurs can flourish (their dreams, visions, and labor will determine our destiny)

GOVERNMENT

For some, the attitude toward government is antipathy; for others, the attitude is enthusiasm. A better attitude would be cautious skepticism. The government needs to perform its essential functions, and it needs to do them well.[1]

If government policy can be twisted to benefit certain groups at the expense of the rest of the public, the beneficiaries could become strong advocates. If a certain policy provides a large benefit for the few while providing a small cost to the many, those few have a strong incentive to advocate the policy. However, a transparent argument to the public ("all of you pay a bit to enrich us") won't be very successful. That means that the beneficiaries of narrow-interest policies will have to use obscure arguments in hopes of confusing the public so they won't realize what is going on. Economic policy can be vastly improved if we can reduce the possibility for narrow interests to rig the system in their favor.

DECIDING ON POLICY

Suppose we're trying to evaluate proposed policy X.

We need to do two things:

Determine the Consequence of the Policy

First, determine what will happen if the policy is implemented. We need to determine an "if–then" statement of the form:

"If policy X, then consequence Y"

This statement is not a matter of opinion. Consequence Y either will or will not happen if policy X is implemented, depending on the nature of reality but totally regardless of whether you personally appreciate or despise consequence *Y*. If you jump off a cliff, you'll crash into the ground below—your feelings of dislike for falling make no difference to the fact you will fall.

It can be difficult to determine for sure what the consequences will be. One problem is that some effects are very visible, but other effects may be harder to observe. A policy that increases employment for some may decrease employment for others, but those who lose their jobs may not see the connection to the policy that helped the others. In the nineteenth century, Frederic Bastiat wrote about the importance of understanding the economic effects of both "what is seen and what is not seen."[2]

To figure out what will happen you have to develop a model. A model is a simpler system that can represent some aspect of a more complicated system. Since language is a way of modeling reality, you always have some model in your mind when you make any statement about what economic policy should be. In order to think clearly it is necessary to make models as clear as possible. Since mathematics provides the language for rigorous analysis of decisions involving any "how much?" question, math is the essential tool.

Since economic decisions inevitably involve questions of "how much?" you have to deal with numbers. It is not uncommon for people to say they just won't do math, but it seems that non-mathematically inclined people had better realize this: economic decisions are too important to be left only to the mathematically inclined.

The risk of a mathematical model is that one can be dazzled and beguiled by the specificity and can confuse the model with reality. Developing adequately realistic economic models is very very hard. No model needs to be (or can be) totally realistic. (A totally realistic model of an aircraft carrier would be as big as the aircraft carrier itself.) However, a model only needs to be adequately realistic, in the same way that a map needs to show adequate detail for its intended purpose. If you're driving from San Francisco to the Washington monument, you'll need both a map of the entire U.S. and the Washington D.C. city map. These two maps show very different levels of detail, but each shows the appropriate detail for its purpose. The U.S. map doesn't show Pennsylvania Avenue, and the Washington D.C. map doesn't show Kansas City. It doesn't make sense to say that one of these maps is more realistic than the other.

Economists often discuss models that have reached equilibrium. A system is at equilibrium when it will tend to stay in its current state. For example, if you pull on a weight hanging from a spring, it will be out of equilibrium—but the force of the spring will tend to pull it back toward equilibrium. In economics, if there are mutually advantageous trades that can be made and profit-making opportunities that can be taken advantage of, the economy will be out of equilibrium. As people take part in these trades and opportunities, the economy will be pushed toward an equilibrium state. Economists often focus on models that are in equilibrium states because they are easier to work with mathematically. Even though the real economy will not be in equilibrium it will be pushed in that direction. Sometimes the economy will move quickly toward equilibrium and other times it will move more slowly. Sometimes it might oscillate about the equilibrium (as the weight on the spring will oscillate about the equilibrium a few times before it settles down).

A model needs to be tested to see if it works. Natural scientists often can test models by conducting experiments. Usually, you can't conduct an experiment to test an economic policy. It's not enough to know just the effect of the policy. You need to compare the effect of doing the policy with the effect of not doing the policy; so an ideal experiment would involve randomly choosing half of the people in the country to live with the policy and the other half to live without the policy—but the voters would never tolerate being experimented on just so economists could see what would happen.[3]

Not all natural scientists can perform laboratory experiments. Astronomers, like economists, are limited to observing things that naturally happen out there in the real universe, not in a laboratory. Astronomers can make very accurate predictions of the future movement of planets in the solar system because we know the rules governing gravitational behavior, and the number of initial conditions is manageable. It is much harder to forecast the weather. Even though the rules governing weather are known, the number of initial conditions that would be needed is enormous and only a relatively small number of observations are available. For economic forecasters, it is even worse: we don't know the complete rules of people's economic behavior, and the number of initial conditions needed is enormous.[4] To make it still worse, the weather affects the economy; so as long as there is uncertainty about future weather there will inevitably be uncertainty about the future economy.

Make a Value Judgment

Even if you could know for sure that consequence Y will result if you implement policy X, this does not mean that economic policy decisions can be made in a totally objective, value-free manner. You can't make a decision about whether or not to do policy X without making a value judgment about whether consequence Y is good or bad.

It's not possible to objectively determine the best policy in a scientific manner without making value judgments, but this doesn't mean we should fall for the opposite fallacy and think that everything is subjective and there are no objective facts.

NOTES

1. This book is about economic policy; so we won't consider other crucial issues such as national security, foreign relations, social issues, or criminal justice.

2. Bastiat, *Selected Essays*, chapter 1.

3. See Karlan (2011) for some ways in which experiments can be used to help find out which policies are more effective in alleviating world poverty, but these experiments don't apply to macroeconomic policy questions.

4. But, to make it worse, not so enormous that some of the approximations that work in statistical mechanics and thermodynamics can be applied.

Chapter 2

Freedom

There is both a fundamental case and an economic case for why a society should provide freedom, but there also are reasons why freedom should not be the sole goal of society.

THE FUNDAMENTAL CASE FOR FREEDOM

Love-Your-Neighbor-Symmetry Principle

Start with this principle: "love your neighbor as yourself" (Leviticus 19:18, Matthew 19:19, Luke 10:25–37).[1] If you become the absolute ruler of society, then this means that you need to design the laws so that any other person is treated the same way that you wish to be treated. We'll use the name "Rosencrantz" to refer to a generic person, who could be anyone else in the society. If you (the ruler) were to trade positions with Rosencrantz, would you still approve of the laws of your society? Call this idea the "love-your-neighbor-symmetry" principle. Another way of stating this is the "no-privileged-ruler" principle: nobody should have the privilege of designing laws for society without also having to live subject to those laws. An example of this principle is Lincoln's argument against slavery: "as I would not be a slave, so I would not be a master."[2]

You need to design the laws so that Rosencrantz is allowed to do anything you would like to do. More than that, you also need to allow Rosencrantz to make the same choices you would like to make. If you don't like playing tiddlywinks, you might think you could ban tiddlywinks—but then after you have switched places and Rosencrantz is now the ruler you need to worry that

Rosencrantz will ban something you like to do. So the symmetry principle requires that people have freedom.

Even if a majority of the voters approve of the laws passed by the ruler, it still doesn't justify restricting freedom in violation of the symmetry principle. Fundamental freedoms should not be subject to majority vote.[3] The tyranny of the majority can be just as frightening as the tyranny of a dictator. However, it is complicated because somebody somehow has to decide what fundamental freedoms the people have. Who will the final arbiters of freedom be accountable to? There is a problem if they are accountable to the majority, but there also is a problem if they are not accountable to anyone. There is no easy solution to this dilemma (see page 177).

Rules-in-Advance Principle

Another principle follows from the symmetry principle. Call this the "rules-in-advance" principle: when deciding what the rules of society should be, we need to imagine that we are designing these rules in advance, before any of us know where we individually might end up in society.[4] For example, at one time the rules of the National Football League did not allow a team to try for a two-point conversion following a touchdown. (The rule was changed in 1994.) Suppose that the rules committee is trying to make a decision about whether to allow two-point conversions. A team has just scored a touchdown at the end of the game which leaves them two points behind. Obviously that team wants to have the option of trying for the two-point conversion, whereas the other team would (at that moment) prefer that two-point conversions were not allowed so their victory was guaranteed. This would be the worst possible moment to ask the rules committee to decide what the rule should be. If they had to decide at that moment, it would be impossible to separate the general question of whether it would be a good rule or not from the specific question of "who would this rule help and hurt at this very moment?" The only way to objectively decide the question is to make the decision during the off-season, when you cannot know whom the rule might help or hurt during the upcoming season.

In order to design the rules of society we have to imagine everyone having an opportunity to get together before they know where or when they will be born. In that case everyone would be apprehensive about designing rules that risked allowing a small group to have the power to limit the freedom of most of the people in the society. If you were considering creating a society where a dictator had absolute power, you had better imagine what the society would be like if that power was in the hands of the vilest person you could imagine. You might be more willing to allow the dictatorship if you knew that you or someone you liked would be the dictator, but in the situation we have imagined you cannot have that information. You need to design the society so that it will be best for the people with the least power, since that may well include you.

The symmetry principle means to provide the most freedom possible provided that all can have the same freedom. Ask this question: if one person has the freedom to do *X*, does that prevent another person from having that same freedom?

No-Injury Principle

What if you want to clobber Rosencrantz with a baseball bat? You quickly realize that you can't allow that because you don't want to be clobbered by the bat after switching places with Rosencrantz. Society must enforce the first essential restriction on freedom: you should not have the freedom to injure others.[5]

Ownership

You need protection from another type of injury: if you're about to eat a slice of bread, you need assurance that someone won't take it away from you. People need to have the right to possess the food they eat, the clothes they wear, and the roof they shelter under.[6] The need for protection of private property for these essential person-specific goods follows from the need to prevent injury.

Conflicts inevitably arise: one person will want to do one thing with an object while another person will want to do something different with it. You may wish to eat a particular apple while someone else wants to eat the same apple. There needs to be a system for determining who gets to decide what will happen—who gets to eat the apple. The need for a decision is inescapable—even deciding to leave the object alone is another type of decision. One system is to let anyone who can grab resources do whatever they want with them. This system (might-makes-right anarchy) fails to meet the no-injury principle. A good society must let people sleep peacefully at night without worrying about being victims of violence.

Someone needs to make decisions about what to do with the resource. That decision maker is (by definition) the owner. Ownership may belong to a person, or a group of people (an organization with a mechanism for making decisions), or the government. The nature of a society depends on how ownership is arranged, but some form of ownership is essential for a society to avoid anarchy. An essential government role is to keep track of property ownership. Hernando de Soto writes about how a lack of legal title to property severely handicaps poor people.

One of the most egregious violations of freedom in the U.S. came when Congress made it illegal for someone to grow their own food on their own farm. The Supreme Court upheld this repression of what should be a basic right.[7] One objection to passing the original Bill of Rights was that if certain rights were listed, then it might seem that other rights were not protected. This case provides an example of that. Since the Bill of Rights does not explicitly protect your right to grow your own food on your own land, that right ended up being trampled upon. How can we remedy this situation? It would help to pass a constitutional amendment to update the Bill of Rights to explicitly protect more rights, based on the experience of two centuries living under the constitution. However, it is difficult to attain a super-majority to adopt a constitutional amendment to overrule a decision taken by a Congress that was elected by the majority. And even if this could be done, there still is the problem that the explicit list of rights leaves open the risk that other rights that people should have but are not listed might be taken away.

The Legitimacy of Property Rights

How far should property rights be allowed to extend? If society protects your property rights to own bread should you have the right to own a wheat field?[8] At least some private property rights are essential to liberty, but it is a complicated question to determine how extensive property rights should be. The economy thrives when substantial private property is allowed, but the right to use private property should not be unlimited.

If the population density is low enough, and people can forage/gather/hunt wild food, then property rights aren't needed for anything beyond a small number of personal possessions. If one group of people can obtain all they need from nature, and nearby groups can also obtain all they need, and there are still bountiful resources left over, then there is no need for anyone to make decisions about how particular resources will be allocated, and hence no need to define property rights.

As population density increases, it becomes more likely that some people will want to use the same resources that are desired by others. If anybody can use a resource, there is a risk called the tragedy of the commons.[9] Too many people use the resource and the supply becomes depleted. A far-sighted individual might realize the danger and decide to cut back on use of the common resource—but this effort will be futile because the conservation effort of the far-sighted person only results in more available for the myopic individuals to use up. Society needs some decision process to prevent people from using up the resource at an unsustainable rate. Ocean fish provide a contemporary example—there need to be international rules to prevent overfishing that could drive the fish population to extinction.

Larger population densities require more food than can be obtained by foraging and hunting, so agriculture becomes essential. Farmers need to work hard at plowing and planting long before they get the benefit of the harvest. Society needs a way to restrict people from harvesting whatever crops they feel like taking. One way is to provide the farmer with property rights to the land, and prevent other people from encroaching on it. Another way would be for the ruler to decide who should plant what land, then who should harvest what land, and finally who should receive the produce. The choice between private ownership and government control of the means of production determines the destiny of a society.[10]

If you buy something, then you will feel that your ownership is legitimate. However, you're assuming that the person you bought it from owned the item legitimately. That person might have bought it from someone else, but was that person's ownership legitimate? If you keep working backward in time to all of the previous owners, you'll eventually reach the original owner and have to ask if their ownership is legitimate.

We might follow the chain of ownership back to the person who made the item. One principle we should follow: if you make something, you deserve to own your creation. Society benefits when people are encouraged to put the effort into making valuable items.

If we're investigating the ownership of land or a natural resource, then we need to trace the chain of ownership back not to the maker but to the first person who claimed ownership of it. In much of the U.S. land ownership can be traced back to homesteaders who created farms and occupied land previously held by Native Americans. Distant descendants of the homesteaders might own wealth that can be traced back to the homesteads. Is a homesteader more deserving of passing on their land wealth to descendants than is someone who did not own as much land but stayed in a more established settlement? There's no clear answer to this question. Certainly the homesteader had to work excruciatingly hard to survive, so they maybe more deserving than the less adventurous non-homesteaders. A hardworking homesteader does seem to be more deserving of owning their land than does a medieval lord or antebellum plantation owner who left the actual work on their land to their serfs or slaves.

Tracing landownership history in Europe becomes even more complicated because records go back so much longer. The original prehistoric settlers in Britain faced waves of subsequent invaders and settlers: Celts, Romans, Angles, Saxons, Vikings, and Normans. A modern family might have ancestors from several of these groups, and some of their ancestors might have been the victims of some of their other ancestors. There's little hope that trying to trace this history will lead to original legitimate land ownership. Even if it were possible to determine when original ownership of land was legitimate and when it was not, it does not seem at all clear whether distant descendants should inherit rights of ownership (or land sale proceeds) based on the actions of their distant ancestors. At least in some cases it would be difficult to correct inequalities arising from the distant past.

What society can (and should) do is try to provide more of an equal start for today's current citizens (see the next chapter).

It is Not Feasible to Make It Illegal to Cause Injury by Non-Action

Suppose you sell potatoes. You realize you will be hurt if Rosencrantz doesn't buy your potatoes; so you promulgate a law requiring that Rosencrantz buy potatoes from you. After switching places, you are now required to buy potatoes from Rosencrantz, which you are willing to do because the price is fair. So, at first glance the no-injury principle would seem to allow this law, to prevent harm to the potato seller.

However, Guildenstern also sells potatoes. Your law forcing Rosencrantz to buy your potatoes hurts Guildenstern. The symmetry principle requires that you can't allow this law since you won't approve of it after switching places with Guildenstern.

In general, the law can't prevent you from hurting someone else by a non-action. Although buying potatoes from Rosencrantz will hurt Guildenstern, you're also hurting every other potato seller who's not Rosencrantz. The law cannot require you to buy potatoes from every single potato seller. In general, the law should prevent an action that injures someone else, but it cannot prevent a non-action from hurting someone, since you cannot feasibly be required to take positive action to the benefit of everyone who might be affected by your non-action.

In some cases, you can be compelled to take positive action to benefit someone else—but there has to be a specific reason why you have an obligation to that person (and not all the other people). For example, parents have an obligation to care for their children. For another example, you have an obligation to fulfill the terms of a contract you have voluntarily agreed to.

Freedom of Exchange

Suppose you (the ruler) make a trade: you give Rosencrantz an apple, and Rosencrantz gives you a house. The problem is obvious: Rosencrantz ends up much worse after the trade. As ruler, you could force Rosencrantz to make the trade, but the symmetry principle forbids this: after you have switched places, you would not like having your house taken away in return for an apple. Therefore, freedom from coerced exchanges is essential.

What if you have two apples, and Rosencrantz has two oranges? Now you consider another trade: you give Rosencrantz an apple, and Rosencrantz gives you an orange. If you both like variety, then you are both better off after the trade, with one of each fruit, than you were before the trade.[11] You'd still agree to the trade after switching places, so this mutually advantageous trade should be allowed by the symmetry principle. Furthermore, if Rosencrantz wants to make a mutually advantageous trade with Guildenstern, you should allow that, because you would want the freedom to do so after you switched places with Rosencrantz. The ruler should not prevent exchanges between two people when they are both willing to make the exchange—the trade makes them both better off.[12]

The exchange-must-be-voluntary principle prevents anyone from confiscating the products of someone else's labor (so no slavery is allowed). When you benefit from the labor of others you need to pay them enough for them to be willing to do the work.

Also, you should have the freedom to voluntarily give resources away. Generosity is good.

Bear the Consequences of Your Own Actions

You should have the freedom to lie on the beach all day every day; however, if you do that you won't grow any food or earn any income to buy food.

In general, people should pay for the damage they cause, care for the children they procreate, reap the harvest from the seeds they sow, and live with the results of the decisions they make.

Should you have the freedom to engage in risky activities, such as hang gliding, parachute jumping, not wearing seat belts, or not wearing motorcycle/bicycle helmets? If others are at risk, the case for restrictions becomes clear; but if you're only putting yourself at risk, the case for freedom is strong. However, what happens if you engage in a wildly risky activity and then do become injured and are rushed to the hospital emergency room? If you can pay the full cost of your medical care, there is a strong case for letting you have the freedom to risk your life and then you pay the consequences. What if your injuries require extensive medical care costing much more than you can afford? One option would be to turn you away at the emergency room door. This option likely seems unpalatable to many people, and there also is a practical difficulty. When a patient is rushed to the ER every moment counts, and it would be better if the doctors did not have to stop and ask questions such as "(1) Did you acquire this injury because you foolishly took a wild risk? If so, (2) Are you rich enough to pay lots and lots of money for your treatment? If the answers are 'yes' and 'no,' then goodbye." Therefore, it is best for emergency rooms to have a rule that they need to treat everyone, no questions asked.

There is a problem for society if people engage in wild risks and then show up at emergency rooms expecting other people to pay the bill. You can understand the desire for the government to ban certain risky behaviors. We should be concerned about the restriction of freedom involved, and also be concerned about the difficulty of deciding which risky behaviors should be banned. People can be injured on staircases, but it seems clear that we should oppose a government ban on climbing staircases.

A compromise between a complete ban and unrestricted permission would be to require that people engaging in certain risky activities purchase special insurance to cover potential injuries. The insurance premium cost would be higher if the activity is riskier (based on a statistical analysis of people undertaking that activity).

Other activities (such as eating salt) are fine in moderate amounts but problematic if overindulged. We could benefit if the people can become more educated about the consequences of overindulgence, but it does not seem that the government should have the power to prevent people from engaging in activities that are fine in moderate amounts.

There is more discussion of health care in chapter 4.

Safety Regulations

Instead of government deciding on detailed safety regulations, an option that can work in some cases is to rely on the court system to enforce liability for those creating dangerous situations. There need to be safeguards so that the innocent are not found liable, and protections are needed so innocent defendants are not pushed into agreeing to settlements because the cost of mounting a legal defense is too high. If these requirements are met and the judgment of the court system can be trusted, then the threat of a severe penalty will force those who create dangerous situations to seek insurance. The insurance companies have every incentive to develop safety rules that must be followed if the insurance coverage is to be maintained. The advantage of having the insurance company make the rules, rather than the government, is that the insurance company is not a monopoly. If you don't like the rules of one insurance company, you can try to get another one. Insurance companies with rules that are too picky will lose customers, but those with rules that are too loose will have to pay too much in claims for careless customers. The insurance companies have a strong incentive to get it right. If the insurance companies are making excessive profits, then new firms will be attracted into the industry and the increased competition will lower prices and profits.

Taxes

If you are forced to pay a 100 percent tax rate, you lose the freedom to own your own food, clothing, and shelter. On the other hand, if there are no taxes, the government won't have the resources needed for police to enforce the no-injury principle and to provide other essential services. How high should tax rates be while still providing freedom?

The symmetry principle requires that if you (the ruler) tax Rosencrantz, then you must be providing government services that are valuable enough that Rosencrantz is willing to pay the taxes—and also, you must be willing to pay the taxes after you switch places with Rosencrantz. The question becomes very complicated because different people have different opinions about the value of the government services. When purchasing products for personal consumption, these differences pose no problem. If you value apples a lot and your neighbor values oranges a lot it is easy for you to buy lots of apples while your neighbor buys lots of oranges. Government services are different: everyone in a jurisdiction gets the same government, so it's not possible to adjust the level of government preferences so that it matches the preferences of every citizen.

RESTRICTIONS ON FREEDOM

Here are specific restrictions following from these principles.

Prevent Actions that Injure Others

If someone severely injures you, you lose your ability to exercise your freedoms. In order to preserve freedom, society must have a criminal justice system to arrest, try, and confine killers and thugs. In a society with an effective criminal justice system, you gain the freedom to walk along the street without fear.

Some other actions that harm others, and should be restricted, include fouling the air or water with pollutants such as industrial waste, spilt oil, untreated sewage, or cigarette smoke.

If people were always good, then much less law enforcement would be needed. Or, if people were always bad, society would be impossible—there would be no way to hire enough law enforcement officers if everyone was committing crimes every day.

The reality is in the middle. Most people are generally good, but there are always some people who are bad, and many people might do bad things on occasion.

Prevent Robbery

The government needs to arrest robbers. If people don't feel reasonably safe from robbers they are more likely to act as vigilantes and society becomes more dangerous.

Prevent Swindling

If I took $1,000 from you in return for promising to give you an ounce of gold, but then give you a gold-painted rock instead of actual gold, it is essentially the same as if I stole $1,000 from you. Swindling needs to be prevented, just the same as robbery is. First, truth-in-labeling laws are necessary. Second, there needs to be a court system with the power to enforce contracts.

Protect Children

A one-year-old can't be granted very much freedom. Toddlers don't have enough sense to avoid getting into situations where they could harm themselves. As children get older, they gradually need to be given more freedom, but they still can't be given all the freedoms of an adult. For example, a six-year-old might wish to skip school, but there are compulsory school attendance laws. Six-year-olds haven't developed the judgment to make long-run decisions, and they should not have the freedom to make a decision at age six that would cause their future selves long-run difficulties.[13]

Also needed are restrictions on adult activities regarding children. Parents don't (and shouldn't) have the freedom to refrain from caring for their children.

SPECIFIC FREEDOMS

You should have the freedom to do something unless there is a law against it. However, some specific freedoms are worth enshrining in the constitution to protect against any future attempt to restrict them.

Freedom of Thought and Belief

Freedom of speech, freedom of the press, and freedom of religion provide the essential foundation of liberty.

Exceptions should be very rare: you can't give false warning that requires immediate action (no shouting "fire" in the crowded theater), and you are liable for damages if you make a harmful false statement about someone (provided you have an absolute defense if what you say is true; or if what you say is a matter of opinion; or if what you say is clearly labeled fiction, such as parody or satire).

Freedom of Privacy in Your Home or Other Private Space

The worst part of the technology in the futuristic novel *1984*[14] was the government's ability to monitor whatever you did in your own home.

Freedom to Make Economic Decisions

The government should not have the power to centrally control the economy. In particular, the state should not have the power to run houses of worship and news organizations.

Freedom to Move

People in the U.S. have the freedom to move around the country. By contrast, totalitarian dictators need literal walls (such as the Berlin Wall) to prevent their subjects from leaving.

The U.S. centennial was commemorated by the Statue of Liberty (a gift from France) with these words:

"Give me your tired, your poor,
Your huddled masses yearning to breathe free,
The wretched refuse of your teeming shore.
Send these, the homeless, tempest-tost to me,
I lift my lamp beside the golden door!"

In the days when the U.S. provided the freedom to move in, many immigrants took the risk of leaving their original homeland. Not only did they find opportunity, they enriched the nation. People sometimes fear immigrants because they fear competition for jobs, but more people also create more demand for workers, and many immigrants have been innovators that have created jobs. (The concern about lack of jobs is discussed in chapter 9.) Returning to more open immigration would hold up the beacon of liberty to the world.[15]

Freedom to Bear Arms

The second amendment protects the right to bear arms, which means criminals need to fear the possibility that their intended victim might be armed. However, we would all be safer if we could make it harder for criminals to get guns, and easier to track crimes committed with guns. A gun company should be liable to be sued by the victims for substantial damage payments if a gun it made is used by a criminal with a previous conviction. This policy will give gun companies a substantial incentive to develop a way to make it harder for criminals to get guns.[16]

ECONOMIC EFFICIENCY ARGUMENT FOR FREEDOM

Surprisingly, there also is a very different case for freedom: people in a free society will be more prosperous than those in an unfree society. Marxists have thought the opposite: that a society will be richer if a central planner controls how the society's resources will be used.

Decision-Making for the Entire Economy

At first glance it seems as if it would be chaotic if a society dispenses with the central planner and lets people produce what they want. However, a kind of order does emerge spontaneously from this chaos.[17] If a product can be produced profitably, it provides a signal that some people value the product more than the cost of its inputs. The profit encourages increased production of that product.[18]

In a free economy nobody needs to look at information about the entire economy. People acting as consumers look at the price of an item selling for $5 and decide if they would rather have the item or the $5. Business decision makers will sell the item for $5 if they would rather have the $5 instead of the item—meaning the $5 selling price is enough to cover the cost of making it. Millions of people making individual decisions make the free economy run far more efficiently than does the economy of the harried central planner.

If you're the central controller for the economy, you need information on what products people need, and also how much they already have. Staggering amounts of information must flood into the central planner's office if these decisions are to be made well.

It's hard enough for the central planners to make all economic decisions when technology stays the same. In reality, technology races forward. Innovative entrepreneurs that come up with new ways to combine resources can increase the final value of the new products compared to the value of the resources that go into making them.

Mutually Advantageous Trades

In a modern economy with millions of people, is there any way for everyone to get in touch with everyone else to see if there are any mutually advantageous trades they can make? Fortunately, it is not necessary for everyone to personally meet everyone else they can do a mutually advantageous trade with. Here's an example of how this works. People in Florida grow lots of oranges, and people in Washington State grow lots of apples. If people prefer a variety, then there is an opportunity for mutually advantageous trade: people in Florida can send oranges to people in Washington in exchange for apples. Although it would be awkward for individuals in the two states to meet in person to conduct these trades, the price signal leads to the same result. If the two states were isolated, the price of oranges would be low in Florida and high in Washington, and the price of apples would be the opposite: high in Florida and low in Washington. The price differential provides a profitable opportunity to buy oranges at a low price in Florida and sell them at a high price in Washington, and buy apples at a low price in Washington and sell them at a high price in Florida. These profit opportunities are only transitory: as people take advantage of the price differential, the increased demand for the low-priced product and the increased supply of the high-priced product will narrow the price differences.

Adam Smith's phrase "the invisible hand" is sometimes applied to this. He writes, "It is not from the benevolence of the butcher, the brewer, or the baker that we expect our dinner, but from their regard to their own interest . . . by directing that industry in such a manner as its produce may be of the greatest value, he intends only his own gain. He is in this . . . led by an invisible hand to promote an end which was no part of his intention."[19]

However, "invisible hand" is an unfortunate phrase if people think of it as meaning the market is a spooky invisible force that controls people. The reality is that a free economy is made up of people making choices. There is no invisible force acting on them. The only thing a little bit mysterious about the process is how prices adjust so that buyers who are willing and able to pay the market equilibrium price can obtain the product, and sellers willing to accept that price can find buyers.[20]

Consumer Sovereignty

As a group, people (acting as consumers) are all-powerful in a market economy. The fate of almost every business is in their hands. Businesses that produce things that people purchase will thrive; those that don't will wither away. (For some businesses, their dependence on consumers is indirect. For example, a company producing jet airplanes is dependent on airlines, and airlines are dependent on the public buying airline tickets. A business selling to the government does not need to worry about whether consumers will buy its products, but it should be indirectly accountable to taxpayers.)

You as a consumer may not feel all-powerful when you step into a store. The reason, of course, is that you have very little power as an individual person. The power belongs to all consumers as a group.

At its best, a voluntary economy can be no better than the preferences of the consumers—whether they are beneficial or destructive. If people want to buy products that damage their health, those are the products that will be produced in a voluntary economy. The results of the voluntary economy may be beneficial or harmful, depending on the preferences of the people. A market system does give people freedom to act for good or for ill. By way of contrast, if people have less freedom then they have less ability to make moral choices of any kind.

Freedom to Not Buy and the Pig-Trough Principle: Beware the Organization with Guaranteed Funding

Just as important as the freedom to buy things is the freedom to *not* buy things. If a business provides lousy service, you will stop buying from it. That freedom to exit spurs better performance by the business (or else the business fails, and other businesses will make better use of those resources).

In general, beware an organization with guaranteed funding, or "breathing money" (money they get just by breathing). Human nature being what it is, an organization would wish to be like a pig with guaranteed access to the pig trough. Society is better off by making sure that the funding for an organization is conditional on its performance. Call this the "pig-trough principle."

WHY A FREE ECONOMY MIGHT NOT BE POPULAR

Despite the human yearning for freedom, and despite the economic advantages of freedom, there are a variety of reasons why a free economy might not be fashionable.

Concern for the Poor

We should be concerned for the poor. If we think that a free economy means more poverty, we will have reason to be against a free economy. However, we need to have a correct diagnosis and efficacious remedy if we are actually to help those in poverty. Poverty is more likely to be caused by exclusion from markets rather than participation in them.[21] Avoid blaming the poor for being poor, although in some cases people are poor because of their bad decisions. However, some people are poor because of *other* people's bad decisions, such as the children of an absent non-supportive father. Some people are poor because of misfortune that could hit anyone, such as a disease or injury.

A free economy with wise government policy is the best way to end poverty. Since a free economy with unwise government policy can mean more poverty, it should be clear that we need to study government policy to determine what policy is best. Good intentions are not enough, since good intentions combined with naive policy lead to bad results.[22]

Should There be a Right to the Necessities of Life?

One reason people dislike a free economy is because they feel there should be a right to certain products that are essential for life: air, water, food, medical care. Fortunately air is available without charge. For other products, it would be meaningless to say there is a right to the product without also saying how that right will be operationalized. If someone has a right to food, then someone else needs to be coerced to provide it. In some cases, that is exactly what is and should be done. Parents are legally compelled to care for their children under 18. In most cases, parents will care for their children because they love them, regardless of the legal compulsion; but when necessary the legal compulsion is there as reinforcement.

We should also care for those that are too old or too disabled to work (see chapter 4).

If some working-age able-bodied adults are obligated to care for other working-age able-bodied adults, you have to ask who determines who is required to be the care providers (taxpayers) and who gets to be the care receivers (recipients). If too many people decide they wish to switch from being a tax payer to being a benefit recipient, there is a problem for that society.

Rather than trying to guarantee a right to necessities, it is better for a society to make sure there is opportunity for employment and then people can work to earn the ability to purchase necessities.

Lingering Marxism

Another reason for an instinctive mistrust of a free economy by some people comes from the lingering effects of Marxist analysis. When Marx wrote in the mid-1800s, the lives of industrial workers were truly dreadful. Marx had good reason to write about the oppression of the proletariat when they (and their children) worked 60 or more hours per week under noisy, arduous, crowded, and dangerous conditions for miniscule pay.[23] If the bourgeoisie had continued to oppress the workers, Marx's prediction of the coming revolution undoubtedly would have been proven right. In reality, when the revolution did take place it was in an agricultural nation (Russia) rather than the industrialized ones. To paraphrase Leon Trotsky, Marx's theory of the inevitable course of history needs to be consigned to the ashcan of history.[24]

One key moment when history diverted from its Marxist course came in 1914, when Henry Ford more than doubled the wages of his workers so they could afford cars and would have an incentive to stay on the job.[25] It turns out that capitalists get richer when the workers are richer and can afford to buy more things. Even the greediest capitalists find it in their interest to enrich rather than impoverish the general population.[26]

Marx correctly identified the ills in a society where the few held most of the property and the masses held little. However, that doesn't mean that his suggestion for eliminating private property is the best answer. An even more obvious solution would be to make sure that the masses have some property for themselves. In other words, people need to be given opportunity.

The irony of Marxism is that the revolutions that took place in his name resulted in societies where the workers had even less power and were oppressed even more. Millions died under Stalin, and literal walls were needed to prevent workers from escaping the grip of those who ruled in Marx's name. One could imagine that actual Marxist governments might have been more truly Marxist, rather than simply brutal totalitarians, but the reality is what it is. In certain circles a kind of Marxism remains fashionable, impervious to these realities.[27]

It is sadly ironic when some artists romanticize an unfree society and claim to be socialists. An artist would be nothing without the freedom to create. Artists may be displeased with the way a free economy requires them to earn a living, and they imagine that socialism is an alternative.

One sinister possibility is that they truly do wish to control what art the public will be allowed to see so they can prevent the work of rival artists from reaching the public.

A more likely explanation is a more charitable one: that the self-professed socialist artists are truly ignorant of the fact that socialism means the government owns all the theatres, studios, galleries, and concert halls, and that the government controls what art is displayed and performed. Some artists like to be nonconformists and challenge whatever government they live under. It is true that being a socialist makes you a rebel if your society is not socialist, but if these rebels get their purported wish and society actually became socialist they would find it is very hard to be a rebel artist criticizing the government in a socialist society. In this case we can hope that once these befuddled socialists learn the true meaning of socialism they will become former socialists.

Some self-proclaimed socialists might say that they're not Stalinists and would still allow private newspapers. That is considerable progress in their thinking, so we can be thankful that such people are not really socialists and don't believe the government should own all the means of production. If they think a bit more perhaps the socialist artists will eventually come to the conclusion that the government should not have the power to control industries that let us move around, that entertain us, and that provide us with basic necessities.

For those inclined to think that socialism provides protection for common people from evil greedy capitalist bosses, here is a way to picture what socialism actually does. Socialism won't get rid of your evil greedy boss; instead, imagine that your evil greedy boss now is not just the boss of your company, but also is the boss of the police force, the boss of all of the news media, the boss of your doctor, the boss of the government tax collector, the boss of the border security people, etc. As you expand this list by thinking of the government running everything, you will eventually realize that the way to protect yourself from an evil boss at a private firm is not to hand power over to even more powerful bosses that run both the government and the businesses.

Pope Francis mistakenly wrote that advocates of a market economy express "a crude and naive trust in the goodness of those wielding economic power."[28] In reality, the reason for supporting a market economy is precisely the opposite of this: people can't be trusted to be good. They have a fallen, selfish nature. That means that it is extremely dangerous when economic power is concentrated in too few hands, as happens in a socialist country where the government runs both the newspapers and the police, both the churches and the military, both the farms and the passport office, etc.[29]

Don't Know Much about History

People who have never lived in societies that lack year-round food, clean clothes, fast travel, instantaneous communication, modern medicine, and on-demand availability of light, heating, cooling, sanitation and plumbing may tend to forget that those benefits did not just happen. There is the risk that people take the economic system for granted and to think that it is the natural state for people to have enough food, for stores to have shelves filled with products, for houses to have refrigerators, air conditioners, telephones and televisions; for information and entertainment to be available instantly wherever you are; and for it to be possible to travel easily wherever you want, both locally and globally.[30]

Joseph Schumpeter wrote that the very success of capitalist economies undermines the attitudes of society needed to support the continuation of that success.

Those who claim capitalism is the cause of poverty and inequality[31] need to learn history. To gain perspective on today's poverty and inequality, study the poverty and inequality under the rule of Khufu, Qin Shi Huang, Mithridates VI, Nero, William I, Genghis Khan, Henry VIII, Shah Jahan, Montezuma, Louis XIV, Dom João V, Nicholas II, Stalin, Mao Zedung, and others.

A capitalist society can produce poverty and inequality if the ownership of resources is highly concentrated, but a survey of world history shows that a free economy is more likely the cause of the reduction in poverty.

Left-Wing, Right-Wing Confusion

Some people become confused by the terms left-wing and right-wing. The terms aren't really that helpful. Some oppressive rulers such as Czar Nicholas or fascists such as Hitler are called right-wing, which makes left-wing seem good because opposition to fascism is good. However, when left-wing is applied to communists such as Stalin, or other advocates of central control, there is no real difference between left-wing and right-wing: they both favor oppressive governments that restrict freedoms—the only difference is over which thugs have the power.

Often so-called right-wing governments can only be removed by a revolution, so freedom-supporting revolutionaries might think they have joined the left-wing. The very difficult part happens after the revolution: will the result be a society with freedom, or a society with different oppressors? The different results of the French, Russian, and American revolutions show how difficult it is to acquire the force needed to win a revolution without letting that force fall into the hands of other oppressors.

Concern for the Environment

The environment would suffer in an unregulated market. The bear-the-consequences-of-your-actions principle means that the government must require those that cause environmental damage to pay for the damage (see page 97).

Concern that Items of Ultimate Value are Mismeasured

Prices don't seem to measure the true worth of items (see page 68).

Dependence on Business

Unless you are a farmer growing your own food, you're dependent on business to survive. People understandably become apprehensive when their survival depends on the actions of others. An individual person will inevitably feel smaller than most businesses, so dependence is compounded by relative powerlessness. Dependency becomes doubled because people need businesses to provide employment as well as provide goods and services. If you feel like a powerless mouse confronting a powerful cat, you might hope for a big dog to chase away the cat. Likewise, people might turn to the government to protect them from the actions of businesses. Sometimes this protection is needed, although there is the risk that you then confront a dog more dangerous than the cat you originally feared.

An alternative way of reducing dependency on business is to make sure you have choices. If you have multiple employers to choose from, then no individual employer has much ability to mistreat you. If you have multiple grocery stores to buy food from, no individual store can overcharge or underperform if it wants to keep you as a customer. We'll use the term *polypoly* when you have many suppliers to choose from.[32]

Do government workers care for you more than workers at a private business? Maybe or maybe not. There are lots of types of people in both government and business, and some of them are more caring than others. The important thing is that workers at a business have to care about providing quality service so you will keep coming back, or their employer may go out of business and put them out of a job.

Business Misdeeds

Plenty of businesses earn the mistrust of the public by a wide variety of nefarious deeds: overcharging, underperforming, underpaying workers, overpaying executives, polluting environments, mistreating workers, influencing government, advertising deceptively, writing legalistic fine print, wild risk-taking, etc.[33]

Businesses (and anyone else) should be made to pay for damage they cause. For example, BP should be (and was) required to pay multiple-billion dollars for the damage caused by its carelessness that resulted in the 2010 Gulf of Mexico oil spill.

You are better protected from business misdeeds when you have choices. If you can walk away from a business that overcharges you and instead buy from another seller, the overcharger has little power over you.

Business Receiving Undeserved Blame

Sometimes business get blamed undeservedly. A poor harvest that drives up the price of crops is not the fault of the grocery store, but the grocer gets the blame.

Misunderstood Government Distortions

There are a variety of economic irritants that might be blamed on businesses when they actually arise from government policies. Taxicabs and rental housing in New York City are hard to get because of government restrictions and price controls. The price of milk, wheat, corn, sugar, and cotton are high because of deliberate government agricultural policy. The price of steel is high because of government-imposed trade restrictions (and the resulting higher prices make it hard for industries that use steel, such as the automobile industry). Oil prices are higher than they otherwise would be because of government restrictions on oil drilling. (The restrictions may be good for environmental reasons, but it is important not to blame the oil companies for the higher prices that result.) Businesses are sometimes blamed for the mortgage crisis when part of the blame belongs to government distortions in the housing market (Fannie Mae, Freddie Mac, Federal Reserve interest rate policy, and bond-rater special legal privileges).[34]

CEO Pay

People become upset if CEOs are paid more than is justified.[35] Especially galling is when CEOs collect lots of money from a company that is losing lots of money. Part of the solution is to require CEOs to be paid in stock that they are required to hold for a certain period of time so they can't grasp the money and skip town leaving a wrecked company behind them. Another part of the solution is to require explicit shareholder approval of executive compensation (since it is the shareholders that are being ripped off when their representatives—the board of directors—pay too much to the shareholder's employee—the CEO) (see page 170).[36]

Economic Instability

The economic instability problem causes considerable distress. The Great Depression of the 1930s (25 percent unemployment) wreaked enormous suffering on people around the world—not because of any natural disaster or war, but because of the malfunctioning of the economy. The inflationary stagflation of the 1970s and early 1980s (with a deep recession [8 percent unemployment in 1975] followed by a deeper recession [10 percent unemployment in 1982]) inflicted widespread misery. The mortgage crisis, financial meltdown, and subsequent recession (10 percent unemployment in 2009) further exacerbated the problem. More details will follow in chapters 8 and 9.

Lack of Thought about the Choice Set

Some people might criticize a free economy, but their thinking might be so muddled that they have not thought about how a centrally controlled economy would be worse. Or maybe they're not aware that the nature of the choices about the role of the government (see Figure 2.1).

| Anarchy | Extreme Libertarian | Small Government | Medium Government | Big Government | Central Control |

Figure 2.1 Role of Government Possibilities

If we want a good society we need to rule out anarchy (where might-makes-right and the powerful can take what they want) and also rule out central control (which is similar to anarchy in that the powerful can take what they want, but in this case the powerful are better organized).

In the extreme libertarian case, there is a high degree of freedom. The government enforces the do-no-injury principle and does little else. However, then society might not provide enough opportunity and security.

That leaves three choices left in Figure 2.1—small government, medium government, or big government—but in reality there is a continuum of different choices for the role of the government. This book will investigate the question of where along this continuum the role of government should be.

Freedom to do Bad Things

When people are free, then they are free to do bad things. No society can make all harmful actions illegal.

Does a society that emphasizes freedom encourage people to be too individualistic and disconnected from the community? In reality, most people naturally choose to be part of families and communities. However, there is an important point here: freedom can't be the only value. People also need to be taught virtue. Society needs to promote teaching both generosity and industriousness.

Freedom itself doesn't answer the question: what do you do with your freedom? The principle of freedom doesn't provide a guide to life. Once you've achieved freedom, what do you do with it?

Stephen Carter writes, "The amorality of markets poses scant threat to a nation that possesses a highly organized set of institutions that do speak in a moral voice, but it is deadly for a nation that has none."[37] A market is *amoral*, meaning that it makes no moral judgments on the goods that are produced, sold, and consumed. If there are institutions, such as families and churches, that teach people how to act morally, then actions in a marketplace will tend to be moral. However, if people are not taught morality, then the results of actions in the market may lead to immoral results.[38]

George Weigel wrote about Pope John Paul II's understanding "a vibrant public moral culture is essential for democracy and the market, for only such a culture can inculcate and affirm the virtues necessary to make freedom work."[39]

Envy

People naturally feel a tinge of envy on seeing others in better situations. The envy is not all bad if it encourages you to work hard to improve your situation (provided you have an opportunity to do so), or if the envy inspires curiosity into whether the other person acquired their riches in a good way or a bad way—and inspires you to work on ways to reduce the opportunities to acquire riches in a bad way. However, envy becomes destructive if it leads you to try to make the other person worse off just because you resent seeing them well off.

Lack of Empathy

One reason for freedom not being popular: people may not be concerned about encroachment on someone else's freedom. The grandchildren of immigrants may not support freedom for other people to become immigrants. Non-entrepreneurs and innovators may not support the freedom of entrepreneurs and innovators.

Fear that People Will Buy from Someone Else

You as a buyer benefit when you have choices of who to buy from, but when you are a seller you would prefer that the buyers not have choices. People understandably fear that their livelihood is at risk in a free economy.

Fear of Change

A free economy will tend to have a lot of change, which understandably causes distress.

No Guarantee of Opportunity

Freedom is not very meaningful without the ability to make a living. What is also essential: opportunity (see chapter 3).

No Guarantee of Security

People crave security. A free economy provides no guarantee of security (see chapter 4).

NOTES

1. Claar and Klay, p65.
2. www.abrahamlincolnonline.org/lincoln/speeches/quotes.htm

3. John Adams, as described by Howe, chapter VI; de Tocqueville, volume I, part two, chapters 7–8; Mill, p140–52.

4. See Rawls, p23.

5. Mill, p125.

6. Sirico, p18, p30, p35; Gregg, p8.

7. *Wickard v. Filburn*, 1942. The purpose of this depression-era law was so that the government could restrict the supply of food and make it more expensive—which is the same policy followed today.

8. For comparison, see the discussion in Rawls, p338.

9. See Hardin and Diamond.

10. Rousseau's argument that the first walling off of land was the first source of conflict is incorrect. See Ferris, p117.

11. People decide for themselves whether they are better off after the trade. There is no external authority that decides for them.

12. This principle also applies to international trade (see page 100).

13. Mill, p9.

14. Orwell.

15. Tanner, p95.

16. Gun companies would likely purchase stolen gun insurance to compensate them for the damages they would have to pay if a previously convicted criminal steals one of their guns from a law-abiding gun purchaser and then commits a crime.

17. Hayek.

18. Also, negative profits lead to less production.

19. Adam Smith, Book I, chapter II, paragraph 2; Book IV, chapter II, paragraph 9.

20. If buyers wish to buy more than sellers wish to sell, then the price generally rises. In the opposite case the price generally falls. The result is a price that reaches the level where the amount people want to buy matches the amount people want to sell (see page 91). Under certain conditions it is possible to find a set of prices that make the quantity demanded by the buyers equal to the quantity supplied by the sellers for all products. The exact nature of the conditions necessary for this to be true is a complicated issue; see online appendix myhome.spu.edu/ddowning/fos.html.

21. See the examples described by Sachs.

22. See Karlan, and see chapters 3 and 4.

23. Factory workers in the mid-1800s may have had the longest working hours ever; Schor, p44.

24. Trotsky's fate was a kind of poetic justice. After doing so much to help create the despotic Russian regime, he learned that dictators have the power to exile and then murder potential rivals.

25. Ingrassia, p17; Schor, p61.

26. See JB Say. By contrast, feudal lords and plantation owners wouldn't mind if the serfs and slaves were poor, as long as they ate enough so they could keep working.

27. Fontova; Collier and Hurowitz; Kantor; Ferris; van den Haag.

28. November 24, 2013, Evangelii Gaudium.

29. Novak, p86–88.

30. The book by Noell, Smith, and Webb provides a concise summary of the causes and benefits of economic growth.

31. For example, see Schnick and Petrequin.

32. The term *polypoly* is a better description of this situation than is the term usually used by economists (see page 220).

33. Van Duzer, chapter 2.

34. See chapter 8.

35. Accurately measuring CEO pay is complicated. See Reynolds.

36. You cannot complain about *both* excessive CEO compensation and excessive fixation on maximizing shareholder returns—more of one means less of the other.

37. *Civility*, p180.

38. Claar and Klay (p26, p215) write about the importance of moral foundations for a society.

39. Eaton, p90.

Chapter 3

Opportunity

Freedom is a hollow blessing without opportunity. Freedom to do something you lack opportunity to do is meaningless. The second crucial test of whether a society serves its people is: do they have opportunity?

Opportunity requires there to be care for dependent children; access to the tools, resources and education needed to make a living upon becoming an adult; an end to discrimination, and the availability of jobs.

FIRST PRINCIPLE OF OPPORTUNITY: CARE FOR CHILDREN

Circles of Care

Care for a child should be provided from multiple sources.

However, not all caregivers have the same degree of closeness to the child. Caregivers can be illustrated as a series of concentric circles (Figure 3.1).

Most care should come from circles closest to the child. Primary care should come from both parents, with extended family and community or church or synagogue or mosque groups supporting the parents as caregivers. The government should provide education.

Losing a parent while still a child is one of the calamities that might befall anyone. Fortunately, the probability of this happening is small in modern societies, and this risk can be insured against (see next chapter).

Welfare and Children of Absent Parents

A harder problem is what to do about children with one absent non-supportive parent? For several decades (the 1930s to the 1990s) the U.S. operated the welfare program Aid to Families with Dependent Children (AFDC).

31

Figure 3.1   Circles of Care

Typically, the recipients were single mothers with children. Either the father and mother were married and became divorced, or they never had been married. In some cases paternity might not have been established.

Providing cash assistance for single mothers in cases where the father simply skipped out turned out to have unfortunate consequences. The problem is not so much that the cash assistance provided an incentive to have out-of-wedlock children. The welfare benefits were meager enough that the resulting lifestyle wasn't lavish and enticing. However, providing welfare benefits acted as an enabler, making independent single-teen-mother households possible.[1]

The 1996 welfare reform act was based on the idea that there needed to be change in behavior: parents need to take responsibility for their children.

Children need to know their parents are committed to caring for them. If the parents are not married, that could cast doubt on their willingness or ability to make a commitment to another person.

We can't take it for granted that society will continue. It takes an enormous amount of work to raise even one child, and society depends for its existence on the labor of parents and others involved in caring for and teaching children. A poor society where people are on the brink of subsistence cannot have much tolerance for dysfunctional family behavior. If children are not cared for in such a society the entire society might die out (call it societal natural selection). A rich society can survive even with greater tolerance of dysfunctional behavior, but such behavior still has a cost when children are unable to develop their potential because their basic needs are not met by their parents.

Throughout most of human history, children lived close to their parents and grandparents and aunts and uncles. When people were much less likely to move to another area to live they would be more likely to live with extended family members, which was a good thing because more people were available to care for the children. One big change has been that people in modern societies are much more mobile. People have lost something important when people move around and children grow up far from grandparents and other relatives. However, they have also gained an important advantage because of the ability to move to new areas. There is a benefit but also a price—as is often the case in economics.

During the great depression, when economic hardship was much more severe than we have seen since, families tended to stay together. Economic hardship historically would force people to rely more on family members. It is only in a rich society willing to enable it that people can decide they can try to live independently of family members. For most of human history a single mother living alone with a baby wasn't a viable household. (This does not mean that there weren't single mothers; it just means that single mothers had to live with extended family members if they were to survive.)

Marriage Vows and Contracts

Should marriage vows be regarded as something weaker than a contract, or the same as a contract, or stronger than a contract? Changing marriage laws in the 1970s often lead to a situation where either person can obtain a divorce just because they want it. This view of marriage makes it weaker than a contract, because a contract cannot be altered without the consent of both parties. Perhaps no-fault divorce laws need reconsideration. If one person wants the marriage to continue and the other person doesn't, the law should give the benefit of the settlement to the person wanting the marriage to continue. If one person tries to make the other person's life unpleasant so they will give up trying to preserve the marriage, then that person should be found to be at fault, and the legal proceedings for the dissolution of the marriage work for the benefit of the victim. In a situation of abuse, or the case of a man abandoning his wife for a "trophy" second wife, the marriage should be dissolved on terms that favor the victim.[2]

If marriage is regarded as a contract, then it could be dissolved when both parties agree to it. However, given the effects that a divorce has on others, especially children, a marriage should be regarded as stronger than a contract.[3] If both parties desire to dissolve the marriage, then it is important for the legal process to give top priority to the benefit of the children.

Welfare and Behavior Rules

The question is: how can welfare be made unattractive enough that it discourages the behavior that leads to it, without hurting the babies and children that depend on it? A total cutoff of unmarried minor parents would be too harsh for the innocent babies, but there should be some rules, such as:

1. Don't provide benefits if the mother does not help establish paternity.

    Here is a value judgment: fathers need to take responsibility to support their children.[4]

    What if the father might be abusive? Being abusive should not be an excuse for a man to avoid child support obligations. If the abuse has been confirmed then a no-contact court order should be established. The obligation to pay child support exists (and should exist) regardless of whether the father has visitation rights to see the child.

    What if the mother wants to care for the child but the father doesn't? The father doesn't get to choose.[5] Supporting his child is legally mandatory. However, prior to 1996 the requirement often went unenforced.

    It will be very hard for parents to support their children if neither one has a job (see chapter 9).

2. Require minor parents to live with their parents. For example, the baby of a teen mother should be living with her parents (the grandparents of the child), and the baby should receive support from the father (and the paternal grandparents if the father is also a teenager).[6]

3. Require recipients to progress toward finishing high school.

    It will be difficult for any job training program to have much success in placing people in jobs with reasonable pay if they have not at least finished high school.

4. Require recipients to be involved with a non-profit caring group, such as a house of worship or some other nonprofit group. This requirement recognizes the important role of the third circle of care.

5. Require that welfare recipients receive treatment if needed for cases of substance abuse.

1996 Welfare Reform

By the 1990s there was a growing feeling that something needed to be changed. Bill Clinton promised to "end welfare as we know it" during his successful 1992 presidential campaign. The result was the 1996 Personal Responsibility and Work Opportunity Act, which had the bipartisan support of a Republican Congress and a Democratic President. This act renamed the AFDC program to TANF (Temporary Assistance for Needy Families), which imposed a much more restrictive set of rules on welfare eligibility, such as a five year lifetime limit in addition to some of the rules mentioned earlier. (See online appendix myhome.spu.edu/ddowning/fos.html for updated information on welfare reform.)

SECOND PRINCIPLE OF OPPORTUNITY: PEOPLE NEED ACCESS TO TOOLS AND RESOURCES

No matter how hard someone works, they can't produce something out of nothing. People need tools and resources.

Agricultural Land

For most of human history the essential opportunity that people needed was access to agricultural land. The Bible provides rules on providing access to land.[7]

Rome's republic had originally fielded armies consisting of small landowners. Gradually more land came under the control of a smaller number of rich Romans who relied on slave labor. Eventually Rome needed more soldiers, and after 110 B.C. the urban poor were allowed into the armies. If the richest Romans had been more sensible, they would have willingly provided land for these soldiers when they retired. Instead, the troops understandably became more loyal to the generals that were trying to get land for them, rather than to the leaders of the senate that opposed giving them land.[8]

During the 1800s, U.S. homesteaders could obtain 160 acres of land, subject to the condition that they live and farm on that land. The land provided an opportunity, but it still required tremendous work on the part of the farmers to make a living. Abraham Lincoln's presidency provided several policies directed toward expanding opportunity: homesteads, land grant colleges, agriculture extension, and the transcontinental railroad bill.[9]

Education

Parents should be encouraged to work hard to provide a better life for their children. This motivation leads millions of immigrants to America to work hard to provide education for their children. However, the unfortunate fact is that some parents will do less well at providing for their children than others. Society also has an interest in making sure that children have a good chance at life even if their parents are unable or unwilling to make the effort to give them a better opportunity. Public education has become the ladder providing opportunity for many. The G.I. bill provided higher education opportunities for thousands of soldiers returning from World War II. Financial aid and loan policies expanded opportunities for college to more and more people.[10]

Two main areas of concern about education are cost and quality. The cost issue is discussed on page 82.

Many public schools do an excellent job (the U.S. would not be where it is now if this were not so). Unfortunately, as most acknowledge, some schools don't teach very well. Education is more of an art than a science. The quality issue is complicated because there are many different schools all over the country of widely varying quality. Since nobody knows for sure what is the best approach to improving education, some room for experimentation is helpful. It would help to provide choices among public schools so people could choose which public school to go to, rather than be assigned geographically. People would have a natural inclination to stay close to home, but if significant numbers choose distant schools it provides an indication of a problem and a need for new leadership at the neighborhood school.

In cases of extremely substandard public schools, students should be able to choose other types of schools (charter schools or private schools). Their share of the money that would otherwise be spent on their public school would be applied to the cost of their education at the school they do choose.[11] College students can choose where they will attend school, which is good because colleges do feel the pressure to make sure they can provide a good experience so students will want to study there.

There is debate about whether private or charter schools do a better job than the traditional public schools, but researching the national average performance of private and charter schools misses the point. If an individual charter school performs poorly, there is a something that can be done: parents won't want to send their children there, and the school will have to close for lack of students. By contrast, if a traditional public school performs poorly, there is no good mechanism for shutting it down or restructuring it. As on page 20, it is good to avoid monopolies with guaranteed funding.

A national goal should be for everyone to graduate from high school. The opportunity to attend college or receive other training needs to be available,[12] although not everyone will need or want to seek additional education. It is a complicated question about how well the U.S. provides access to college. Community colleges and public colleges provide more affordable access to many students, but those costs have been increasing lately. Private colleges post higher prices but often make financial aid available so that each student faces a different price.[13] The problem many U.S. college graduates face is substantial debt. The Universal Opportunity Loan proposal later in this chapter would provide one way to ease this burden.

THIRD PRINCIPLE OF OPPORTUNITY: PEOPLE NEED JOBS

Receiving care as a child, receiving a good education, and showing a willingness to work still won't be enough if jobs are not available. Making sure jobs are available turns out to be very difficult (see chapters 8 and 9).

The Problem of a Guaranteed Job

Although at first glance it seems appealing, providing a guarantee that people can keep their job is not the way to ensure employment opportunity. If people have an ironclad guarantee that they will keep their job, regardless of their performance, then at least some of them will recognize this provides an opportunity to avoid working very hard. If the guarantee was truly absolute, so that people kept their job even if they never showed up for work, then some people would take advantage of that and not show up. A concern about chronic absenteeism and slack work effort was one of the reasons Mikhail Gorbachev worked on reforming the Soviet economy in the late 1980s.[14]

Why can't society promise easy living? Although society might provide for a lie-on-the-beach lifestyle for some, it can't promise that for everyone. If everybody enjoyed easy living than nobody would be working. The symmetry principle requires that society should not promise for a few what can't be provided for all.

POVERTY AND INEQUALITY

Should we be more concerned about inequality or about poverty? Since this is a matter of opinion there is no right answer, but it seems that it is more important to be concerned about poverty. In a recession, many people suffer a loss of income, but high-income people suffer larger losses. Inequality therefore declines in a recession, but that does not mean we should hope for more recessions.[15]

If these are the incomes in society A:
90, 100, 100, 100, 110
and these are the incomes in society B:
500, 600, 1000, 1500, 2000

it is clear that society B has much more inequality, but society A has much deeper poverty. Which would you prefer? Again, this is an individual value judgment, but it seems perverse to prefer a society where everyone is poor (as in A) over a society where some people have gotten very rich while others are somewhat rich (as in B).

A lower-middle-class person in an industrialized country today has access to products to make life healthier, more comfortable, and more interesting than the lives of the richest nobility prior to 1800.[16]

If a country used to have all of its people being extremely poor, and now it has half of its people much better off while the other half is still extremely poor, do you lament the fact that the country is now much more unequal than it used to be, or do you celebrate that many people are now less poor (and then wonder about how to help the rest of those people become less poor)?

When you think about the *Titanic*, do you think it would have been better to have a result with equality where all 2200 people died, or was it better to have a result with inequality where 700 people survived? Hopefully you realize that the problem was that *1500 people died*, not that there was inequality in the result. Imagine someone writing, "Inequality on the *Titanic* increased rapidly during the period when some people left the sinking ship to board floating lifeboats."

Piketty[17] actually does write, "Chinese inequality increased very rapidly following the liberalization of the economy in the 1980s and accelerated growth in the period 1990–2000. . . ." There are two problems with this statement. Is it really true that China under Mao had equality? It is true that just about everybody was desperately poor, but one person had unlimited power. A society with one person with everything and everybody else with nothing is an example of the maximum possible inequality.[18] For the sake of argument, leave aside this point and focus on the fact that in China before Deng Xiaoping just about everyone was poor. Under Deng and his successors, literally hundreds of millions of people have become fairly rich. China is such a populous country that there still are hundreds of millions that are poor, but does it really make sense to focus on the growing inequality as if that was the problem, rather than focusing on the fact that so many people are no longer poor?[19]

Piketty and the *r, g* Model

Piketty writes that inequality inexorably increases when the rate of return to capital exceeds the growth rate of the economy. However, elsewhere he warns against too much reliance on mathematical economic models, so it should be clear that a model with only those two parameters is not adequate to predict what will happen. In particular, the rate of saving plays a crucial role. See the online appendix for a model where the parameters can be adjusted so that the share of income going to labor might decrease, increase, or stay the same.

In a traditional society where land is the only significant form of productive wealth, the only way rentiers[20] (landlords) can convert their rents into increased wealth is by buying more land, which transfers rents from one landlord to another without affecting the overall distribution between workers and landowners. They could also hold wealth in the form of gold, but they collect zero rent from that investment. When productive capital investment opportunities are available, then the rentiers can spend their rental income on capital investment—except they will find that this is not as easy as collecting land rents. They will have to become entrepreneurs, or venture capitalists that fund entrepreneurs, and in either case there is considerable risk of failure. If they succeed, then the real income of the workers is likely to increase as the productive capacity of the economy increases, even if the worker's share of national income does not increase. In reality wealth holders probably don't just accumulate more and more wealth. Call this the "what's the point principle:" why just accumulate more and more wealth without finding ways to spend it?[21] Most likely wealthy people will spend money on lavish lifestyles or buying political influence[22] or whatever. If society is fortunate they will spend some of their wealth on charitable donations.

If those that think the problem is *inequality* rather than *poverty* win the debate on policy, the result will be people becoming poorer. For middle income people becoming poorer will be an inconvenience; for the extreme poor around the world becoming poorer will be life-threatening.

If, one day, a team of people develops a cure for Alzheimer's, the world will become much better off even if that team earns billions of dollars for their discovery. We can hope that most people won't prefer to see people suffer from Alzheimer's rather than see a team of researchers become rich. One reason people may not like the rich is envy, but envy is not an admirable quality in a person. We undoubtedly all feel it to some extent, but it is not an emotion to be encouraged.

On the other hand, if there are incentives for activities that are not as productive for society, and people become rich in ways that do not benefit society, that is a problem. The problem of influence-buying and CEO pay is discussed in chapter 12.

In summary: the problems are poverty and unjust riches—not inequality.

The Rich Get Richer and More People Get Rich

It is also important to distinguish a situation where the rich get richer from a situation where more people become rich.

For example, suppose the richest 100 people in a 1,000 person society have an average income of $300,000, the next richest 100 people have an average income of $100,000, and the other 800 people have an average income of $50,000.

Number of People	Average Income
100	$300,000
100	$100,000
800	$50,000

The richest 200 people (or the richest 20 percent of society) have an average income of $200,000.

Now suppose the richest 100 people have their average income increase to $500,000, with no change for the other groups.

Number of People	Average Income
100	$500,000
100	$100,000
800	$50,000

In this case the average income of the top 20 percent becomes $300,000. This is a case of the rich getting richer.

Alternatively, suppose the second richest 100 people have their average income increase from $100,000 to $300,000, with the average income of the richest 100 staying at $300,000.

Number of People	Average Income
100	$300,000
100	$300,000
800	$50,000

In this case the average income of the richest 20 percent also increases to $300,000, not because the richest group has become richer but because more people have become rich. In reality both of these effects have happened.[23]

Another complication is that income inequality cannot be measured by looking at tax return data over a period of time when there has been a major change in the tax structure. Before 1986, tax data would make the income of the rich seem to be less than it really was because the rich had many tax shelter opportunities. When the 1986 tax reform act cracked down on tax shelters in return for lower tax rates, the reported income of the rich increased significantly, partly because more of their income was reported to the IRS even in cases where their income had not actually increased. That wasn't some obscure side effect; the whole point of the crackdown on tax shelters was to get the rich to report more of their income so it could be taxed.[24]

Another major problem with measuring income from tax return data is the failure to account for the shifting of filing status from corporations to individuals. After 1986 there was an increase in income reported on individual tax returns that did not represent an actual increase in income because it was simply a shift away from income that had previously been reported as corporate income.[25]

Rawls' Difference Principle

Rawls makes an important contribution to the theory of a just income distribution with the *difference principle*, in which income inequalities should be allowed, but only to the extent that they improve the well-being of the *worst-off* person in the society. Rawls suggests that people would choose to design society for the benefit of the worst-off person if they were designing it from an original situation where nobody knew what their own condition would be (which is Rawls' version of the symmetry principle). This principle provides a reason for why the poor would benefit if some inequality is allowed. If, by contrast, one imagined a government that enforced perfect equality of income by taking 100 percent of income above the average, people would have very little incentive to work hard. If someone earned an extra dollar, their take-home pay would only go up by $1/n$ if there are n people in the society, which will be a trivial amount if n is large. Given a choice, too many people would tend to choose to be recipients rather than taxpayers and there would end up being little income to tax.

Everybody benefits if there are incentives to work hard, so Rawl's difference principle allows for this. However, it would not allow for any inequalities that do not result in improvements for the worst-off person.

There are a couple complications with Rawls' difference principle.

The Free Economy is also the Fair Economy

Jobs are different. If some jobs are challenging, unpleasant, dangerous, or arduous, then few people would want to take those jobs—unless they were paid enough extra to compensate them for the difficulties of the jobs.[26] There are also pleasant jobs that pay well, because there are other factors that determine pay (such as having a rare skill). Suppose that the differences in pay between jobs only occur to encourage people to be willing to do all of the unpleasant jobs. In this case it would be incorrect to view the lowest-paid person as the "worst-off" person, because that person has the most pleasant job. Rather than there being "differences" that are accepted because of their benefit to the worst-off person, in this case there actually are *no* differences in overall economic status. Some people are paid more, but the people that are paid more are those doing the unpleasant, dangerous, and arduous jobs. Pay would also have to be higher for jobs (such as doctors) that require years of expensive training. Even if income varies, the true situation is essentially one of equality if pay inequality exists only to compensate for job-condition inequality.

Therefore, the *free* economy is also the *fair* economy, provided people have opportunity.

Bad Decisions

Some people make bad decisions. Someone making bad decisions (injuring themselves while thrill-seeking, driving while drunk, turning to crime, refusing to work, defrauding customers, polluting the environment, colluding to raise prices) should not be considered when Rawls' difference principle is applied. If they end up worse than the difference principle would allow, there's no way to put it more diplomatically other than to say: it's their own fault. This certainly does not mean most poverty is the fault of the poor. People who lose their jobs in recessions or are hit by drunk drivers or contract cancer can't be blamed for their economic misfortune, and children can never be blamed for the circumstances of their upbringing.

Other Reasons for Inequality: Talent, Luck, Attachment, Families

Whether or not we should do something to deal with inequality depends on the reasons for the inequality. Creators (artists and inventors), hard workers, the naturally talented, heirs, the lucky, and looters and riggers are some groups that will end up with high incomes. We all benefit from the hard work of others, so we should be glad when the hard workers earn enough to encourage them to continue their hard work.

It does seem unfair that some people are born with natural talent that others don't have, but it is hard to know what we can do about this. For one thing, it is hard to distinguish the effect of hard work from the effect of natural talent. Usually a talented person can only develop their talent by hard work. If we could somehow measure natural talent and somehow find a way to handicap the talented so that they would not be able to earn any more than average, we would all suffer. If this handicapping prevented a medical researcher from finding a cure for a deadly disease, more people would die earlier. If this handicapping presented a performer from entertaining us, our lives would be much duller. One good thing about the riches of an actor, a musician, or an athlete is that they earn their money by receiving payments from a lot of different people (their viewers, fans, and spectators). You may think that a particular entertainer doesn't deserve their high income, in which case you can avoid paying for any of their works. If most people agree with you then the entertainer's income will shrivel. However, if most people disagree with you and are still fans of this entertainer, there's no reason why you should be able to impose your preferences on the rest of the people and prevent them from enjoying (and paying for) the work of the entertainer.

Some people inherit their wealth, or are otherwise lucky. Unlike the case of those with natural talent, the rest of society doesn't benefit from the good fortune of these lucky people. Theoretically we could have a "pure luck" tax to somewhat reduce this type of inequality, but that would be difficult to do. Perhaps the estate tax could be increased but then modified so that it would not apply to people who continued to work at a farm or business they inherited, but it would apply to other people who inherited a large amount of wealth. However, it would not be easy to distinguish an heir who really worked at the business from one who only pretended to do so.

Other people become rich by rigging the system in their favor (see chapter 12).

There is another reason skilled workers are paid more: employers become attached to skilled workers. Finding workers with specialized skills can be very expensive for an employer. The search process is complicated if there are a lot of applicants that need to be reviewed and it takes considerable effort to determine if an applicant really has what it takes to succeed at this job. Even after all that effort, you can't be sure how the worker will perform until they actually have the job and you can see what happens. This means that when an employer has current employees who are performing adequately in high-skill jobs, the employers want to keep them so they can avoid the cost of finding a replacement worker.[27] As a result, these workers will likely be paid somewhat more than just their productive value to the employer. Their pay will be increased by the amount the employer saves by not having to search for their replacements. This tendency reinforces the trend for higher-skilled workers to be paid more.

Furthermore, family income, not individual income, is the relevant measure. A baby has zero income, but that's not relevant—the family income is what determines what care the baby will get. As more women work at higher paying jobs, it is more likely that two high-income people will be married to each other.[28] This effect amplifies the differences in family income. In the 1950s, a family with a man earning $2x$ dollars would earn x dollars more than the family of a man earning x dollars. Today, a family with a husband and wife both earning $2x$ dollars will earn $2x$ dollars more than a family with a husband and wife both earning x dollars. There is no economic policy that can reverse inequality that increases for this reason, but it becomes even more crucial for policy to make sure that the opportunity to gain access to higher paying jobs is open to all.

The Importance of Workers Having Alternatives

Workers can't count on their boss' altruism. Many bosses will continue to treat workers as poorly as they can get away with.[29] The way to improve wages is to make it so employers can't get away with paying low wages. When workers have alternatives, then the employers will have to pay high enough wages to keep them. Workers have alternative employment opportunities when the economy is growing and the workers have skills and the other employers have capital tools sitting around waiting to be used.[30] The workers can also earn higher wages when they are harder to replace, because they can tell the employers they won't work unless they get a pay raise. This strategy won't work when the employers can find other workers with the same skills.[31] If the incumbent workers lack special skills, they can try to intimidate the employers into not hiring any other workers, but if this strategy is successful it only works for the benefit of the incumbent workers, not for the workers who don't get the jobs.

A Tale of Two Bureaucrats: Minimum Wages and Price Ceilings

Suppose bureaucrat Rosencrantz is charged with raising child caregiver pay, and is empowered to issue a regulation requiring that caregivers be paid at least $200 per hour.

Bureaucrat Guildenstern is charged with making health care affordable, and is empowered to issue a regulation requiring that doctors charge no more than $10 per hour.

Instead of well-paid caregivers, the result is that people can't afford to hire caregivers, and the caregivers become unemployed. The high pay doesn't do the workers any good if they don't have jobs.

Instead of affordable doctor visits, the result is that people can't afford to become doctors. The affordable cost doesn't do the patients any good if there are no doctors available.[32]

Creative people attempt to find ways to get around the regulations. Some doctors offer to give haircuts which happen to include conversations about medical care. Some housecleaners offer to keep an eye on the children in between housecleaning tasks. When the bureaucrats realize that people are taking advantage of these loopholes, they consider hiring monitors to make sure every barber cuts hair rather than discusses medicine, and every house-cleaner doesn't watch the children. When they realize this drastic proposal would be insanely expensive, the bureaucrats revise the rules so that all work-ers must be paid at least $200 per hour, and all workers can charge no more than $10 per hour. When these contradictory edicts arrive. . . .

The government can't successfully require both higher pay and lower prices, since the two are inherently connected.

The government might drop the price ceiling policy but stick with the mini-mum wage policy. One could object to the $200 minimum wage story by call-ing it a straw man argument, since nobody advocates a minimum wage that high. However, there are people who do argue that the way to help low wage workers is to raise the minimum wage. It is important to realize when this will work and when it won't work. When workers without alternatives are under-paid by monopsony employers, then a minimum wage will help them get higher wages.[33] By contrast, if the minimum wage is raised above the level consistent with productivity, then profit-seeking employers will respond by hiring fewer workers. The same concept applies to workers trying for higher wages by forming a union: when workers without alternatives are underpaid by monopsony employers, then a union will help them get higher wages. By contrast, if the union wage is raised above the level consistent with productivity, then profit-seeking employers will respond by hiring fewer workers.

If low wage workers have alternatives then they won't have to remain stuck in low wage jobs. Employers will have to pay them more to keep them working in those jobs. If low wage workers don't have alternative jobs, then the absence of a legal minimum wage means they have low wages; the existence of a legal minimum wage will mean they have no jobs. In either case the workers are in good shape if they have alternatives (with or without a legal minimum wage) and they are in bad shape if they do not have alternatives (with or without a legal minimum wage).

Suppose the current workers are able to prevail upon the employers to pay them more than before. Then the question becomes: are there other qualified workers out there that are willing to do the job for that wage (or less)? If not, the higher wages are secure. If there are other workers, then the current workers can only keep their higher wages if they can find some way to keep the other willing qualified workers locked outside the factory gates. A neutral observer trying to judge the morality of the situation would have no reason to regard the current workers as having a greater moral claim to the jobs than those that don't currently work there.

More recently there has been a movement advocating increasing the minimum wage closer to the level of a living wage for a family, whether or not a specific worker has a family to support. (Call these LWMW advocates, for living-wage-minimum-wage advocates.) LWMW advocates could do something constructive by actually hiring low-skill workers at higher wages, rather than advocate that other people be required to increase wages (that may not actually get paid to the workers if the workers lose their jobs). However, the LWMW advocates might find it is easier to stay on the sidelines shouting orders to businesses than it is to actually try to run a business themselves.[34]

It is odd that some people castigate business as being greedy while also being in denial about the fact that businesses will respond to incentives. If a minimum wage increase reduces the profitability of hiring low-skill workers, then a greedy business will reduce low-skill-worker employment.

Actually measuring the employment-deterring effect of the minimum wage is challenging because of the difficulty of conducting controlled experiments in economics. Empirical studies of variation in the minimum wage across time or across locations cannot reliably make an extrapolation prediction about the effect of a significant increase in the minimum wage. The fact that youth unemployment is always much higher than adult unemployment indicates that hiring low-skill workers poses a challenge for employers. Even if this difficulty is not caused by the minimum wage, it suggests at the very least that the minimum wage for workers with absolutely no employment experience should be lower than the minimum wage for workers once they have acquired some experience.

Some jobs are pleasant low-skill (PLS) jobs, and other jobs are unpleasant low-skill (ULS) jobs. The only way to get people to do the ULS jobs would be to pay them more than the PLS jobs. Now suppose the minimum wage is raised to the level of the current pay for ULS jobs. The pay for ULS jobs would likely have to increase or else nobody would want to do them. The result could be a ripple effect as the pay for other jobs increases. Eventually the same relative wage structure might be restored, and the Federal Reserve might expand the money supply to keep unemployment from rising. The result is that the price level rises about the same as the wage scale increased. The result: if the minimum wage goes up 40 percent, and all other wages and prices go up 40 percent, the effect of the higher minimum wage gets cancelled out by higher inflation. The good news is that the inflation will reduce the employment-deterrent effect of the minimum wage increase, but then there also will be no benefit because there will not be an increase in the real wages for the workers.

Suppose that the minimum wage for baby-sitters was set at $15 per hour. Clearly the price that parents pay for baby-sitters would go up to $15 per hour (in this case the price the customer pays is exactly the same as the wage the worker gets). The situation becomes more complicated when the customer pays an employer and the employer pays the worker, but the idea is the same—the higher wage most likely pushes up the price to the customer (either that or it squeezes out some other item that the employer needs to buy). The customers may buy less of the item with the higher price, creating a deterrent to hire workers. Even if the customers spend more to buy the same amount as before, some other spending will get squeezed out and there will be an employment deterrent in some other area.

Paradox of Government Power

Here is a further warning that we should be cautious of income redistribution. The problem if the government has enough economic power that it can redistribute income is that it may start with well-intentioned plans to benefit the needy, but in practice that power is likely to be hijacked for the benefit of the powerful. Call this the "paradox of government power." Corporate CEOs, subsidy recipients, and tax loophole beneficiaries can sometimes persuade the government to enact policies that further enrich the rich (see chapter 12).[35]

A government with less ability to control the economy would provide less opportunity for narrow interests to twist the rules in their favor at the expense of the rest of society.[36]

DISCRIMINATION

Discrimination can deny opportunity to people. Discrimination has a long ugly history dating back to the days of slavery. One of the many pernicious rules was that slaves were not allowed to be taught to read.[37]

The Constitution had to be a set of compromises and unfortunately some of the biggest compromises were with the slave owners. Slaves were counted as 3/5 of a person for the census for determining the members of the House of Representatives allocated to each state. Slave owners had wanted each slave to count as 1 person because that would increase the number of representatives from the slave states, thereby increasing the power of the slave owners and making it harder to eradicate slavery. The slaves would have been better off if the census had counted them as zero so that the slave owners would have less power and it would have been more likely that slavery could have been ended earlier.

The cost to end slavery was enormous. More than three hundred thousand soldiers died in the union army during the Civil War. Legally mandated segregation continued for a century after the end of the Civil War and the end of slavery.

Politicians were able to suppress voting rights for African Americans and could keep winning elections by appealing to the segregationist vote. The tide began to turn in the 1950s with the *Brown v. Board of Education* decision in 1954 overturning the separate but equal doctrine (established by the Supreme Court in the 1896 case *Plessy v. Ferguson*). Rosa Parks refused to give up her seat on the bus, and Martin Luther King's "I have a Dream" speech in 1963 helped push for change.

Progress was painfully slow. As recently as 1968 an avowed segregationist candidate won 45 electoral votes in the election for president. African Americans were legally prohibited from working in textile factory jobs in South Carolina until the 1960s.[38]

Eliminating mandatory segregation enforced by law was the essential first step, taken with laws such as the voting rights act of 1965. After the end of legally mandated segregation, changing attitudes becomes the next step. People need to learn to avoid judging people by stereotypes.[39]

The profit motive helps eliminate discrimination. In a very competitive market a company that discriminates against qualified workers will be at a disadvantage. However, if the customers of a business expect discrimination and they want the business to discriminate against other groups then a profit-seeking company might have to discriminate even if it doesn't want to. For example, there was a time in the 1960s when certain sports teams had to make sure they did not have too many black players because their bigoted fans would not support teams with too many black players.[40] This type of discrimination gradually fades away when the imperative of winning forces teams to consider how to get the best players. Fans who want to win cannot tolerate a team that would release quality players just because of their race. In 2014 a sports team owner was rapidly driven out of the league after making racist comments.[41]

One way for an employer to reduce hiring discrimination would be to make sure that hiring managers remain unaware of the race of candidates as long as possible. For example, symphonies conduct auditions behind a screen so the evaluators can judge the candidates only on the quality of their music, not on their appearance.[42]

Simply looking at percentages does not provide information about discrimination. If group *a* makes up *x* percent of the population, that does not mean that you should necessarily expect group *a* to make up *x* percent of the workers at a job or the students at a college or the qualifiers for a loan.

Instead of looking at percentages, a better way to test for the presence of discrimination would be for researchers to submit test applications to employers. Discrimination would show up in these tests if employers choose less-qualified white applicants over more qualified black applicants. Evidence of discrimination would be found if the hired black applicants on average have higher qualifications than the hired white applicants. That would indicate that race was acting as a handicap that needed to be overcome. Similarly, lending discrimination could be measured by submitting test applications to lenders, and if the approved blacks were on average better credit risks than the approved whites, that would be evidence of discrimination. Furthermore, if employers and lenders knew that these test applications were going to be submitted, they would have an incentive to make sure that their approval processes were truly fair and did not consider the race of the applicants.

As a temporary measure in the early stages of the end of discrimination, those groups that were previously denied opportunity need to be given extra opportunities. In 2003 the Supreme Court ruled that these opportunities could last for an additional twenty-five years.[43]

In the long run, greater socializing and intermarriage between different groups provides the best hope for improving attitudes among the public, as it did when immigrants from various European nations gradually intermarried and subsequent generations would lose their tendency to look on those from other nations as being the "other."[44]

Fair Pay

What is fair?

Laws require equal pay for equal work, but it is hard to determine how pay should be different for different work.

Settling pay questions in court would not be a great way of doing this, because there are many factors involved in determining pay and it ultimately comes down to the question: is the person willing to work for this amount, and is the employer willing to pay this. A court of law is not the place to decide how much extra compensation someone should receive for a job with an X percent higher chance of serious injury, in comparison to someone in a job requiring Y more years of education. Transparency in pay amounts would help because then it would be clear to everyone when someone was paid more.

We need to be concerned about discrimination in access to jobs. That used to be so common that it was thought to be normal, and clearly there is much less of that now. Fifty years ago many jobs simply were not available to women. That was a big factor in keeping pay for women low. Fifty years ago men had the vast majority of both high-education jobs and high-danger jobs, and were paid considerably more. Now, men still have a majority of the high-danger jobs (there is serious inequality in the rate at which men and women are killed on the job).

Once women started to find more jobs accessible to them after the 1960s, a slow process of change began. Women now outnumber men in college enrollment, and women are now almost half of all medical students.[45]

As the number of women becoming doctors increases, this causes an increase in the average wage for women not just because more of them are becoming doctors, but also because the pay for nurses has to increase in order to recruit women (who now have more opportunities). This will be a slow process, because the work force at any time consists of people of many different ages. A change in college enrollment patterns this year will still be affecting the economy for the next forty years.

Even after enough years have passed for the increased opportunities for women to be reflected in the labor force, there may still be differences in pay if men and women still have different interests. These differences will work in favor of women if they gradually become a majority of higher-paying doctors and college graduates, but men will still have a pay advantage if women are more likely to choose part-time work or avoid some non-medical technical fields (such as engineering, computer science, and math). We should avoid assuming that women will always have different vocational interests than men, but we should also avoid assuming that women will eventually have exactly the same interests as men. As long as everyone has opportunity, everyone should be free to set off on their own path.

UNIVERSAL OPPORTUNITY LOAN

To move closer to the world where opportunity is the reality for everyone, the U.S. should establish a universal opportunity grant in the form of a no-interest loan. Under current policy the U.S. taxes workers to provide social security benefits for retirees, which is a valuable policy when you consider a person's life cycle: a working-age person has more income available while a retired person has more financial need.[46] However, a policy focused on life-cycle needs will also transfer funds from people during peak working years to those that are just starting their working careers.

In this proposal, everyone who turns 18 and graduates from high school receives a restricted $30,000 grant, which can be used for one of these three things: (1) higher education, (2) partial payment for a house, or (3) investment in a diverse portfolio.[47] Those who choose to invest the money can transfer it to education or a house at any time; otherwise, they must keep the money in savings until they reach age 35. Then, beginning at age 35, the person needs to repay $1,000 per year for the next 30 years (with an automatic $1,000 added to their tax bill). In the end the entire $30,000 will be repaid to the government, so the amount becomes a zero-interest loan from the government.

The grant would not replace financial aid for college, but it would mean that students would be less dependent on that financial aid. It also helps with another problem created by financial aid, which can act as an enabler to let colleges raise their prices even faster, so much of the benefit to the aid recipient is cancelled out by the higher tuition. Since people will have other choices about what to do with their universal opportunity loan the colleges will have to think more about the value that they provide for the students. Other recipients will choose the portfolio investment until they are ready to purchase a house. This system would be a more efficient and equitable way of subsidizing home ownership than the current system of home interest deductibility (which disproportionately benefits rich borrowers) and costs about $100 billion.[48]

With about 4 million people turning 18 each year, the initial cost of the program would be $30,000 \times 4,000,000 = 120,000,000,000$ (120 billion dollars), which is affordable, given the size of the U.S budget. Once the first recipients turn 35 and start repaying, the net amount that needs to be spent on the program falls each year. If the population was stable then eventually the net amount spent on the program would be zero (as the total repayments equal the total benefits for that year). In the case of a growing population there would need to be a continuing appropriation for the program, but in that case there would also be a growing number of taxpayers to support it. The program can be justified on the principle of helping provide opportunity, but it might have substantial additional practical benefits if it encourages teenagers to stay engaged with society and finish high school.

NOTES

1. Perkins, p10.

2. Wilson (2002) presents a detailed summary of research on changing attitudes toward marriage and divorce and the effects on children. There is no clear answer to the problem.

3. Morse, chapter 4, p104.

4. Mothers need to support their children as well, but in practice the more common problem has been nonsupportive absent fathers. For this purpose "child" means someone under 18. Once the child turns 18 the parents should (and do) have the legal right to kick them out to live on their own (although it would be sad if they do this).

5. The father did have a choice about whether or not to become a father, but after conception it is too late to make that choice.

6. Exceptions to this rule would be needed if the parents have been abusive or if they are substance abusers.

7. Leviticus 25; Claar and Klay, p189.

8. For example, Julius Caesar as consul advocated providing land for Pompey's soldiers in 59 B.C. In opposition were a group of elite senators such as Cato. See Goldsworthy, p28, p164–70.

9. Kevin Brady and Lewis Lehrman, Wall Street Journal, February 12, 2013.

10. Noah, p88; note economist Milton Friedman advocated student loans to expand opportunity.

11. Personal note: As a student in public schools from kindergarten to 12th grade, and as the child of a long-time public school district administrator, I know that public schools can do a great job. This makes it even more important that the poorly performing schools not be allowed to sully the reputation of public schools in general.

12. See Piketty, p306.

13. Piketty's statement (p307) that the most prestigious schools tend to favor students from privileged social backgrounds no longer applies to elite U.S. schools such as Yale and Harvard.

14. Hedrick Smith, p186.

15. Reynolds, p44.

16. Cox and Alm; Goff and Fleisher.

17. Piketty, p327.

18. Maximum possible inequality means a Gini coefficient of 1.

19. See online graphs.

20. A *rentier* is someone receiving income from economic rent—i.e., the opposite of a *renter*.

21. Someone who loves wealth so much that all they do is accumulate is called a *miser*. The most famous miser is the fictional character Ebeneezer Scrooge (pre-transformation), who lived a miserable pathetic life because he did not even spend his hoarded wealth on things to make his life more comfortable.

22. Society might be better off if they just accumulated the wealth rather than spend it on influence buying; see chapter 12.

23. Reynolds, p47–48. The percentage of U.S. households with real (inflation-adjusted) incomes higher than $50,000 rose from 24.9 in 1967 to 44.1 percent in 2003.

24. See Reynolds. Piketty's statement (page 282) that the tax-avoidance correction for tax-based inequality measures would be similar in different periods is incorrect when there has been a significant change in the tax code, as in 1986.

25. Reynolds, p82; Bartlett, p146.

26. Sirico, p104.

27. Okun, p49.

28. Noah, p55.

29. Noah, p189.

30. See chapters 5 and 9.

31. See page 165.

32. See page 91.

33. "Monopsony" means one buyer.

34. One argument is that businesses will actually benefit from a higher minimum wage because they will face less turnover. However, in that case the employers don't need to be required to pay more—they need to be educated so they'll voluntarily pay more.

35. See also Buchanan and Tullock.

36. Rose-Ackerman, p227.

37. Douglass, p146.

38. Rivoli, p81.

39. The terminology used in statistics may unintentionally encourage discrimination. If a statistical study finds evidence that there is even a slight difference in the average measurement for two groups, this difference is called a "statistically significant" difference. This just means that the averages are not the same, but they are not necessarily very far apart. In everyday usage, the word "significant" means about the same thing as "important," but in statistics a "significant" difference can be so small that it is not very important.

40. Wolf, p291.

41. Donald Sterling was forced out as owner of the Los Angeles Clippers in May 2014.

42. Goldin and Rouse.

43. *Grutter v. Bollinger*, opinion by Justice Sandra Day O'Connor.

44. When my mother was a child, a member of her close-knit community of Swedish immigrants would have been discouraged from marrying a non-Swede. That attitude changed by the time she was grown up.

45. Claar and Klay, p201.

46. In chapter 11 there is a discussion of how to protect social security and make it sustainable.

47. Veterans could use their veteran's educational benefits for education and then apply the $30,000 to a house or investment.

48. Bartlett, p112.

Chapter 4

Security

Life is risky.[1] We all face the danger of a sudden unexpected illness or accident. We can reduce some risks by being careful. For example, avoiding drinking before driving will make it much safer for you on the road, and avoiding smoking significantly reduces your chance of cancer. However, some natural disasters can strike you no matter how careful you are.

RISK POOLING AND INSURANCE

One way we can partly protect ourselves is by pooling (sharing) the risk. There are three possible institutional mechanisms to provide for risk pooling: charities, private insurance, or government. Each has advantages and disadvantages, so there should be a combination of all three.

If m people out of the n people in the population will suffer a particular type of injury next year, and each person that suffers the injury will need medical care costing $\$D$, everyone can be protected if they all pay mD/n dollars into the pool, and that amount will be distributed among the m people that suffer the injury.

Figure 4.1 shows the probabilities for a society with $n = 1000$ people, with probability of injury equal to 0.01. On average, the expected number of people suffering the injury in a year is $m = np = 1,000 \times 0.01 = 10$.

There are four major problems that make risk pooling more difficult.

The Problem of Non-Independent Risks

Previous calculations are based on the assumption that everyone is independent: so if an injury hits one person, it won't have any effect on the other

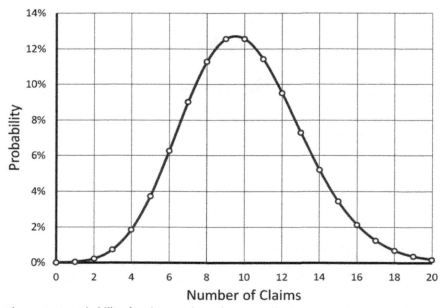

Figure 4.1   Probability for the Number of People Filing an Insurance Claim, Out of 1,000 People, with 0.010 Probability of Each Person Filing a Claim. The horizontal axis measures the number of claims, and the vertical axis measures the probability for each possible number of claims. Most likely there will be about 10 claims (there is about a 12 percent chance of this). The chance of there being more than 20 claims is very small.

people. For many ordinary injuries, this is a reasonable assumption. However, if a single disaster can strike everyone, then risk pooling does not work so well. Suppose $p = 0.01$ (same as previous example), only this time there are only two possibilities: everyone suffers the disaster with probability p, or nobody suffers with probability $1 - p = 0.99$.

If the disaster strikes everyone, then the total cost of the damage will be 1,000 people times $10,000, which equals $10,000,000 (10 million) dollars. Since the probability of this disaster hitting in a particular year is only $p = 0.01$, on average the disaster will hit only once every $1/p = 1/0.01 = 100$ years.

Our society could plan for this disaster by saving ten million divided by one hundred $= 10,000,000/100 = 100,000$ (one hundred thousand) dollars each year, which can be split among the people so that each person pays $100,000/1,000 = 100$ dollars per year.[2] After saving $100,000 every year for 100 years, society has $10,000,000 saved, and is ready to pay for the damage caused by the disaster.

However, just because this disaster will only strike once every hundred years on average, that does not mean it will regularly hit once every hundred years. If society is fortunate to have a gap of more than 100 years between disasters, then it can save up more than what is needed. However, if the disaster strikes more often than once every hundred years, then there is a serious problem. If the disaster strikes before the full 10 million dollar fund is accumulated, the society would have to liquidate other assets, or borrow from other societies. This illustrates why hurricane or earthquake insurance is hard to obtain.

Moral Hazard

Imagine that you were guaranteed that whenever you lost money on a stock market investment, your insurance company would reimburse you for the full amount of your loss. You would have no reason to care about the risk of the investment. You would prefer very risky investments with a slight chance of a large profit, since you either win with a successful investment or else receive the full reimbursement from the insurance company. Or if you had insurance that would automatically replace your cell phone (with the newest model) if you lost yours, you would have no incentive to be careful about not losing it. The general problem that people might be less careful to avoid risks they are insured against is known as *moral hazard*. This becomes less of a problem in some contexts; for example, even if your stay in the hospital is completely paid for you would still wish to avoid the pain of suffering a major accident or illness. However, even here there is an issue: if you have a choice of treatments that vary in expense, you have no incentive to try to economize on cost if someone else is fully paying for it.

Insurance companies do try to reduce the problem of moral hazard through deductibles (you will have an incentive to be careful if you have to pay part of the cost of your loss) or risk-based premiums (you will have an incentive to be more careful if your insurance premiums will depend on how risky your behavior is).

Adverse Selection

The next problem is that insurance does not work if the people susceptible to the loss are identifiable in advance. People who live on high ground won't purchase flood insurance since they know they are safe. People who live in a river flood plain will want to purchase the insurance, but no insurance company can successfully provide insurance when the only customers are those who are sure to file a claim. This problem is known as *adverse selection*.

The Probabilities May be Unknown

Another difficulty occurs if nobody knows the relevant probabilities. There is an advantage in having insurance companies estimate the probabilities because they have a strong incentive to get it right. If they are too optimistic and underestimate the probability of a certain risk, then they will lose money as they will need to pay out more in claims than they expected. If they are too pessimistic and overestimate the probability of risk they will charge premium rates that are too high, which means that another insurance company with a more accurate estimate of the risk will be able to charge a lower premium and attract more customers.

WORKER RIGHTS

The fear of losing a job creates serious insecurity. Although workers can't be guaranteed that they will never lose their job, they should be guaranteed certain rights.[3]

1. All workers need a written contract.
2. The employer needs to specify if there are any actions that would cause a worker to be immediately fired. Some of these would be obvious—for example, if the worker steals from the business or commits some other crime. Employers need to have the freedom to define what acts could get a worker be fired—but these actions need to be clearly specified in advance.
3. A worker needs to have due process rights in case there is a factual dispute about whether the worker committed an act or not. It should be legal for the employer to decide that doing X will cause a worker to be fired, but it would clearly be wrong if an employer fires a worker for doing X if the worker didn't actually do X.
4. If an employer wants to fire an employee for poor performance, then they should be required to first provide a performance evaluation for the worker, and provide the worker with a chance to improve. Only after the worker has failed to improve following such feedback would the employer be allowed to fire the worker for poor performance.[4]

Making it too difficult for employers to fire workers has an unintended consequence: employers will be reluctant to hire workers if they know they run the risk of being stuck with them even if they perform poorly. If employers are reluctant to hire then society suffers from less job growth. However, making it too easy to fire a worker makes it too hard on the workers.

HEALTH CARE

Health Insurance

We're all vulnerable to the risk of being struck by a sudden serious illness or injury. As with the risks discussed earlier in this chapter, the best way to provide some protection from these risks is through pooling. Therefore, people should have health insurance.

Another advantage of the insurance is that it spreads the costs around to different years. It is easier to pay a reasonable amount each year than it is to pay a huge amount in one particular year when you actually suffer from a disease or injury.

Insurance does not work if people don't buy the insurance until they need the care. The solution is to establish a mandate that requires everyone to buy medical insurance. The alternatives to such a mandate are (1) turn people away at the hospital door if they have chosen not to have insurance and can't pay the bill on their own—which is not a very humane alternative, or (2) treat everyone whether or not they have insurance, which is unfair to those that do pay for insurance.

The 2010 health care law included a mandate, but the problem is it required costly medical policies with a list of many items that had to be covered. People should be able to buy such a comprehensive policy if they choose and can afford it, but they should not be required to do so. The mandate should be changed so that it would only require that people buy coverage for major care (which would be more affordable). A major-care policy would require a large deductible, which would make the insurance premiums more affordable—but people would have to pay directly for normal health care.[5] For comparison, auto insurance pays for damage from collisions. It does not pay for a normal expense like gas. If an insurance policy did pay for gas, it wouldn't really be an insurance policy—it would be an expensive prepaid gasoline program.

People would pay attention to the cost of normal care if they were paying it themselves, rather than expecting the insurance company to pay for it. That would help in making the system more efficient, but it is debatable over how much this will help with holding down costs. If people could buy insurance on a nationwide market (so state lines would not matter), it would be possible to find out if people would choose insurance plans covering more advanced treatments or if they would choose more affordable plans covering fewer advanced treatments.

In 2012 the Supreme Court[6] ruled that Congress cannot use the powers provided by the constitution's Commerce clause to mandate that people buy insurance, but it can use its taxing power to require insurance. The best way to do this would be to establish a tax credit for the purchase of health insurance. A tax credit means that a taxpayer could subtract the amount spent for health coverage (up to a certain limit) from their tax liability.

If you have been faithfully paying your premiums for the years when you've been healthy, you have the right to expect the insurance company to be there to cover the cost when you finally do get sick. However, this also means that health insurers can't be free to raise their prices whenever they want to. If you become sick and they decide to increase your annual premiums to $1,000,000 that would be equivalent to them denying coverage to you, which violates the promise they had been making to you during all the years when you have been paying premiums. This issue is not as much of a problem for other types of insurance. If your car insurance company drastically raises rates you can find another car insurance company. (The loss of customers will hit the expensive insurance company where it hurts—their bottom line—so they will have to compete to win back customers.) However, you won't be able to switch to a new health insurer if you've just become seriously ill. When insurance companies won't insure people with existing conditions it is not because they are being heartless, it is because that is the way insurance works.[7]

Trade-offs

Health care decisions inevitably involve making choices about trade-offs. Suppose procedure X to treat disease Y is expensive. How should this choice be made? One approach is to have a single decision maker (as in the 2010 law). However, it would be better if there were alternative decisions possible, so that if the national decision board denies coverage for procedure X it is not the final binding decision for the whole country. Some people may choose not to do this procedure, but other people may be willing to make extensive sacrifices so they could make this choice.

Different insurance plans should be able to make different decisions about whether or not to offer coverage for procedure X. These decisions should be spelled out in advance, so that nobody will be surprised when they learn that their health insurance will or will not cover a certain procedure. There should be independent raters that would rate insurance companies so potential customers could tell if they were getting into a plan that covered a lot of procedures, or one that did not cover as much. Then people could make a choice. One complication: new procedures are developed after you've made the decision about whether to sign up for the insurance, so these ratings for different insurance plans would need to be revised as time goes by.

One reason why health care does not function like other markets is that people seldom have the information needed to make good decisions. Unless you've gone to medical school, it is very hard for you to make decisions about what would be the best treatment for a particular condition. You can retrieve information from different medical sources, but if they conflict you do not know who to turn to.[8]

Another possibility would be to provide the option to buy supplemental insurance that would just cover procedure X. If you like a general insurance plan but it does not cover procedure X you could still get the general plan you like but then get the supplemental plan that covers procedure X. If you are young, and your chance of needing procedure X is small, then this supplemental plan would not be very expensive. It is better to make decisions about whether you should have coverage for procedure X before you are actually suffering from disease Y.

The Strange Case of the Accidental Connection between Employment and Health Care

The system would work much better if health insurance was not connected to employment. The employment-based system did not develop because someone thought that connecting employment to health care would be a rational system; it happened through a weird historical accident when some employers began offering health care as a way of avoiding wartime regulations on wage increases and then pressure grew to make the value of employer-provided health insurance be non-taxable.[9] With employer-provided health coverage non-taxable, employees understandably asked for generous health insurance programs since one non-taxed dollar spent on health insurance is worth more than one taxable dollar provided as cash compensation. People's choices are seriously limited since their employer-provided plan is paid for by pre-tax dollars, but any plan they might buy on their own is paid for with after-tax dollars.

One main disadvantage of employer-provided insurance is that it becomes difficult for workers to change jobs when it also means changing health insurance.

Another disadvantage is that two-career couples would be better served by having their employers provide them with the equivalent money rather than providing two different health insurance programs. Another problem is that some naive people with employer-provided health insurance are probably under the illusion that they are receiving the insurance because the employer is generous. The reality is that (for tax reasons) they are having some of their wages diverted into a less flexible form than would be the case if they were just given the money.

Furthermore, since health care benefits that are provided to a worker do not depend on hours worked, employers have a perverse incentive to hire fewer full-time workers but make them work more overtime hours.[10] Also, by requiring employers with 50 or more employees to provide health care for full-time employees, and full-time is defined as those working 30 hours per week,[11] there is a perverse incentive to hire workers who work 29 or fewer hours, or to hire 49 or fewer workers.

Government

Should the government run all of health care? The no-monopoly principle[12] argues against this. One of the issues that often arises in government-run systems is that care is allocated by making people wait for care. A government-run system works better when people do have choices, such as having surgery in other countries.[13]

The Independent Medicare Advisory Board

There is no easy solution to the issue of health care cost, but we probably would be better off if multiple decision makers test out different possibilities, and people can choose coverage plans from multiple providers with different options. People who choose coverage that includes more expensive procedures would need to pay more. Directing health care subsidies to the person would help with affordability while still leaving the person with choices.

The 2010 health care law tended to move in the direction of centralizing health care decisions in one place (at least for Medicare). This will work fine if people are happy with the decisions the board makes for what to cover and what to not cover, but there are no other options available for cases where people disagree with the decisions of the board. (See the online appendix myhome.spu.edu/ddowning/fos.html for the text of this section of the law.)

Richer Societies Will Spend More on Health Care

Part of the reason for increasing cost is inflation; part of the reason for increasing cost is higher quality; part of the reason for increasing cost is new hope[14]; and part of the reason for increasing cost is the productivity issue inherent in the fact that providing health care is a service (see page 83).

Most likely, the share of national income devoted to health care will continue to increase. This will happen because a richer society will most likely decide that it is worthwhile to do this. This means that average-income individuals will end up paying an increasing amount for health care in the future, regardless of what system is used. They will either be paying for care or insurance directly, or they will pay indirectly with taxes.

Match Costs to Specific Risks: Crime, Vehicle Accidents

It would help to lower the general cost of health care by identifying certain types of health needs and assigning the cost so that it matches the source of the problem. For example, worker's compensation funds currently provide coverage for those injured on the job. Here are a couple other examples where this concept could be applied. Victims of violent crime (and their insurance companies) should not have to pay anything for health care related to the crime. Who should pay in that case? The obvious answer is: criminals. This is probably hard to do because criminals don't have a lot of wealth, but the government does collect fines in some criminal cases that could be applied to crime victim health care; otherwise general tax revenue should be used.

It also would help if there was a separate fund for health care related to motor vehicle accidents. This care would be best paid for by revenue from gasoline taxes.[15] The cost of general health insurance would be less if it was clear that such a policy would not have to pay for care in cases of crime or vehicle accidents.

Also, participants in certain dangerous thrill-seeking activities should pay for special insurance to cover potential medical costs if they are injured in action.

Is There a Right to Health Care?

Should there be a right to health care? There can only be a right if someone is coerced into providing it (see page 21).

It is only relatively recently that health care has advanced to the point where it is beneficial. In previous centuries there were cases where you would be better off not being at the doctor because the doctor's treatment (such as bleeding) would cause more harm than good. In Dickens' time, it would not have been possible to provide Tiny Tim with a right to an MRI scan. If Tiny Tim had really been able to go to a doctor in the 1840s it is not clear if medical care at that time would have even had a positive effect, let alone be able to cure him. James A. Garfield died in 1881 because of incompetent medical care. He might have recovered from his gunshot wound had he not been infected during the medical examination—and as president of the U.S.he presumably received the best medical care in the world at that time.

Today we can't provide everyone a right to diagnostic tricorders and holographic emergency doctors and other medical advances provided on *Star Trek*.

Government Paying Large Health Care Bills

Another way to reduce the cost of general insurance would be for the government to pick up all of the health care bills for an individual when the total amount is over a certain large limit (perhaps $250,000 per year). The limit would have to be adjusted to make sure it only applied to rare cases. There would be a moral hazard problem for the rest of the year once someone's health bill hit that limit, since the government would pick up all of the additional cost. One could hope that the moral hazard problem would not be insurmountable because of the large limit would act as a very large deductible.

Health Care for Low-Income People

It would be fair to provide a subsidy with high and middle income people paying taxes that can be used to subsidize the health care of low-income people, but it would be very controversial to determine what the level of subsidy should be. Such a subsidy should not have a single cutoff point so that people whose income exceeds the cutoff suddenly become ineligible for the subsidy; instead, it needs to be phased out gradually as income increases.

There is a haphazard subsidy for low-income people because they can turn up at the emergency room and receive care. The cost of this care is then spread across other patients who have insurance. The result is a kind of subsidy (but not a well-designed subsidy). It is also not the best way to provide care, because it means that people put off getting care (because they can't afford it) until they have to go the emergency room. If they could be treated earlier it likely would be less expensive. There also are explicit subsidies: Medicaid for low-income people and Medicare for elderly people.

It is also important to make sure children have health care. You can't expect children to work to earn money to pay for things they need. This would be best provided by the parents, but there needs to be a subsidy for low-income parents (as provided by medicaid).

AGING POPULATION

Regardless of what system is adopted for financing health care, the increase in the number of elderly people will lead to significant increases in the total national cost of health care in the future (see the online animation). It would help for the government to offer enormous prizes to those that come up with significant cures for major illnesses associated with aging. By providing strong incentives for researchers to develop these cures we might hope that society can thrive as the growing number of elderly people become an asset to society rather than an increasing burden.[16]

NOTES

1. Note: This chapter is about personal economic security, not national security.

2. The job of saving is easier if you can collect interest on the accumulated balances, but the math becomes slightly more complicated. Also, considering the effect of inflation adds another complication that does not change the basic implications of this story.

3. Very small employers should be exempt from these requirements.

4. See Alexander Hill, p164.

5. A major care plan might also cover preventive health care, because it might be cheaper to pay for early preventive care rather than major care after problems become worse. The important point is that there is no single best model for all health care plans.

6. *National Federation of Independent Business v. Sibelius.*

7. The 2010 health care law prevents insurers from denying coverage in cases of pre-existing conditions. At the time of this writing it is too early to tell how this will affect the insurance market when the law is fully implemented.

8. In an episode of the television series *Downton Abbey*, an aristocratic doctor provides different advice from the local doctor. How could the characters know who they should believe? Did the aristocratic doctor have a better education? Or did his status allow him to make it through medical school without working very hard?

9. Gratzer, p5.

10. Schor, p66.

11. Public law 111–48, section 1513.

12. See page 20.

13. For example, Newfoundland premier Danny Williams had heart surgery in Florida in 2010 (Macleans, February 23, 2010).

14. In the old days it was relatively cheap to treat someone hopelessly ill because all the doctor could do was tell them there was nothing that could be done.

15. However, there would need to be a way to tax electric cars based on mileage driven.

16. See the discussion of social security in chapter 11.

Chapter 5

The Reality Constraint

Average Real Wage Equals Average Productivity

Any proposed public policy confronts its moment of truth with the question: can this really be done? Call this fundamental limitation the *reality constraint*.

PRODUCTIVITY DETERMINES DESTINY

Consider a society with one person and one good (for example, Robinson Crusoe consuming nothing but clams). The number of clams Crusoe can consume per day equals the number of clams he can harvest. Suppose he can dig three clams per day.

consumption measured in clams per day

equals production in clams per day equals 3

The expressions involving "per" can be written as fractions:

$$\text{consumption measured in } \frac{\text{clams}}{\text{day}} = \text{production in } \frac{\text{clams}}{\text{day}} = 3\frac{\text{clams}}{\text{day}}$$

The productivity ratio (clams produced divided by the amount of time needed to produce them) determines Crusoe's living standards. In economics, productivity determines destiny. A society with high productivity will be rich; a society with low productivity will be poor.

Working more hours does not mean you are more productive. Instead, it means you will have more of the good(s) you work for (in this case clams), but you have less free time. You may be willing to make this choice, but it depends on the situation. If you are working a huge number of hours per week, you would likely be better off by working fewer hours, sacrificing the consumption of goods in order to have more free time. On the other hand, if you are slacking off a lot now, you might be better off working more and being able to consume more goods.

Now introduce money into Crusoe's world. (Although this would be silly for a one-person economy, it does take us one step closer to reality.) The total amount spent equals

$$(\text{price}) \times (\text{clams per day})$$

In this case all of the money collected by the clam seller is paid as wages to the only worker:

$$(\text{price per clam}) \times (\text{clams per day}) = (\text{wage per day}) \times (\text{one day worked per day})$$

The wage rate will depend on what Crusoe uses for money. If Crusoe uses big rocks for money, and there are 12 big rocks on the island, he could arrange to have a wage of 12 big rocks per day. The price of clams then would be 4 big rocks:

$$4\left(\frac{\text{big rocks per}}{\text{clam}}\right) \times 3\left(\frac{\text{clams per}}{\text{day}}\right) = 12\left(\frac{\text{big rocks per}}{\text{day}}\right)$$

From now on we'll leave out the word "per" in the fraction:

$$4\left(\frac{\textbf{big rocks}}{\textbf{clam}}\right) \times 3\left(\frac{\textbf{clam}}{\text{day}}\right) = 12\left(\frac{\text{big rocks}}{\text{day}}\right)$$

When units written as fractions are multiplied, they will follow the same cancellation rules as ordinary fractions. In this case, the "clam" in the denominator of the first fraction cancels out the "clam" in the numerator of the second fraction.

In general, write this relationship as:

$$\text{price} \times \text{productivity} = \text{wage}$$

Alternatively, Crusoe could use pebbles for money. If the beach contains 12,000 pebbles, Crusoe could arrange to have a wage of 12,000 pebbles per day. He could momentarily delude himself into thinking he is richer because his wage has increased from 12 to 12,000, but then he finds the price of clams has now shot up to 4,000:

$$4,000\left(\frac{\text{pebbles}}{\text{clam}}\right) \times 3\left(\frac{\text{clams}}{\text{day}}\right) = 12,000\left(\frac{\text{pebbles}}{\text{day}}\right)$$

The numerical value of your wage doesn't determine how well off you are. The important thing is what you can purchase with that wage.

THE REAL WAGE EQUALS PRODUCTIVITY

The reality constraint is represented by this equation:

$$\frac{\text{wage}}{\text{price}} = \text{productivity}$$

(Obtain this equation by rewriting equation from the previous page) The ratio of the wage to the price is called the *real wage*, because it determines the real purchasing power of your wage—in other words, what you can actually buy with it, after correcting for the effect of inflation.[1]

Increasing the real wage means you must increase productivity. Workers are more productive when they learn new or better skills, or when they have more or better tools (capital) to work with.[2]

What if productivity does increase but the benefits flow to profits rather than to the workers?[3] A solution is for workers to receive part of their compensation in the form of stock in their company so they will share in the profit (see page 80).

THE JOHN KENNEDY QUESTION

One possibility is that everyone's real wage equals their productivity. However, if someone has their real wage exceed their productivity, then someone else has to have their wage be lower than their productivity. In order to increase your wages, it comes down to two choices: either improve your productivity, or find a way for your share of consumption to exceed your share of production. The catch is: the only way your share of consumption can exceed your share of production is for somebody else to have their share of consumption fall short of their share of production.

Upon this choice much of economic destiny depends. Will people strive to increase their productivity, or will they attempt to exploit weaknesses in other people to increase their own share at the expense of others? Call this the John Kennedy question: "Ask not what your country can do for you, but what you can do for your country."[4]

It's not surprising that some people have consumption exceeding their productivity. For example, children need food, clothing, and shelter, but they're not expected to earn them for themselves—their parents care for them. Others are deserving of support from society—those that are disabled, or have lost their job.

JUST PRICES AND AUTHENTIC PRICES

Sometimes a price might seem too high, so you wonder if it is really a just price. Other times a price might seem too low, so you might wonder if that price is just.

One possible answer to the just-price question is that a price should measure the true worth of a product. Water, being the product most essential to life, should be the most expensive good, and diamonds (pretty and sparkly but hardly necessary) should be cheap. Shakespeare plays, having the greatest literary value, should be the most expensive literature, while trashy novels should be least expensive. However, that doesn't seem right. The most valuable products should not be the most expensive; that would make it very hard to live. Fortunately, prices do not represent the true worth of goods, nor are they intended to.[5]

Buyers benefit from low prices, but sellers benefit from high prices. It is impossible to make a moral judgment on what a just price should be without deciding whether you are partial to the sellers or to the buyers. The product might be an essential product purchased by poor consumers, so at first glance it might seem the just price should be low. On the other hand, it might be a product produced as the sole means of livelihood by a group of poor workers, so it might seem that the just price should be high. It can't be both low and high.

Instead of measuring the true worth of products, prices measure trade-offs. In order for prices to measure trade-offs, they need to be authentic prices in the sense that it is possible for buyers to obtain the good if they are willing to pay the price, and it is possible for sellers to sell the good if they are willing to sell at that price. This tends to be true in a free economy, because the prices tend to adjust up or down if they are not initially at the level where supply and demand balance.

You might be excited if you hear that you can buy a house on Atlantic City's Boardwalk for $200, but then you will be quickly disillusioned when you realize this is not an authentic price—you cannot buy a real house on Boardwalk for this price.[6] If you cannot obtain the item at a certain price, then that price is an irrelevant fantasy price.

In a free economy prices depend on the interaction of buyers and sellers. If a good is more attractive to the buyers, then, other things being equal, it will have higher demand and higher price. If the sellers are more willing to sell it, then it will, other things being equal, have a lower price.[7]

In some cases, prices in an uncontrolled market will not correctly measure trade-offs. This would be the case when there is environmental pollution, or some other form of externality. In that case the government should take action to make sure that those who cause the pollution pay the price. Government action is needed because of the "bear the consequences of your own actions" principle (see page 97).

NEXT TASK: HOW CAN PRODUCTIVITY INCREASE?

In summary, the only way to increase prosperity for society is to increase productivity. A group of people has another way to increase their prosperity: by increasing their share of society's resources at the expense of other groups.[8]

Next, turn to the question: how can productivity be increased? Two complications will arise: in some industries productivity is very difficult to measure; in other industries it is very difficult to increase.

NOTES

1. The real wage has units of items per time, the same units as productivity. Higher real wages means producing more things per unit time. The unit of wage is $\frac{\text{dollars}}{\text{hours worked}}$. The unit of price is $\frac{\text{dollars}}{\text{unit of output product}}$. Then the unit of real wage is:

$$\frac{\dfrac{\text{dollars}}{\text{hours worked}}}{\dfrac{\text{dollars}}{\text{unit of output product}}}$$

$$= \frac{\text{dollars}}{\text{hours worked}} \times \frac{\text{unit of output product}}{\text{dollars}}$$

$$= \frac{\text{unit of output product}}{\text{hours worked}}$$

so real wage has the same units as productivity.

2. "Capital" here means a durable good used to produce other goods, such as a factory, an airplane, a truck, a computer, an office desk, or a printing press. Capital eventually wears out, but it is not used up in the production process. Confusingly, the word "capital" is also sometimes used to mean "equity" (see page 108) or sometimes to refer to financial assets instead of physical assets.

3. Sweeney, p37, "The Great Productivity Heist."

4. John Kennedy's 1961 inaugural speech.

5. Gregg, p57.

6. You can buy a pretend Boardwalk house with $200 of pretend money in the game *Monopoly*.

7. See page 41 for how wages relate to working conditions of different jobs.

8. Some (such as Noah, p176) have argued that the wages of average workers has been significantly falling behind productivity growth. These arguments miss the gains to workers in broader measures of compensation (see page 71).

Chapter 6

Productivity and Prosperity

What can we do to increase productivity and prosperity?

A RICH COUNTRY

The U.S. is extremely rich. That fact is important to keep in mind. Even though the financial crisis and recession in 2008 and following caused enormous hardship, the U.S. is still rich (more about the crisis in chapters 8 and 9).

There has been a widespread myth that the average person in the U.S. did not do well economically during the three decades before the crisis. Some confusion arose because of statistics that exclude non-wage benefits and mixed part-time and full-time weekly earnings. A better measure of what people actually consume shows an increase of 74 percent from 1980 to 2004.[1] You can also make a list of items owned by a greater percentage of *poor* households in 2001 than were owned by *all* households in 1971: air conditioner, color television, refrigerator, clothes dryer, microwave, DVD player or VCR, personal computer, and cell phone.[2] The average size of new homes increased as the home ownership rate increased,[3] and the amount of travel on airplanes significantly increased.[4] Furthermore, the fact that so much of U.S. spending is on nonessential items such as entertainment indicates that a lot of people have more than enough for their needs. Also, Americans have more free time compared to previous decades (although less free time than people had in medieval times, and less free time than people in Europe have today[5]).

One reason people might think their economic living standards have been stagnating is because they get so used to having new things that they just think of those new things as normal. It takes effort to recall earlier decades

71

when there were no home computers, pocket calculators, web pages, cell phones, smart phones, satellite communication, GPS devices, jet planes, flat screens, digital cameras, measles vaccinations, or ultrasound examinations. It takes effort to recall a time when color televisions were rare and expensive and homes typically only had one television that received only three or four channels with no way to record shows, and airline travel was a luxury for the rich rather than a common experience for ordinary people. How can we measure improvements in medical care since the days when doctors did not even understand the nature of infections?[6]

PRODUCTIVITY

In economics, productivity determines destiny. Skills, resources, tools, and innovation determine productivity. For Robinson Crusoe, further practice with the skill of clamming will increase productivity. Digging along a beach abundant with clams will increase productivity. Building a new tool following an existing design increases productivity. Designing and building a new and improved type of tool (innovation) increases productivity.

More than anything else, the productivity of farmers determines the economic fate of society. In the days when each farm family could barely grow enough food to feed themselves, most of the people in society had to be farmers. Technological advances that increased agricultural productivity freed more people for other jobs.[7]

Although improving productivity is essential for improving economic well-being, these efforts sometimes bring resentment. The term "featherbedding" applies to efforts to resist productivity gains.[8]

Sometimes complex contracts deliberately suppressed productivity with rules preventing people working outside their job classification, or required payment even in the absence of doing any work.[9]

DO ADVERTISERS MANIPULATE PEOPLE?

Can advertisers mold the preferences of the people, so they buy what the advertisers want them to buy, allowing giant firms to permanently dominate the economy? This seems more likely to work with clothes and cars, but less likely to work for food, music, and movies. Companies would not spend money on advertising if it did not seem to be effective, so that fact lends support to the preference-manipulation hypothesis. However, much of this advertising provides information, such as letting you know about a new movie opening this week, or what hours a store is open or a church service is held.

A strong-willed consumer who would never let their preferences be manipulated might still appreciate advertising that provides this type of information.

John Kenneth Galbraith discussed the preference manipulation hypothesis in the 1950s and 1960s. In *The New Industrial State* (1967), Galbraith describes a world where General Motors sold half of all cars (p30) and the economy was dominated by companies such as A&P (p82), Montgomery Ward (p91), Sears (p82), U.S. Steel (p82), Bethlehem Steel (p84), Continental Can (p95), AT & T (p393), Western Electric (p395), and Chrysler (p395). Looking back, it is a bit amusing to see the list of entrenched companies that he thought would be able to effectively control the consumers so there would be reliable demand for their products (p200). All of the companies listed have since gone bankrupt, been acquired, or otherwise lost their once-dominant position. The economy did not develop as Galbraith predicted. Instead of the giant firms from those days continuing to dominate the economy, there came the rise of firms such as Intel, Microsoft, Apple, Google, Facebook, Starbucks, Amazon, FedEx, UPS, DirecTV, Staples, Nike, Southwest Airlines, Alaska Airlines, Netflix, Toys R Us, Nordstrom, Whole Foods, Gamestop, WalMart, and Costco (all of which were founded or significantly expanded since the 1960s). Furthermore, a host of global competitors shook up many complacent formerly powerful firms.

Even if advertisers can't control people they can affect them. Carter (p171) doubts that advertisers can brainwash people, but they can have bad effects by assaulting human dignity. Lindblom (p217) writes, "The problem posed by the steady flow of seductive communications from market elites, then, is not that they decide for consumers what they are to buy. It is that they degrade the mind."

WILL TRADE BALANCE?

Americans buy a lot of things made in China and Japan. Why isn't this trade balanced?

Imagine a bank in the middle of the Pacific, with a big paper stack of dollars, and another paper stack of Japanese yen (in reality, this is done by changing numbers on computers representing bank accounts, but the picture is more vivid if you imagine large paper stacks of bills) (see Figure 6.1). Suppose the U.S. buys cars from Japan and sells airplanes to Japan.

To buy from Japan, an American hands the bank dollar bills and receives yen. The bank tosses the dollars onto the dollar stack and takes yen from the yen stack.

If the trade is balanced, then at roughly the same time someone from Japan arrives at the bank with yen which they exchange for dollars in order to buy

Airplanes

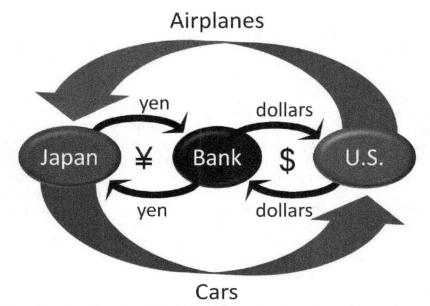

Cars

Figure 6.1   Flow of Trade and Goods for Trade between the U.S. and Japan

American products. The heights of the two stacks stay about the same as both dollars and yen flow both in and out.

What if the trade isn't balanced? What if Americans buy a lot more Japanese goods than Japanese buy American goods? The dollar stack at the bank continues to grow as Americans bring in dollars, while the yen stack continues to decrease as Americans take out yen. The rising dollar stack isn't a huge problem for the bank (other than the need to find room to store the dollar bills, or make sure its computers can handle very big numbers). However, the falling yen stack does pose a problem: if the bank runs out of yen, then it will no longer be able to offer yen in exchange for dollars, and it will be out of the foreign exchange business. In order to prevent this from happening, it will have to somehow encourage more people to bring yen to the bank, and discourage people from bringing as many dollars. To do this, it offers a higher price for yen and a lower price for dollars. This means the exchange rate value of the dollar falls against the yen, or the value of the yen rises against the dollar (these two mean exactly the same thing; the only difference is your perspective when you observe the change).

Is the falling value of the dollar good or bad? It depends on what you are trying to do. If you are an American consumer planning to buy Japanese goods, then the fall in the dollar is bad for you: you will find the Japanese goods more expensive. On the other hand, if you are an American business hoping to sell to Japan, the fall in the value of the dollar is good for you: your goods will become more affordable to people in Japan.

The general effect of the fall in the dollar is to discourage Americans from buying Japanese goods while encouraging Japanese people to buy American goods, which will mean fewer dollars and more yen arriving at the foreign exchange bank, which will help bring the bank's money stacks, and the U.S. trade deficit, back into balance.

Asset Trade and Exchange Rates

The story of U.S. trade with China is similar to trade with Japan, although the trade with China has not been going on for as long. The recent boom in exports from China to the U.S. only began in the 1980s. See the online graphs.

If the exchange rate would tend to adjust so that the trade would balance, why has the U.S. trade deficit with China persisted?

The flow of funds between countries is more than just payments for exports and imports; it includes trades in assets. The reason the U.S. is able to buy so much merchandise from China is because of Chinese purchases of U.S. assets, which keeps the value of the dollar higher than it would be if merchandise trade alone mattered. China purchases assets such as U.S. real estate and stocks, and it also purchases U.S. bonds—which is another way of saying that China is lending the money to the U.S.

The inflow of funds keeps U.S. interest rates lower, and U.S. investment higher, than they otherwise would be. At some point the flow of funds will be more likely to balance out, as China eventually will want to convert its dollar assets into products it can use and let its currency value rise.

If China and the U.S. were isolated from each other, and if China had a higher savings rate than the U.S., then China would tend to have lower interest rates and the U.S. would tend to have higher interest rates. Lots of people in China would bring funds to banks, so the banks don't need to pay very high interest rates to attract deposits, and they have lots of funds to lend so they will offer low borrowing rates to attract borrowers.

On the other hand, in the U.S. borrowers will be competing for a limited amount of savings, so banks will offer higher rates to depositors to try to attract more funds while charging higher rates for loans because they can profitably charge high rates to borrowers that need access to the limited funds that are available.

Suppose that one day these two previously isolated nations come in contact with each other, and find no obstacles to trading goods or assets with each other. The savers in the high-savings rate country (China) will realize that the interest rates are higher on savings in the low-savings rate country (the U.S.), so they will send their savings across the ocean by buying assets (bonds, stocks, bank deposits, real estate) in the other country. This process will continue as long as the interest rates in one country are higher than the other. Money will flow from the high-savings country to the low-savings country (not to buy goods or services, but to buy assets or make loans).

If there was no trade in goods between the countries (or the trade was balanced), then the foreign exchange bank would find lots of Chinese yuan flowing in and dollars flowing out, so the result would be a fall in the value of the yuan and the corresponding rise in the value of the dollar. The change in exchange rates would encourage Americans to buy Chinese goods.

The flow of currency between the two countries can stay balanced with Chinese purchase of U.S. assets and U.S. purchase of Chinese goods. The result is a persistent U.S. trade deficit. U.S. consumers benefit because of interest rates being lower than they otherwise would be, and the price of products from China being lower than they otherwise would be. Chinese workers benefit because of jobs being available to produce goods to sell to Americans. However, at some point China will likely figure that it would help to do something with its dollar assets rather than continue to accumulate them.

Is it good or bad that the U.S. borrows so much? That depends on what the money is being borrowed for (see page 139). The U.S. should look at China's willingness to lend money as an opportunity that will be tremendously helpful if the U.S. invests in assets that improve productivity, but it will be a missed opportunity if the borrowed money is used to finance current consumption.

In summary: borrowing from another country will, other things equal, push up the value of your currency, which leads to more imports into your country, and fewer exports out of your country, leading to a larger trade deficit for your country.

Empirical Case for Trade

The empirical case for trade is based on the experience of formerly isolated countries that have become less isolated.

Countries excluded from trade were poorer.[10] Countries hurt by trade are those that were excluded from trade in manufactured goods as colonial powers pillaged their natural resources while restricting their development of industry.[11]

Japan once had low wages. The U.S. started buying large amounts from Japan in the 1950s when Japan was a low-wage country making cheap products. The result in subsequent years was not job loss in the U.S. but higher wages in Japan, and Japan became a producer of high-value cars and electronic products.

Both India and China were desperately poor countries when they were isolated and they both have become richer as they have traded more with the rest of the world. (See the online graphs.) India's reforms beginning in the 1990s lead to more open trade and less poverty.[12]

The U.S. enforced a trade embargo against China in the 1950s and 1960s. The U.S. embargo didn't help China, but that was not the main reason for China's poverty at that time. Low wages in China lead to a rapid increase in U.S. imports from China starting in the 1980s. China will not continue to be a low-wage land. As its wages increase, American fears of losing jobs to low-wage Chinese workers will fade away (as they have with Japan, which is now a high-wage country), and more American jobs will relate to selling things to China.

The U.S. has long maintained a trade embargo against Cuba. Opponents of U.S. policy argue that the embargo hurts Cuba (and they oppose hurting Cuba); proponents argue that the embargo hurts Cuba (and they support hurting Cuba). Neither side argues that the embargo helps Cuba.

INCREASING WAGES: THE OPTIONS

What can be done to increase the wages of workers?

The options can be divided into two categories: increasing revenue or increasing the share of revenue paid to workers. To increase revenue, either the price has to go up or the quantity produced has to go up. Increasing quantity means either higher productivity or more hours worked.

The simplest case is where workers sell directly to customers (for example, a barber, hairdresser, taxi driver, or baby sitter). The wage the worker earns per hour is equal to the price they charge times the number of customers per hour. For a barber who can serve four customers per hour, the wage is four times the price. For a baby sitter who takes care of two children, the hourly wage is twice the hourly price that is charged per child.

In this case, there are only two ways for the wage to increase: (1) increase productivity or (2) charge a higher price. Again, the reality constraint appears. Raising the price won't work as a strategy to increase the general level of wages for all workers, because the higher price will cancel out the benefit of the higher nominal wage, and the real wage would stay the same.

If the price of product X increases (and the prices of other products do not), the result is unpredictable. The best situation for product X workers would be if people buy the same amount of X as before. However, the higher price means that people will have to spend more dollars to get the same amount of X. If the income of the customers has gone up, they can afford to pay more for product X without decreasing spending on anything else.

This means that even if some workers are in industries where productivity is stagnant, they can benefit from productivity increases for other workers. In that case the high-productivity workers can afford to buy the same amount of the low-productivity workers' services even at a higher price. For example, the pay of baby-sitters in high-wage areas will go up because the high-wage workers still need baby-sitters and can afford to pay them more.

However, if income stays the same when the price of X increases, and the customers buy the same amount of X despite the price increase, they will have to spend more dollars on X and they will have less money to spend on something else. That result will not be good for the workers who make whatever it is that people will buy less of, but it is hard to predict which product(s) that will be. Alternatively, people might save less so they can buy the same amount of X, which will mean less savings will be available to be used for investment for society.

When the price of X goes up, most likely people will buy less of it. People might continue to spend the same total dollar amount on X, but because the price is higher they will be buying a smaller quantity. Employment in the X producing industry will fall, so even if the remaining X workers benefit from the higher wage there will be some X workers that will lose their jobs. There will be less of an effect on other industries in this case because the amount spent on X stays the same (so the amount available to spend on other products doesn't have to change).

It would be even worse for the X workers if the product X price increase causes people to spend less total dollars on X, so some X workers would most likely lose their jobs. (However, this situation would be better for workers in whatever industry where people will now spend more because they are spending less on X.[13])

The reality constraint is more subtle in the typical case where a worker works for an employer who sells the product to the customer.

These are the options for how to increase the wage (the first two options are the same as the case of the direct sellers discussed previously):

1. Increase productivity.
2. Increase the price of the product.
3. Decrease the amount spent on raw materials or intermediate products, leaving more money available for workers. If the business can make more productive use of resources (raw materials and purchased intermediate products), it can reduce the amount spent and direct more money to workers. It also benefits if the prices of resources go down, but the price of resources is beyond the control of the business.
4. Increase the wages of some workers while lowering the wages of other workers. In this case it would be possible to increase the wages of

low-wage workers without changing the total revenue or the total share of revenue that goes to all the workers. However, if the wages of hard, dangerous, unpleasant, and/or high-skill jobs are not high enough, workers will not want to do those jobs. Employers will find they have to compensate these workers enough to entice them to do the jobs, so if the difference in wages became too small it would tend to be pushed back up again to attract people back into doing the hard jobs. The level of CEO pay is a complicated problem (see section 12.6), but even if the CEO was paid a thousand times the pay of the other workers, if there are ten thousand employees in the company it would only be possible to raise the pay of the other workers 10 percent if the CEO worked for free and all of that amount was divided up among the rest of the workers.

5. Decrease interest payments. However, interest payments for past borrowings can't be reduced to fund higher worker pay. Possibly future borrowing or future profit could be reduced to increase worker pay, but the worker-capital paradox arises. Although workers and capital owners compete with each other for a share of the revenue from selling the product, the workers need there to be capital investment in order for productivity to increase (and ultimately for real wages to increase).

6. Decrease the rate of profit. Somebody, either labor or capital owners, has to bear the risk of the uncertainty of future returns for a business (see section 12.5). It is less stressful for the workers if their pay is fixed and the capital owners bear all of the risk, but in that case it is in the worker's interest to make sure that the capital owners earn enough of a return that they will continue to invest in productivity-enhancing improvements for the business. The result will be maddening for the workers during good times when they see the capital owners raking in the money, but it will be easier for the workers in bad times when the business makes a loss instead of a profit and the owners are the ones who suffer. Assume that business owners are greedy and will want to take advantage of opportunities to earn profits. If capital is abundant and workers are scarce, the business owners will find it profitable to pay the workers lavishly enough to entice them to come to work. If capital is scarce and workers are abundant, the owners will find it profitable to let a mere trickle of money flow to the workers. The problem with any policy that reduces the return to capital is that it reduces capital formation and ultimately makes workers poorer. Krugman is correct that we should be skeptical when businesses claim they need tax cuts to create more jobs,[14] but we also need to realize that if taxes are too high it will negatively impact job creation.

One unfortunate tendency is for workers to try to raise their wages by making labor scarce by discriminating against other workers, by opposing freer immigration or blocking access to jobs by members of an "outsider" group. We should view all people as equally worthy, so we need to try to overcome these attitudes.

The best solution will probably be for the workers to share some of the risk, so their pay increases as the enterprise prospers. There is no clear answer to the question of how much of worker's compensation should be in the form of profit sharing—too little and the workers don't share in the good times, but too much and the bad times cause too much hardship for the workers. The government should provide a tax incentive for some compensation to be paid to workers in the form of stock in their employer.[15] Workers who are guaranteed to share in the profits will also have incentives to improve productivity, which ultimately is the necessary step to increase the average real wage. Many businesses already know this and provide profit sharing programs for the workers.

Summary: ways to increase worker pay for the workers who make product X

I. Increase the revenue to the sellers of X.
    I.1. Increase the price charged for product X.
        I.1.A. If the income for the customers increases, they can afford to pay a higher price for product X.
        I.1.B. If the revenue to the sellers increases (because of inelastic demand), but income for the customers does not, then more revenue is available to increase worker pay, but people will spend less money on some other product(s) and the overall effect on wages is unpredictable.
        I.1.C. If the revenue to the sellers decreases (because of elastic demand), then even the price increase will not add to the total revenue, and most likely employment will fall—hurting some workers even if the remaining workers get a wage increase (although some other unpredictable sector of the economy will benefit because people are spending less on product X).
    I.2. Increase the quantity produced.
        I.2.A. Increase productivity—the only way to increase average real wages.
        I.2.B. Work more hours—this increases total income but not the hourly wage.
II. Increase the share of revenue paid to workers.
    II.A. Increase share paid to workers by reducing spending on resources.
        II.A.1. Increasing resource productivity (the amount of output that can be produced for the amount of resources used) makes it possible to increase wages.
        II.A.2. A fall in the price of resources would make more funds available to pay workers more, but this won't happen just because

we would like it to happen (and if the price of resources increases, there is less money available to pay workers).

II.B. Increase the share paid to low-wage workers by paying less to high-wage workers—this might work in some cases, but in other cases the high-wage workers will leave for other jobs unless their pay is enough to entice them to stay.

II.C. Increase the share paid to workers by paying less to capital owners— his could possibly be a problem if there is less willingness to invest in productivity-enhancing improvements to the business.

II.D. Compensate the workers partly with stock in the company, so the workers receive a share of the return to capital owners—has the disadvantage of increasing the risk for the workers, but has the advantage that the workers know they will benefit when the business prospers.

PRODUCTIVITY RISES FASTER IN SOME INDUSTRIES

Productivity rises faster in some industries rather than others. Here's a very simple model with only two industries and productivity equaling wage over price[16]:

$$\text{industry 1 : productivity} = v_1 = \frac{w_1}{sp_1}; \text{price} = p_1 = \frac{w_1}{sv_1}$$

$$\text{industry 2 : productivity} = v_2 = \frac{w_2}{sp_2}; \text{price} = p_2 = \frac{w_2}{sv_2}$$

Suppose the share of revenue paid to labor (s) stays the same in both industries. One possibility is that the wages in the industry with greater productivity rise faster than the slow-productivity industry. However, if too many people desert the slow industry for the growing industry, the shortage of workers in that industry will tend to push their wages up. If the general skill and working conditions of the jobs are the same, then the wages would be the same in both industries.

$$p_1 = \frac{w}{sv_1}$$

$$p_2 = \frac{w}{sv_2}$$

The price of the product will increase faster in the slow-productivity-growth industry.

Service Sector Productivity

Some types of industries have experienced huge productivity gains, such as in agriculture and manufacturing. Factory worker productivity increased dramatically, from Ford's introduction of the moving assembly line to modern factories using robots. Farm productivity has skyrocketed with mechanized equipment and improved fertilizers.

However, productivity in the service sector increases more slowly (if at all) than in manufacturing and agricultural sectors.[17] Education and medical care are examples of industries with slower productivity growth and rising costs.

Productivity in Education

The annual cost of education (C) for students is determined by this equation[18]:

$$C = \frac{W s_s [rps]}{[acs][cpt] s_T}$$

W = annual average pay (wage) for teachers
s_S = share of revenue paid by the students
$[rps]$ = number of classes taken by each student (registrations per student)
$[acs]$ = average class size
$[cpt]$ = courses taught per year per teacher
s_T = share of revenue paid to the teachers

Therefore, to lower cost to students, there are six options[19]:

1. Lower the teacher's pay W (the opposite of what society needs to do in order to attract more qualified people into teaching).
2. Lower the share of the revenue paid by the students (s_S), by finding other sources of revenue: donations, interest on endowments, government funding, etc. (For public K12 education, the cost to the students is zero because the cost is paid for by taxpayers.)
3. Lower registrations per student $[rps]$ (that is, the number of classes taken by each student per year, but this wouldn't really help—either the students would take more years to graduate, or they'll take fewer classes and won't learn as much).
4. Cutting non-teacher costs; for example, by having fewer administrators and support staff. This will increase the share of revenue paid to teachers (s_T). This would work if there are more support staffers than are needed, but cutting too many workers would be bad.

5. Increase the average class size [*acs*].
6. Increase the number of classes taught by teachers [*cpt*].

The last two items relate to productivity—the number of students taught by each teacher. The basic question about increasing productivity is how quality will be affected.

Is it a lot more efficient for a teacher to teach thousands of students over the internet? If the teacher is providing one-way communication to the students, it doesn't much matter if there are 30 or 700 students in a lecture hall or several million watching a movie of the teacher. If the teacher is truly providing an interactive experience for the students, then there is a limit on the number of students it is possible for a teacher to teach. This is true regardless of whether the students are physically in the same classroom or if they all interact with the internet.

Medical Care Productivity

For a doctor, productivity is measured by the number of patients seen per hour. There are limits on how many patients a doctor can see. If the pay for doctors goes up at the same rate as other wages, the price of medical care inevitably goes up. There are three basic options:

1. Spend less on health care as it becomes more expensive (society is less likely to choose this option).
2. Spend a greater share of income on health care (society can afford to do this if it continues to become richer because of productivity gains in other areas).
3. Work on improving health care productivity as much as possible without reducing quality. Some of this happens as new technologies are developed. For example, less invasive surgical techniques make it possible to both increase quality and decrease cost (because the patient recovers from the surgery more quickly). When drugs are developed that can take care of problems that previously would have required surgery or more extensive treatment, then health productivity improves. Or, it might be possible that artificial intelligence systems will be able to replace doctors for diagnosing and recommending treatment for simpler ailments (thereby freeing the precious time of doctors for treating more difficult ailments). However, if the symptoms are subtle it is hard to know if it really is a serious case, so it may not be possible to find a way to replace the face-to-face patient-doctor meetings if quality is to be maintained.

Productivity and Creativity

In some industries the situation is exactly opposite the situation for teachers and doctors: productivity has skyrocketed. For example, the productivity of entertainers has dramatically increased with technological developments such as microphones and speakers, records, compact discs, digital music players, television, and movies. Singers and actors traditionally could entertain only those within the sound of their voice. After Edison's invention of the phonograph, millions can be entertained by a music performer, and the pay for a select group of entertainers zoomed upward.

However, a different problem arises in this case. The reason the productivity is so high is because there is close to zero marginal cost: that is, once the first copy of a song has been created, there is very little cost to make each subsequent copy. That is why one singer can entertain millions who listen to the recorded song. Up until recently, there was some cost of recording: you needed a blank record or tape. With digital recording the marginal cost truly approaches zero. The problem is: how does the creator get paid if the product can be copied at zero marginal cost? In this area the future is unclear.

NOTES

1. Reynolds, p57; Feldstein 2008.
2. Reynolds, p67; see also Cox and Alm; Goff and Fleisher.
3. Reynolds, p66.
4. Cox and Alm, p12.
5. Cox and Alm, p55; Schor, p2, p44.
6. See page 61 for a note about medical care improvements.
7. Landes, p41–42.
8. How many featherbedders does it take to change a light bulb? One to change the bulb; one to verify that all the workers required by the work rules are present; one to supervise these two; one to supervise the supervisor; one to supervise the supervisor of the supervisor; etc.
9. Ingrassia, p8–9, p48, p119, p169.
10. Bhagwati, p65.
11. As was the case for Brazil; Neuhouser, p40. See also Stiglitz, *Making Globalization Work*, p87.
12. Bhagwati and Panagariya.
13. When the price of product X increases, the change in total spending on product X depends on a quantity known as the *elasticity of demand*, which is the percentage change in quantity sold divided by the percentage change in price. If elasticity is exactly 1, then a higher price will cause a fall in quantity sold of the exact amount that total revenue stays the same. If elasticity is more than 1, the buyers are more flexible and will turn to other products so much that revenue falls even though the price has

increased. If elasticity is less than 1, the buyers are less flexible and the higher price will cause an increase in the amount spent on the product.

14. Krugman newspaper column, May 8, 2014.

15. See Weitzman, *The Share Economy*.

16. As in the previous chapter, derive this equation by starting with $wL = spQ$, where s is the labor share.

17. This result is known as Baumol's law. See Baumol 2012.

18. For derivation, see online appendix myhome.spu.edu/ddowning/fos.html. This equation shows tuition only. Room and board costs and revenues need to be accounted for separately.

19. The education cost equation is an identity, meaning it is true by definition. Therefore, any method for reducing the cost of education to the student will fit in one of the six categories listed.

Chapter 7

Government Action
and Economic Policy

What role should the government fill in a successful economy?

THE ROLE OF THE GOVERNMENT

Some essential tasks for government include:

1. Provide a justice system and police protection against crime.
2. Provide security against terrorists and invaders.
3. Enforce contracts and make sure people have accurate information about goods they are considering buying.

   A crucial role of the government is to enforce contracts so that if party A fulfills their part of the contract today they can have some assurance that party B will fulfill their part of the contract tomorrow.
4. Provide for a stable monetary system and macroeconomic stability (see chapters 8 and 9).
5. Promote competition with antitrust laws to prevent sellers from collaborating to raise the price.
6. Regulate certain industries known as natural monopolies. If an industry relies on a distribution system where a pipe or wire must be connected to each house, it is most efficient for there to be a monopoly distributor. Because these industries lack shop-around-ability, the government then should regulate the monopoly to keep it from charging too high of a price (see page 165).
7. Prevent negative externalities such as environmental pollution by making sure polluters have to pay for the damage they cause.

8. Regulate certain resources that cannot feasibly be privately owned, such as wild fish. (In an unregulated market, there would be a tendency to overharvest the fish since no individual acting alone could conserve them; other people could take them instead.)
9. Provide *public goods*. These are goods where it is costless to extend the benefits to other people once they are first provided, and it is not feasible to exclude non-payers from enjoying the benefit of them. Examples include city streets and national defense.
10. Provide education for children to provide opportunity. Also, other people in society benefit when the people around them are educated.
11. Provide for children whose parents are absent or unable to care for them.
12. Provide insurance for the disabled and elderly (social security).

ROLE OF GOVERNMENT: CONCERNS

There are two reasons why you should be concerned about government taking over too many responsibilities. The first concern is the monopoly nature of government power. When dealing with a private company you usually have a choice about who to deal with. This gives you the chance to turn to someone else if you receive poor service, and it provides the organization with an incentive to do better because it has to compare itself with other businesses.

The second concern is the difficulty of measuring government performance. A private company needs to sell products and pay expenses, and the profit it makes in doing so provides a way of measuring its success, and also provides important discipline because a private company cannot stay in business if it suffers a prolonged spell without profit. For government programs, measuring success is much more complicated, and the funds needed to sustain a program aren't necessarily tied to whether or not the program is a success.

A central feature of the political divide is this: some people have greater antipathy to business, and some have greater antipathy to government. In order to bridge the differences, we need to acknowledge some truth to both of these views.

THE U.S. CONSTITUTION: ENUMERATED POWERS

The U.S. constitution includes a list of powers of Congress. If the framers had intended that Congress has the power to do anything it wants, the constitution would not have included the list and simply said "Congress has the power to pass whatever law a majority of each House votes to approve."

Should someone then have the power to overrule Congress when it over-steps its boundaries? Whoever has that power has to be someone who is not accountable to the majority of voters, but how can we trust them to make the right decisions? There is no easy answer to that question. In the U.S. the Supreme Court has the power to overrule Congress if it acts outside the limits prescribed by the constitution.

Here is the list of powers provided in article I, section 8:

The Congress shall have Power. . . .

1. *To lay and collect Taxes, Duties, Imposts and Excises, to pay the Debts and provide for the common Defence and general Welfare of the United States; but all Duties, Imposts and Excises shall be uniform throughout the United States;*

    This paragraph has been modified by the 16th amendment (1913): *The Congress shall have power to lay and collect taxes on incomes, from whatever source derived, without apportionment among the several states, and without regard to any census or enumeration.*

2. *To borrow Money on the credit of the United States;* (see page 139)

3. *To regulate Commerce with foreign Nations, and among the several States, and with the Indian Tribes;* The most important part of regulating commerce is to make sure that sellers accurately represent their products to potential buyers, so the government needs to establish consumer protection laws. Second, the government needs to regulate the sale of goods that are hazardous to bystanders. The government should regulate the price of products that need to travel by pipes or wires along public roadways (the case of natural monopolies; page 165), but it would help to amend this clause to state that Congress or states do not have power to regulate prices in other cases.[1]

4. *To establish an uniform Rule of Naturalization, and uniform Laws on the subject of Bankruptcies throughout the United States;*

    Bankruptcy courts are needed to deal with cases when a debtor can't repay debt. One approach that has been used is to put debtors in prison, which is a bad idea both because the punishment (prison) does not fit the "crime" (not repaying a debt) but also because it is not in the creditor's interest to have their debtors in prison where they will be unable to earn any income to repay even part of the loan they owe. However, bankruptcy shouldn't be too easy on debtors and therefore give people an incentive to evade payment of their debts (which would result in it becoming harder for anyone to get credit). On the other hand, bankruptcy shouldn't be too easy on creditors—they need to have an incentive to be careful about who they lend money to.

5. *To coin Money, regulate the Value thereof, and of foreign Coin, and fix the Standard of Weights and Measures;* (see the next two chapters)

6. *To provide for the Punishment of counterfeiting the Securities and current Coin of the United States;*

7. *To establish Post Offices and post Roads;* A road is an example of a public good. It is impractical in most cases to charge users because it is too expensive to prevent nonpayers from using the road. Also, one person can use the road without preventing another person from using that road.

8. *To promote the Progress of Science and useful Arts, by securing for limited Times to Authors and Inventors the exclusive Right to their respective Writings and Discoveries;*

   This provision provides an important incentive to invent and create.

   The next eight provisions relate to lower courts and the military, and then comes the provision for the district of Columbia:

9. *To exercise exclusive Legislation in all Cases whatsoever, over such District (not exceeding ten Miles square) as may, by Cession of particular States, and the Acceptance of Congress, become the Seat of the Government of the United States, and to exercise like Authority over all Places purchased by the Consent of the Legislature of the State in which the Same shall be, for the Erection of Forts, Magazines, Arsenals, dock-Yards, and other needful Buildings;–And*

   See page 184 for the D.C. issue.

10. *To make all Laws which shall be necessary and proper for carrying into Execution the foregoing Powers, and all other Powers vested by this Constitution in the Government of the United States, or in any Department or Officer thereof.*

There clearly needs to be an elastic clause in the constitution to give Congress the authority to deal with situations that cannot be foreseen. For example, the constitution explicitly authorizes Congress to establish an army and navy, but it does not authorize an air force (for obvious reasons).

How should this clause be interpreted? Does it mean Congress has the power to create all laws which are both "necessary *and* proper," or does it mean Congress has the power to create laws that are "necessary" and it also has the power to create laws that are "proper?" Since the "both necessary and proper" requirement sets a higher standard than the either "necessary or proper" requirement, it matters. If the "necessary and proper" clause is interpreted to mean Congress has the power to do anything, then the enumerated power list becomes meaningless. However, how could a court tell whether or not a law is proper? There is no easy answer to this question (see page 177).

Three important economic statements appear in Article I, section 9:

- *No Tax or Duty shall be laid on Articles exported from any State.*
- *No Preference shall be given by any Regulation of Commerce or Revenue to the Ports of one State over those of another; nor shall Vessels bound to, or from, one State, be obliged to enter, clear, or pay Duties in another.*
- *No Money shall be drawn from the Treasury, but in Consequence of Appropriations made by Law; and a regular Statement and Account of the Receipts and Expenditures of all public Money shall be published from time to time.*

From section 10:

- *No State shall enter into any Treaty, Alliance, or Confederation; grant Letters of Marque and Reprisal; coin Money; emit Bills of Credit; make any Thing but gold and silver Coin a Tender in Payment of Debts; pass any Bill of Attainder, ex post facto Law, or Law impairing the Obligation of Contracts, or grant any Title of Nobility.*

You might be surprised to see the "gold and silver coin" clause is still in the constitution, even though its meaning was ignored in a Supreme Court case shortly after the Civil War.[2]

- *No State shall, without the Consent of the Congress, lay any Imposts or Duties on Imports or Exports, except what may be absolutely necessary for executing it's inspection Laws: and the net Produce of all Duties and Imposts, laid by any State on Imports or Exports, shall be for the Use of the Treasury of the United States; and all such Laws shall be subject to the Revision and Control of the Congress.*

The next few sections discuss some specific economic policy issues.

PRICE CEILINGS AND EMPTY SHELVES

People become upset when prices are high. (Actually, buyers are the ones that get upset—sellers are happy when prices are high.) Sometimes the buyers will prevail upon the government to pass a law making it illegal to raise prices. Price controls are not common in the U.S., but there was a

comprehensive price control system during World War II, and again briefly
in the early 1970s.

Supply and Demand

Sellers like higher prices and buyers like lower prices. Represent this information on a diagram showing sellers willing to sell more at high prices, and
buyers willing to buy more at low prices (see Figure 7.1).

Traditionally the buyer's curve is called the "demand" curve (which is not
the best name because it implies the buyers are holding a gun to the sellers
head and demanding that they sell, which is not the case). The seller's curve
is called the "supply curve" (see Figure 7.2).

If the price is very high, the sellers eagerly come to the market with a large
quantity of goods, but then they are in for a rude shock when they realize
there aren't that many buyers at that high price. The high price results in
excess supply, and the sellers usually have to lower the price (see Figure 7.3).

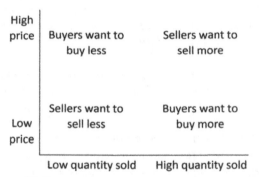

Figure 7.1   Buyers and Sellers

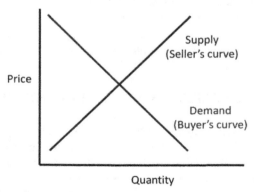

Figure 7.2   Supply and Demand Curves

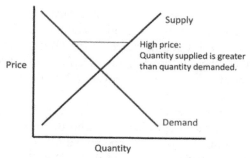

Figure 7.3   High Price: Excess Supply

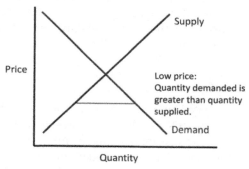

Figure 7.4   Low Price: Excess Demand

If the price is very low, the buyers eagerly come to the market expecting bargains, but their rude shock comes when they realize that the shelves are empty because the sellers are not willing to sell at the low price. The low price results in excess demand, and prices usually will increase (see Figure 7.4).

In some markets the price can change quickly. In other markets prices change slowly. In the stock market prices can change every minute; in grocery stores prices might change every week; in labor markets the prices might only change once per year.

If the price is at the level where the supply and demand curves cross, then every buyer willing to pay the market price will get the product, and every seller willing to take the market price will find a buyer. The system for allocating goods can be called *willingness and ability to pay*: if you are willing and able to pay the price, you get the product. When the price is at the level where supply and demand cross, it is called the equilibrium price because it will tend to stay there (at least until one of the curves shifts).

The buyers would prefer lower prices, and they might think they would benefit if the government imposes a price ceiling (as they did in 1971). However, the sellers won't sell as much as the buyers want to buy at that low price, and the ceiling will prevent the price from adjusting upward (as in Figure 7.4). Buyers like low prices. However, it doesn't help the buyers if the price is low but the shelf is empty.

In the case of the price ceiling, there will need to be some other system for determining who gets the product and who doesn't. Some possibilities include seller discrimination (only the people the seller like get the product); government rationing (as was done during World War II); or first-come, first-served (as when people had to wait in lines in their cars to buy gasoline during the gasoline price controls of late 1973 and early 1974). Another possibility is that there will be illegal transactions (buyers who cannot otherwise get the good have an incentive to offer a price higher than the legal ceiling; the sellers have an incentive to take the higher price; and they both have an incentive not to report their illegal transaction to the police).

Government Rationing

The government considered imposing gasoline rationing during the price-ceiling-shortage of 1973–1974. If they had, they first would have had to decide: should gasoline be distributed equally to everyone (in which case some people would get less than they needed and other people would get more than they needed); or should they decide which uses of gasoline were more important and which were not (workers driving to work? students driving to school? patients driving to doctors? people driving to arts, entertainment, or sporting events?) Should more gas be allocated to people that lived further from work (creating a perverse incentive), or should less gas be allocated to people that took public transit (creating another perverse incentive)? Should gas be denied to people without cars (what use would they have for it? but it would seem to be harsh to tell people who were too poor to have a car that they also can't share in the gasoline)? Would gas be given to someone that was willing to make major sacrifices by buying less of other things in order to have enough gas to visit their ailing out-of-town grandmother every weekend? In each case the government would have to make decisions that would be unpopular with those that were denied the gas.

If the government just distributed the gas equally to everyone,[3] they would have to decide whether people would be allowed to sell any extra gas they had to someone who was willing to pay for it. If the government did not allow people to sell the gas, they would have a difficult enforcement problem and they would have created strange inefficiencies such as an elderly neighbor who drove little being unable to help the two-career-three-children family next door that drove a lot. Could the elderly neighbor drive the next-door family places in exchange for some money? Could the elderly neighbor rent her car (with its full gas tank) to the family? If the government truly insisted on preventing any sale of gas it would somehow have to enforce a ban on all of these activities. Given the difficulty of enforcing a ban on selling gasoline, it might allow people to sell their extra gasoline rations—but if it does that, it has re-introduced a market for gasoline. That policy would be odd—if the government wanted to allocate gasoline in a market all it would have to do would be remove the price control. It would seem weirdly perverse if the price-control-with-resalable-rationed-gasoline policy let everyone except the gasoline suppliers sell the gasoline for a higher price than the control price.

The gasoline rationing problem is even more complicated, because individual drivers aren't the only users of petroleum fuels. How much fuel would be allocated to buses? taxis? ambulances? trucks? farm tractors? pizza delivery drivers? trains? boats? airplanes? helicopters? home heating? emergency generators? lawn mowers? An equal distribution would not even make sense for all of these uses. The government would need an unfathomable amount of information to make these decisions well, and they would need tyrannical powers to enforce their decisions. After thinking through all this, the government decided not to impose gasoline rationing in 1974.

During World War II people realized it was an emergency situation and were committed to supporting the war effort. People understood that the rationing system needed to prioritize war-related products, and were willing to put up with rationing-related complications that they would be less likely to accept during normal times.

In general the government should not impose price ceilings. Although the buyers initially like the idea of low prices, only the buyers able to get the product will benefit. Those buyers not able to obtain the product won't walk away from the empty shelf consoling themselves by thinking, "at least the price was low."

The exceptions where low-price ceilings would help are cases where a product lacks shop-around-ability (like taxis) or where it is a natural monopoly situation (where pipes or wires need to be connected to every house, as with water, electric power, natural gas, or traditional wired phones; page 165).

The best way to reduce price is with increased supply. For example, the price of housing becomes more affordable when more housing is available. What do landlords fear? Vacancies—because vacancies mean they have no rental income coming in. Lowering the rent to attract more renters is better for the landlords than keeping the rent high and having vacancies for a long time.

RESOURCE CONSERVATION: EFFICIENCY,
INVESTMENT, AND SACRIFICE CONSERVATION

Society always faces the choice about how to make sure that people don't use more resources than are available. (Actually, nature will enforce that limitation—but society makes choices about the mechanism by which people will make decisions about using resources.) Suppose that society faces a difficult situation because a crucial resource is in short supply. People need to conserve (they will have to conserve one way or another). There are three general types of conservation:

1. Efficiency conservation: stop wasting as much. This is the easiest type of conservation because you can achieve it without sacrificing anything. If you habitually leave water dripping from your faucets, all you need to do is turn the faucets off and you will conserve some water at no cost to yourself.
2. Investment conservation: devoting some resources today to obtain something that will reduce resource use in the future. For example, if you add insulation to your home, buy a thicker sweater, buy a fuel-efficient car, install solar power panels, or buy energy-efficient light bulbs, you will save resources in the future. You aren't sacrificing any benefits in the future: your house will still be warm, you can still drive, you still have electricity and light. However, you do need to sacrifice resources today in order to pay for the investment, so you need to know the nature of the trade-off between your sacrifice today and the benefits tomorrow.
3. Sacrifice conservation: giving up something you value in order to use less of the resource. For example, you may appreciate nice long showers, but you choose to take shorter showers because you are concerned about saving water. This is the hardest type of conservation.

One way to make people conserve resources is to order everyone to make a percentage reduction in use (for example, 10 percent). This is the worst way to require conservation, because it perversely rewards the people that wasted a lot last year, and penalizes the people that have already been trying to conserve.

There could be a mandatory limit on the amount each person can use, or a requirement that everyone install a particular device such as a low-flow shower head. Although less perverse than requiring everyone to reduce the same percentage, the problem with enforcing particular limits is that it doesn't recognize the nature of the choices involved. If someone really wants a regular shower head, and they are willing to save water by taking shorter showers as long as they have adequate water pressure, they should be able to do that. If someone else really wants to take nice long showers, and they are willing to make many other sacrifices so they can have the benefit of the long shower, they should be able to make that choice.

There still needs to be a way to limit the amount of resources that people use. The purpose of the price of a resource is to make sure that the amount that people are willing to buy matches the amount that is available. If someone is willing to sacrifice X kilowatt-hours of electricity so they can enjoy the benefits of Y additional gallons of water, the price system provides a signal that determines whether or not actual resource availability allows people to make that choice.[4]

ENVIRONMENTAL DAMAGE: MAKE THEM PAY

Greed is not good in itself, but it can be harnessed to lead to good results. In the case of environmental damage, it's best to follow this rule: make those that cause the damage pay for the damage. In that case their greed will push them to cause less environmental damage.

The main problem with regulation as a way to prevent oil spills is that regulators won't know the best way to do it. If there is massive, clear liability for those that cause the spill, they will have a very strong incentive to find the best way to prevent it. It is necessary to carefully measure the amount of oil that is loose each day, being sure to add to the total as more oil escapes each day, but then subtract from the total any amount that is cleaned up that day (to make sure that there is a strong incentive to clean it up). The cost should be specified in advance, so there is no uncertainty, and no need for litigation about the amount. The company has two choices: either pay for insurance, or post a bond to cover the amount. The insurance company has an incentive to come up with good safety rules as a condition of maintaining the insurance; however, if it comes up with rules that are too restrictive then the company may turn to other insurers, or they may choose the other option of posting the bond. A company posting the bond has a huge incentive to be safe because its own money is at risk.

VEHICLE FUEL EFFICIENCY STANDARDS

Improving vehicle fuel efficiency is good, but government mandates for fuel efficiency are conceptually flawed. Imagine that government fuel efficiency standards applied to all vehicles. Consider a hundred-car freight train, which might get mileage of about 0.04 miles per gallon. Freight trains would be completely shut down if they were required to meet a 35 mile per gallon standard. Something seems bizarrely wrong with this scenario, and a moment's thought makes it clear: it's nonsensical to apply the mileage standard to the vehicle without considering what it is actually moving. The hundred car freight train might be moving 10,000 tons of freight. The relevant mileage figure is that one gallon of fuel moves one ton of freight $10,000 \times 0.04 = 400$ miles (so mileage should be measured in units of ton-miles per gallon).

A bus might get only 6 miles per gallon, but again this isn't the relevant figure. The bus might carry 50 people, so it can move each person $50 \times 6 = 300$ miles with a gallon of fuel (so measure mileage in person-miles per gallon).

Six people riding in a van that gets 15 miles per gallon have a fuel economy of 90 people-miles per gallon, so the manufacturer should not be penalized for producing the van—in this case it is more fuel efficient than one person riding in a car that gets 35 miles per gallon. It is true that one person riding in the van alone isn't very fuel efficient, but the corporate average fuel economy standards don't provide any helpful incentives in this case.

To the extent that the government corporate average fuel economy standards do recognize that vehicles are different, they have a perverse effect by encouraging people to buy vehicles that are classified as trucks. Clearly a truck is necessary when you need to haul things, but the government shouldn't encourage the production of trucks for people to use just for normal driving around.

Congress might think it can keep improving fuel efficiency by continually raising this standard, but they will eventually learn the lesson of King Canute about trying to command the tides: the laws of physics will not obey the laws of government.[5]

The best policy to encourage less gasoline use is a tax on gasoline use. This tax provides an incentive to make cars with better gas mileage, but it also provides an incentive for people to find ways to drive less or carpool more–which may be better ways to save gas in some situations.[6]

Although there may not be uncertainty about the scientific reality of the atmospheric greenhouse effect of carbon emissions, there is considerable uncertainty about the magnitude of the effect. The best policy to deal with the situation would be a tax on carbon emissions, which would need to be set at a rate that balances both the benefit and cost of emission reductions. Alternative energy sources all have limitations, so reducing carbon emissions will come at a cost that should not be ignored when policy is determined. Unfortunately actual policy relies more on narrow-interest-driven mandates and subsidies that benefit certain individuals rather than providing incentives focused on efficiently reducing emissions.

AGRICULTURAL POLICY

Farmers live with tremendous risks—the risk of bad weather devastating the harvest, or, paradoxically, the risk that too large of a harvest leads to prices that are too low. Ideally, farm policy would be aimed at easing the risk faced by farmers. Instead, actual U.S. farm policy since the 1930s tries to decrease supply or increase demand to try to keep prices high. The main effect of these programs is that a few people benefit a lot, and a lot of people are hurt a little.[7]

As you might expect, higher prices are good for the sellers (farmers) and bad for the buyers (everyone who eats). However, only some farmers are helped. Why growers of some crops should benefit and others should not is hard to figure out.[8]

One unintended consequence is higher land values. If Rosencrantz owned a farm before subsidies began, he will see the value of his farm increase when the subsidy is established. He can now retire and sell the farm for a high price to Guildenstern. Most of the benefit of the program goes to the retired farmer (Rosencrantz). The current farmer (Guildenstern) needs the subsidies to keep the prices high enough so he can pay for the loan needed to buy the expensive farm, so he would be severely hurt if the subsidy suddenly ended even though he doesn't really benefit from the subsidy.

Some aspects of farm policy are rather bizarre, such as paying non-farmers not to grow crops,[9] or requiring farmers to pay grandchildren of former farmers for licenses to grow their crops.

Sometimes the government lets the crop it buys rot. If it sold it, or gave it away, it would have the effect of lowering the price, which would be beneficial for the public but which would cancel out the effect of buying the crop in the first place.

The best way for the government to help farmers would be to focus on the main risk that an individual farmer faces: the risk of crop failure, with a tax credit for the purchase of crop failure insurance.

ETHANOL

Should we use corn to produce ethanol to blend with gasoline in motor fuel? Compare the cost of petroleum gasoline (including purchasing, transporting, and refining crude oil) with the cost of ethanol (including the cost of inputs needed to grow corn, break the corn starch down to sugar, and ferment the sugar to ethanol). The cost calculations cast doubt on the economic value of using ethanol as a fuel, but the reason ethanol is used in the U.S. is because of government subsidies and mandates.

Harmful side effects of U.S. ethanol policy include higher food prices, and other types of environmental damage such as deforestation, river pollution, and voracious water consumption.[10]

Compounding the resource misdirection problem is U.S. tariff policy. Ethanol can be produced more cheaply from sugar than from corn, and Brazil is willing to sell sugar-produced ethanol to the U.S., but for many years was prevented by a 56-cents-per-gallon tariff.[11]

An odd example is the requirement that a minimum amount of ethanol must be derived from cellulose. It would be great if energy could be derived from cellulose plant fiber, because the energy could be produced from grass and old woodchips and other non-edible crops. However, it is hard to break down the long chains of glucose in cellulose, which is why people can't digest grass and other cellulose plant fibers. (Starch in food products such as corn can be broken down more easily, but growing corn requires more resources.) Breaking down cellulose can be done (for example, cows can digest grass). There are ways to create fuel out of cellulose, but so far none of them have proven to be economical for large quantities of production. So the mandate requires that companies buy a product that doesn't exist. The logic of this policy is the same as if the government decided that the way to reduce the fuel used in airplanes was to require that 10 percent of all air passengers must fly by flapping their arms very hard, and then airlines were fined if the desperately flapping passengers were unable to get off the ground.[12]

TRADE RESTRICTIONS: TARIFFS AND QUOTAS

In 1845 Frederic Bastiat submitted a petition to the French government on behalf of the candlemakers[13]:

We are subjected to the intolerable competition of
a foreign rival who enjoys such superior facilities
for the production of light that he is enabled to
inundate our national market at so exceedingly
reduced a price that the moment he makes his appearance
he draws off all custom from us. This rival
is no other than the sun.

Our petition is to pass a law whereby shall be directed
the shutting up of all windows, dormers, skylights,
shutters, curtains, openings, holes, chinks, and fissures
through which the light of the sun penetrates into our
dwellings. Our country cannot leave us to struggle
unprotected through so unequal a contest.

If the government had adopted this petition it would have helped the candlemakers, since people would buy more candles to have light in their opaque houses. It is no mystery why it benefits some people (the candlemakers) if you put restrictions on their competitors (the sun).[14]

Bastiat's petition seems a rather drastic way to help the industry. You can probably tell it is in fact a satire, but for the moment pretend it is meant to be taken literally. It is easy to make the case for protectionist trade restrictions when you are talking to those that will benefit (the candlemakers), but it is much harder to defend the policy when you are talking to those that would be hurt by the trade restriction policy (everyone else). It's not acceptable for advocates to say that they just hope that the people hurt by the trade restrictions won't notice that they're being hurt. People hurt by tariffs should not be valued less just because they are less visible than the people that are helped by the tariffs.

Here's one example. U.S. policy toward cotton leads to higher prices for cotton in the U.S. because of subsidies. The U.S. produces more cotton then is demanded at that price, so the rest is exported (dumped) at lower prices to the rest of the world. (You can't just buy cotton from the rest of the world and bring it back to the U.S. because of import quotas.) Lowering the prices of cotton in the world market hurts cotton farmers in other countries.

Brazilian cotton farmers protested these policies, so in 2002 they turned to the World Trade Organization (WTO), which provides a forum to resolve trade policy disputes between nations. Countries that have joined the WTO agree not to do certain types of restrictive policies, which is equivalent to agreeing to a treaty with other nations. Brazil and the U.S. argued over the case, and the WTO dispute reconciliation process lead to a decision that the U.S. should stop subsidizing cotton. The U.S. government was reluctant to comply. The WTO doesn't have any direct way to enforce one of its rulings against a sovereign nation, but it has one possible course of action; it authorized Brazil to retaliate against the U.S. by imposing restrictions on imports of U.S. products to Brazil, and to freely copy items protected by U.S. intellectual property. Normally a WTO member will have agreed not to do these things, but the WTO specifically allows a country to do these policies if it authorizes the country to retaliate against another country that is itself violating its WTO agreement.

If you're a U.S. industry that is about to have its exports to Brazil restricted, or its intellectual property freely copied in Brazil, you will understandably be upset—and when you learn that the reason for your distress is so that the U.S. can continue to keep the price of the clothes you buy higher so the cotton farmers will be subsidized, you will become irate. The government becomes caught between the pressure from the cotton growers to continue their subsidies, and the pressure from the other industries that don't want to be hurt. So, in 2010, the U.S. government reached an agreement with Brazil in which the U.S. would subsidize Brazilian cotton growers, and in return Brazil dropped its plans to impose the restrictions on the U.S. products.[15] U.S. taxpayers might wonder why they are now subsidizing Brazilian cotton growers (not that people in the U.S. should have anything against Brazilian cotton growers, but they still might question why that one particular group out of all the people in the world should receive a special subsidy from U.S. taxpayers).

THE GENERAL INTEREST AND NARROW INTERESTS

These examples of questionable policies typically arise because a relatively narrow group is able to prevail upon the government to establish a policy providing a large benefit for the small group and a small cost for members of the large group (everyone else). In chapters 13 and 14 we'll look at ways to make it harder for narrow interests to prevail upon the government to enact narrow-benefit policies.

NOTES

1. Taxis are a special case, because shopping around for taxi services is particularly inefficient (they lack shop-around-ability). It's best for taxis to be part of a central dispatch system, and for them to all charge the same rates.

2. *Knox* v. *Lee* and *Parker* v. *Davis*, decided in 1871, supported the issuance of paper money (greenbacks) during the Civil War, reversing the decision in *Hepburn* v. *Griswold* from the year before (see page 107).

3. They would still need to decide if "everyone" meant every driver? every adult? every person? every car?

4. See page 97 and the online appendix myhome.spu.edu/ddowning/fos.html.

5. See page 100 for another example of Congress mandating something regardless of whether it is physically possible.

6. What rate the gasoline tax should be is a matter of opinion with no clear right answer.

7. In 1996 Congress cut back some of these programs, but in 2002 they were returned to the way they have been since the 1930s.

8. Bovard, p321.

9. Non-farmer columnist Nicholas Kristof receives some of these payments, which he admits is inane (newspaper column August 5, 2007).

10. Biello, 2011.

11. The tariff expired at the end of 2011. See Harmonized Tariff Schedules of the U.S. on internet.

12. In 2013 a Federal Appeals court struck down the cellulose ethanol mandate (*American Petroleum Institute* v. *Environmental Protection Agency*).

13. Bastiat, *Economic Sophisms*, p56–57.

14. Bastiat was writing before the invention of the electric light bulb, which provided even more competition for the candlemakers.

15. *Wall Street Journal* online, April 25, 2011; Rivoli, *The Travels of a T-Shirt in the Global Economy*, 2nd ed., 2015, p263.

Chapter 8

History of Financial Crises

There was, alas, no past golden age where people could sleep serenely with no worries that their financial savings were secure.

THE WAR OVER THE AMOUNT OF MONEY

The Bimetallic Standard

When the U.S. government was first established, the dollar was defined by setting a price for gold and a price for silver. You could bring gold or silver to the mint and have it made into coins at the specified rate (this process was called free coinage). These were full-value coins, meaning that you could melt down a coin and the market value of the resulting metal matched the face value of the coin. The coins today are token coins, where the value of the metal is less than the face value.

By fixing the price of both gold and silver, the U.S. was on the bimetallic standard. However, in practice the supply and demand would shift, and the price of one of the metals would rise above the official price. In that case, people would have an incentive to melt down all of the coins of that metal and sell the metal for its market value. That would cause coins of that metal to disappear from circulation.[1] The result was that in practice the bimetallic standard acted as a single metal standard. In the early decades, this was effectively a silver standard. In 1834, Congress increased the official price of gold, which reversed the gold/silver attractiveness, causing people to bring gold to the mint for coinage. The silver coins disappeared from circulation, putting the U.S. on what was effectively the gold standard even as it officially remained on the bimetallic standard.[2]

The Bank of the United States 1 and 2

Throughout the 1800s, U.S. economic policymakers engaged in fierce money wars—the debate over how much money there should be. On one side was the hard money side, who were concerned that the money maintain stable value, meaning it could not be in too great of supply. The hard money side was strongest in the northeast. The easy money side was concerned that there was enough money so that credit would be readily available. The easy money side was strongest along the wild western frontier (places such as Kentucky), where farmers were clearing land and establishing new farms.

In this debate, neither side was "right" while the other was "wrong." In reality there are serious problems if there is too much money or if there is too little money, so a balance is needed.

The first controversy in the money war was the debate over the Bank of the United States. The U.S. government did not issue any paper money before the Civil War, partly because of bad memories of the paper money issued by the Continental Congress during the American Revolution. Although these notes plummeted in value, they were successful for their purpose of financing the revolution.

The only paper money in the U.S. in the early 1800s was issued by state-chartered banks, which would accept gold or silver coin in exchange for the notes they printed. People were willing to take these notes because they were more convenient to carry around than gold, and they trusted that the bank would redeem the notes for gold whenever someone asked it to. Other people were willing to take the notes as payment for goods or services because they trusted that still other people would take the notes, and they also trusted the banks to redeem the notes for gold on demand. The banks then printed more notes to make loans. This is called fractional reserve banking, which banks still follow today (except they take deposits rather than print notes).

The hard money side wanted tighter restrictions on the issuance of bank notes, which the Bank of the United States provided by demanding payment in coin from a state chartered bank whenever it received a note printed by that bank. The easy money side was against the Bank of the United States, partly because of its control on the money supply and partly because it also acted as a competitor for the other banks.

The original Bank of the United States had a twenty-year charter, from 1791 to 1811. Congress did not renew the charter, but then in 1816 it created the Second Bank of the United States, also with a twenty-year charter. When Congress voted to renew this charter in 1836, the bill was vetoed by President Andrew Jackson (the first president from the western frontier). The result was that there were plenty of bank notes issued in the two decades before the Civil War, which is what the easy money side wanted. However, the fact that there were thousands of different bank notes made it difficult to conduct business.

Wartime Greenbacks and Post-war Deflation

All that changed during the Civil War. The hard money side controlled Congress, which passed the National Banking Act. This act taxed state-chartered bank notes out of existence. The act also established nationally chartered banks, which could issue notes but they were tightly controlled. However, the need for money during the Civil War lead to Congress issuing the first U.S. government paper money notes, called the greenbacks after their color (and starting a U.S. tradition of green paper money). Not surprisingly, extensive issuance of paper money lead to inflation (which is often the result of wars). Following the war the hard money side supported deflation to bring the price level down so that the greenbacks could be redeemed for gold at their original value. Deflation is particularly hard on debtors, so the post-war deflation was very controversial.[3]

The Free Silver Movement

Another front in the money war opened after 1873, when Congress ended the free coinage of silver and put the U.S. officially on the gold standard. (The U.S. had been on an official bimetallic standard, but in practice a gold standard, since 1834.) Since nobody was bringing silver to the mint to be coined, nobody objected. It would be as if the government said, "we're no longer going to let you bring in 11 dimes in return for a one dollar bill." Nobody cared if they were no longer allowed to do something they didn't want to do anyway.

After 1873, increasing silver mining in Nevada and elsewhere tended to push down the price of silver, to the point where the price of silver fell below what had been the official price. If the bimetallic standard had still been in place, then silver would have been brought to the mint, the gold coins would have been melted down, and the officially-bimetallic-but-in-practice-gold-standard would have shifted to an officially-bimetallic-but-in-practice-silver-standard. Since the amount of silver mined was enough to expand the money supply, the easy money side fought hard for the return of free coinage of silver. The movement became known as the free silver movement, and its best remembered speech is the "Cross of Gold" speech by presidential nominee William Jennings Bryan in 1896.

The free silver movement never was able to reestablish the free coinage of silver, but Congress did pass some compromise measures to purchase some silver with paper money (silver certificates). After the Alaska gold rush began in 1896 this issue became less important as the inflow of gold caused an expansion of the money supply even under the gold standard.

It turns out that the U.S. was officially on a gold standard for exactly 100 years: from 1873 to 1973.

THE ERA OF BANK PANICS

The balance sheet of a bank shows its assets and liabilities. Here is an example:

ASSETS		LIABILITIES	
reserves	$100	deposits	$950
loans	$900	Total	$950
Total	$1,000	OWNER'S EQUITY (CAPITAL)	
		Total	$50

A bank's liabilities (deposits) can be redeemed on demand, but its assets are largely in the form of loans with long repayment periods (such as 30-year home loans). It runs the risk that someday so many people show up to withdraw their money that the bank does not have enough liquid assets on hand. If word gets out that the bank might not be able to pay back its depositors or note holders, then people realize they had better rush to the bank to get their money back before the others beat them to it. That creates a run on the bank. If runs occur at many banks it is called a panic. Panics were a fairly regular occurrence in the U.S. for many decades: panics took place in 1819, 1837, 1857, 1873, 1884, 1893, 1907, 1921, and 1929.[4] If banks cause so many problems, why do we put up with them?

WHY LEND TO BANKS?

If we are able to earn more than we spend, we can accumulate savings. That brings up the question: what to do with the savings?

Life is risky, and no option is 100 percent secure. However, some options are more secure than others. Physical storage has its risks. If you hold gold or dollar bills in a vault or under a mattress, there is the risk of theft or destruction. Most people prefer to hold savings with the financial system, but there are other risks there.

Shakespeare's Polonius advised "neither a borrower nor a lender be,"[5] but for most people that is not great advice. Polonius does have a point about the risk, though. Entrusting someone else with your savings inevitably makes you a lender, and there is a risk of not being paid back. Two options for savers/lenders are (1) direct lending and (2) lending to an intermediary. Direct lending means finding someone who needs to borrow the money. Intermediary lending means going to a bank, and the bank will lend the money to someone else. For a variety of reasons, there are advantages to lending to the bank:

1. Information: if you will lend directly, you will have to find the borrower. It is much easier to find the bank (although modern information technology does make it easier to find people).
2. Diversification: if you lend directly, and your borrower is hit by a bus or suffers some other catastrophe preventing repayment of your loan, then you are out of luck. A bank will pool the funds of a large number of depositors and then lend them to a large number of borrowers. This spreads the risk, since the chance of all of the borrowers suffering catastrophe is usually much less than the chance for an individual borrower. (However, the exceptions to this are crucial; see page 120.)
3. Loan amount intermediation: if the borrower does not happen to need the exact amount you have available to lend, it becomes much more difficult to do direct lending. The bank will accept your deposit for whatever amount, and then make whatever loan amounts are needed. If you want to deposit a $4,000 paycheck, but all the potential borrowers want to borrow $300,000 to buy a house, you'll have a hard time arranging a direct loan to one of them.
4. Maturity intermediation: when borrowers buy houses, they probably want a repayment schedule with equal monthly payments spread out over a long time (such as 30 years). You might not want to receive your repayment this way; in fact, you might want to have access to your savings at any time. The bank can take short-term deposits and make long-term loans, which benefits both borrower and lender (but it creates significant risk for the bank).
5. Expertise: if you don't happen to have experience in evaluating credit and writing loan contracts, you will find it complicated to become a direct lender. Since the bank makes its living doing precisely those activities, they will be very experienced at them.
6. Insurance: the above reasons indicate why lending to a bank is safer than lending directly, but even so bank deposits are not safe if the bank fails. Since 1935 the U.S. government has insured bank deposits, which almost completely eliminates the risk to bank depositors. (However, deposit insurance creates other problems; see page 113.)

Banks can't make a living by providing these services for free, so the price you have to pay for doing business with a bank is taking lower interest rates on your deposits than the borrowers have to pay on their loans. Some lenders and borrowers avoid dealing with intermediaries, as when a company sells bonds. However, for most ordinary individuals it is hard to avoid dealing with banks.

THE GREAT DEPRESSION

After the 1907 panic, the government sets up a commission to try to develop a solution to the bank run problem.

A bank that is short of funds for the day's withdrawals has a liquidity problem. The reason for the liquidity risk is that the bank promises that people can obtain their checking account funds whenever they want, but the bank doesn't keep this money in its vault (or electronic equivalent)—instead, the money is lent out. As Jimmy Stewart's character says in *It's a Wonderful Life*, "your money's not here—it's in Joe's house. . . ."[6]

How can we solve the liquidity problem? Some of the bank's assets are fairly liquid—securities that can be sold—so in a liquidity crunch the bank can sell some of these. If it needs more funds it can borrow from other banks. There is a well-organized market for banks to borrow short-term from other banks on an overnight basis. Their third option is to borrow from the central bank (the Federal Reserve, which acts as the lender of last resort).[7] In this case all the bank needs is access to temporary funds to keep paying the depositors.

Tragically, the Federal Reserve failed its first major test, when it let the money supply collapse in the early stages following the stock market crash of 1929.[8]

The Great Depression was a calamity of severe magnitude: unemployment peaked over 25 percent, and high unemployment lasted for a decade.

Looking back, two major policy mistakes seem clear. The Federal Reserve let the money supply collapse. Society can have a big problem if there is too much money (causing inflation), but it can also have a big problem if there is too little money (causing deflation). The great depression was a crisis of deflation, which hammered borrowers who saw the real value of their debts increase to unpayable levels. Depositors lost millions when banks failed, and many people became unable to pay bills. A vicious multiplier effect ensued: the grocer who can't be paid is then unable to pay the farmer; the debt-oppressed farmer is unable to pay suppliers, and more and more people lose their jobs.

The Federal Reserve seemed to be determined not to follow the path of Germany (which printed tons of money in the 1920s to pay World War I reparations, and thereby triggered massive hyperinflation causing the price level to increase literally a trillion times). Although it would make sense to avoid sleeping next to a fire on a burning hot summer night, it doesn't make sense to let your memories of summer heat lead you to sleep outside on a snow-covered winter night. The Federal Reserve successfully avoided any inflation by helping plunge the economy into a crisis of deflation. The Fed seemed to think that less money would be needed as the economy collapsed, when providing more money would have helped ease some of the ravages of the deflation.

Another policy mistake was an increase in tariffs (the Smoot-Hawley bill).[9]

KEYNES

Our understanding of the economy has improved since the 1930s. A major contributor was John Maynard Keynes, whose 1936 book *A General Theory of Employment, Interest, and Money* described how an economy could flounder because of not enough spending, or demand.[10] Keynes viewed his theory as being more general than previous "classical" economic theories that assumed full employment because his theory allowed for an economy to be in a slump caused by lack of spending.

Keynes correctly points out the importance of investment opportunities. A society building cathedrals might benefit from an additional cathedral, but a society that already has a railroad from point A to point B might not benefit from a second railroad along the same route. As Keynes would have expected, a serious economic downturn is typically related to a decline in investment. As a new technology is introduced, often numerous investment opportunities will arise. However, after time passes, many of these new investment projects will have been completed, and there might be fewer new investment projects available. Then after some time another new technology opens a whole new wave of investment opportunities. The result is that investment inevitably has ups and downs.

Unemployment evaporated with the military buildup for World War II, indicating that when there was enough spending there were enough jobs (including enough jobs for a much larger labor force as adult women took jobs in factories). Nobody seeking a job had trouble finding one during the war. Keynes' analysis of the importance of aggregate demand is supported by the experience of my mother, who was a college student during World War II. At this time there was a huge amount of spending on the war, and employers were avidly seeking workers to fill jobs—the exact opposite of the situation as she was growing up during the depression of the 1930s. Her summer job was running elevators in downtown Seattle, for which she was paid 50 cents per hour.[11]

In general, big wars provide a cure for unemployment. That doesn't mean wars are good—it just means that unemployment usually is not one of the problems faced by a nation when many of its citizens are in the armed forces during a big war.

THE ECONOMY BECOMES MORE COMPLICATED:
KEYNESIAN DEMAND-SIDE POLICY IS NOT ENOUGH

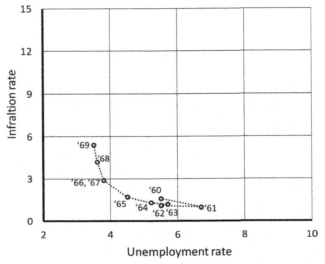

Figure 8.1 The Relation between Inflation and Unemployment in the 1960s (The Phillips Curve). *Source*: Figure based on data obtained from the Federal Reserve Bank of St. Louis

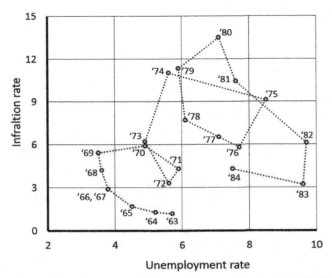

Figure 8.2 The Relation between Inflation and Unemployment From 1964 to 1984 (Spirals). *Source*: Figure based on data obtained from the Federal Reserve Bank of St. Louis

In the 1960s, many economists were cautiously optimistic that economic fluctuations could be moderated if the government stabilized demand (spending).[12] Too much spending would mean inflation and too little spending would mean unemployment, and there would be a trade-off between these two along a curve known as the Phillips curve (see Figures 8.1 and 8.2) However, this Keynesian view of the economy broke down in the 1970s. It turned out that Keynes' general theory was not general enough. Under certain circumstances an economy could suffer from both inflation and unemployment at the same time. A demand-side theory could not account for that. Those who have forgotten the miserable economic history of the 1970s sometimes promulgate a myth that the financial system worked well at that time.[13]

In the early 1980s, the debate in macroeconomics was about how to bring down double-digit inflation. One view (known as the rational expectations view) was that a credible and resolute disinflationary monetary policy could lower inflation quickly and easily.[14] By contrast, some Keynesians expected it would take years and years of high unemployment to beat down inflation momentum.[15] In this case the policy experiment was carried out by the Federal Reserve under Paul Volcker beginning in 1979. The truth was somewhere in between the two views: the inflation did decrease from double digits in 1980 to the 4 percent range by 1982, within two years, but the cost was a severe recession with unemployment exceeding 10 percent.

After the inflation was subdued by the early 1980s, it remained reasonably low (4 percent or less) for the next three decades. Unemployment remained below 8 percent for a quarter century (from 1983 to 2008), so there was a sustained period of relative macroeconomic stability. But there were other problems.

DEPOSIT INSURANCE

As discussed on page 110, a lender of last resort can solve the bank-run-liquidity problem. For all the better assurance, we can further reduce the risk of runs by reassuring people that they don't need to run to the bank. If they know that their funds are safe, there's no point in trying to beat the other people to the teller's window.

Deposit insurance, created in 1935, has been very successful at achieving its objective: ending bank runs. However, there is a much worse problem a bank might find itself in: what if its borrowers can't pay their loans back? Any bank knows that a small number of its borrowers won't be able to pay back their loans, but if loan defaults become so widespread that the bank's continuing existence is in danger it has an insolvency problem.

In the absence of insurance, depositors would tend to want to avoid banks that made excessively risky loans (although it would be difficult for depositors to have the information needed to make good judgments about bank riskiness). When deposits are insured, the depositors have no incentive to care whether the bank makes risky loans. The moral hazard problem reappears (see page 55).

The bad-loan problem is harder to solve, as the savings and loan crisis demonstrated.

The Effect of Inflation on Borrowing and Lending

Savings and loan associations (S&Ls) do the same basic things banks do: they take money from depositors and lend it to borrowers. Unlike banks, traditional S&Ls made only one type of loan: home mortgages. Life was simple for S&Ls in the 1950s and early 1960s. Follow the 3-6-3 rule: pay depositors 3 percent, collect 6 percent on home loans, and close the office and hit the golf course at 3 pm. This peaceful time was not to last.

The roots of the mortgage crisis go back to the inflation of the late 1960s, which began with government spending and monetary expansion during the Vietnam War.

As inflation increased, interest rates were pushed up (see online appendix myhome.spu.edu/ddowning/fos.html). However, if interest rates increase so that depositors now expect 9 percent, the S&Ls lose money with a negative interest rate spread. They still collect 6 percent on the loans made in earlier more peaceful times. They could charge higher rates to new borrowers but it takes time for all of those 30 year, 6 percent loans to be paid back. They were not allowed to pay more than 5 percent to depositors in the 1970s because of a depression-era limit on deposit rates.

The rise in inflation in the late 1960s was unexpected. Unexpected inflation helps borrowers and hurts lenders. Rising interest rates hammer long-term fixed-rate lenders, such as the S&Ls. Falling interest rates would have the opposite effect: hurt the borrowers and help the lenders, except home mortgage borrowers have one option: they can refinance the loan. There are costs involved with refinancing, so it's not worth it for the borrowers to refinance for a trivial fall in rates. However, the option to refinance does protect the borrowers from the effect of a significant fall in interest rates.

Lenders, not surprisingly, are disturbed by the asymmetry of fixed rate loans: the borrowers have protection from falling rates, but the lenders have no protection from rising rates. So, during the 1970s, adjustable rate loans became more common. In an adjustable rate loan, the loan rate changes periodically (typically once per year). The change needs to be specified by a rule (obviously the borrowers could not agree to a contract that let the lenders change the rate to whatever level they felt like in the middle of the loan period). The rule typically states that the mortgage loan rate will adjust to being a fixed percentage above a standard rate such as the rate on U.S. treasury debt.

Since the adjustable rate loan provides more protection for the lender than it does for the borrower, the borrower is unlikely to agree to this type of loan unless they are given some sweetener, such as a low interest rate. This means that typical adjustable rate loans will have starting rates lower than for fixed rate loans.

1980: Deregulation of Deposit Interest Rates

The 1980 Depository Institutions Deregulation and Monetary Control Act (DIDMCA, signed by President Carter) allowed banks to pay interest on checking deposits, and phased out the interest ceilings on other types of deposits.[16] By this time removing the ceilings became inevitable. There were several ways to evade the deposit rate ceilings, once interest rates became high enough that banks had strong incentives to do so. Banks that could not pay interest to depositors could give them gifts, such as toasters or lower loan rates. Or they could have a customer open a zero-interest checking account and an interest-bearing savings account, and let them transfer funds from savings to checking by phone. That was almost as good as an interest bearing checking account; and if the bank decided to spare the customer the need to make the phone call by automatically transferring funds from savings to checking whenever the customer wrote a check, the result was just as good as an interest bearing checking account. Or a bank could let a customer open a higher-yield time deposit, but then decide to be nice and not charge the normal early withdrawal fee if the person wanted the money back early. Another more brazen option was to issue savings accounts with withdrawal slips that could be handed to someone else (called negotiable order of withdrawal, or now account). A NOW account withdrawal slip looked and acted just like a "you-know-what"; just don't call it a check.

It was naive to think the ceilings would help the S&Ls by letting them get away with paying their depositors such a low amount. Depositors found other alternatives, so the risk to S&Ls if the ceilings had been kept in place would be that they would not have depositors at all. Depositors could avoid banks altogether by investing in money market mutual funds, which held liquid short-term low-risk securities that were not insured but were safe enough.

The DIDMCA law also required all depository institutions (S&Ls as well as banks) to meet the Federal Reserve's reserve requirements. The Federal Reserve required member banks to keep a certain percent of their deposits with the Fed (or in vault cash; the exact percentage depended on the size of the bank). The Fed did not pay interest on these deposits (until 2008); so holding the reserves became a serious drag on bank profitability when interest rates were high. Banks discovered that they could avoid this requirement by leaving membership in the Fed. The Fed could have chosen the carrot approach (pay interest on reserve deposits to encourage banks to stay), but instead with the 1980 law Congress chose the stick approach (require that banks keep reserve deposits with the Fed whether or not they are Fed members).

S&Ls Turn to the Wild Side

In the pre-1935 era, failing deposit institutions would have been a major problem for the depositors. In the current era, that risk gets shifted to the taxpayers who ultimately are responsible for the deposit insurance fund.

S&Ls were allowed to diversify their loan portfolio after 1982. They were hoping that income from new loans would grow enough to cover their losses.[17]

Through a combination of (1) a lack of expertise in commercial lending among the S&Ls; (2) a lack of expertise in commercial lending in their regulatory agency, the Federal Home Loan Bank Board (FHLBB, which acquired the unfortunate pronunciation of "flub"); and their deposit insurance agency, the Federal Savings and Loan Insurance Corporation (FSLIC); (3) plummeting oil prices in 1985 that hurt oil-producing regions of the U.S. and caused loans to go bad, particularly in Texas (this is ironic, considering that the seeds for the crisis were planted by the inflation of the 1970s, and the seeds for the inflation were partly planted by *rising* oil prices); (4) political and regulatory desire to avoid recognizing the loan losses, delaying the problem in hopes that the problem could be passed on to successors, while letting the problem get worse in the meantime.

The S&L owners hope to make a profit off the difference between the amount they collect on loans and the amount they pay depositors (also, they have to pay their operating expenses). If they do make a profit, their equity in the business goes up (although they may withdraw some as dividends). If the business loses money, the owners' equity in the business goes down.

S&L loans started going bad.

Here is an example of what the S&L balance sheet looks like initially:

ASSETS		LIABILITIES	
reserves	$100	deposits	$950
loans	$900	Total	$950
Total	$1,000	OWNER'S EQUITY (CAPITAL)	
		Total	$50

Now here's the balance sheet after they discover that $30 worth of loans cannot be repaid. The balance sheet has to stay balanced (by definition, since assets equal liabilities plus equity). Since depositors won't stand for the value of their deposits being reduced, the owner's equity must be reduced[18]:

ASSETS		LIABILITIES	
reserves	$100	deposits	$950
loans	$870	Total	$950
Total	$970	OWNER'S EQUITY (CAPITAL)	
		Total	$20

As long as the owners have some of their own money at risk, they're not likely to be too wild about taking risks. However, suppose there are $20 more in bad loans which need to be written off, so the assets decline to the point where assets = liabilities, and net worth is zero.

ASSETS		LIABILITIES	
reserves	$100	deposits	$950
loans	$850	Total	$950
Total	$950	OWNER'S EQUITY (CAPITAL)	
		Total	$0

The owners won't be pleased if their equity goes negative, but they aren't at risk of losing more than their initial investment. They can lose every penny of their original investment, but not a penny more. The creditors of the corporation can't go after the personal assets of the shareholders to settle the corporate debt.

At the moment that the S&L equity becomes zero, the owner might think of two possibilities:

1. Play it safe; don't issue more risky loans. There's little hope of a big recovery but there's nothing more to lose if equity becomes even more negative.
2. Take wild risks; make risky loans; providing hope for a big recovery, and there's nothing more to lose if equity becomes even more negative.

The company has no reason to avoid option 2 with its wild risks. The owners have already lost everything.[19] By analogy, if a football team is narrowly behind in the final minute of the fourth quarter, it will risk trying for a first down on fourth and long. Because it has nothing to lose, it will take wild risks that it normally would not consider.

This is where the taxpayers can start to worry. Another $100 of bad loans is written off, and the owner's equity is now negative 100.

ASSETS		LIABILITIES	
reserves	$100	deposits	$950
loans	$750	Total	$950
Total	$850	OWNER'S EQUITY (CAPITAL)	
		Total	$-100

The value of the assets can't cover the value of the deposits. Since the depositors are insured, the deposit insurance agency (read: government (read: taxpayers)) pick up the tab.

You may think you don't care if business owners make a profit. However, these business owners may have borrowed money from banks, and you may have deposited money in those banks. In that case you do have an interest in whether or not the business can repay its loans. You might naively think that deposit insurance protects your deposit even if the business can't repay its loans. Although this is true, there is a problem if everyone has this attitude and they favor policies that prevent businesses from succeeding. If a large number of businesses fail, the deposit insurance fund will not be able to cover the losses and the only way for depositors to get their money back would be if taxpayers (that is, everybody) picks up the cost.

In 1989, Congress passed the S&L bailout bill, appropriating about 200 billion dollars to protect the depositors of the failed institutions. Many of the loans were collateralized by office buildings and shopping malls, so the government took control of these and gradually sold them off, earning back some of the cost of the bailout. By 1996 the market was peaceful again, and would stay that way for another decade while the seeds of the great mortgage crisis were slowly being sown.

THE MORTGAGE CRISIS

At the core of the problem: lenders made loans that weren't paid back. Why would they do that?

One possible explanation: greed. Greed did play a role as mortgage lenders become speculators. Their profits depended on winning their bet that housing prices would continue their ascent. By making more loans they did more business and therefore made more money. However, lenders don't make money from loans that aren't paid back, so the correct explanation has to be more complicated than simple greed. Somehow there was a flaw in the system that meant the lenders didn't need to care about whether the loans will be paid back.

There is another reason why it is implausible that greed itself is the cause of the crisis. It is quite plausible that business people have always been greedy, but it is not very plausible that they suddenly became much more greedier in 2006 than they used to be.

The Spring-Trap Loans

The lenders and borrowers expected that borrowers would be able to pay back the loan. The problem loans started with a low monthly payment. In some cases, the payment was so low that the monthly payment wasn't even enough to cover the interest so the remaining principal that the borrower owed was increasing each month (instead of decreasing as it should be). Obviously the lenders could not stay in business if this situation continued very long, so the problem loans were adjustable loans where not only the interest rate but the monthly payment jumped (sometimes drastically) two or three years after the loan origination. The trap was sprung.

Part of the problem seems to be that there were some unsophisticated borrowers that truly did not understand the nature of these spring-trap loans with their skyrocketing future payment amount. However, some borrowers did understand the issue and they had a plan for how the loan could be repaid: by being refinanced. Here's an example of how this might have worked.

A borrower buys a $300,000 house. Traditionally the borrower would have been expected to pay a significant down payment, but imagine that this borrower in the middle of the housing craze about 2005 was able to get this loan with no down payment. A couple of years later, the monthly payments are scheduled to zoom up. However, if things had gone according to the original plan, the market value of the house would have been steadily escalating. Suppose it is now $400,000. Also suppose that the monthly payments for the first two years had been just enough to cover the interest, but no principal, so the borrower still owes $300,000. Here's the key difference: when the borrowers originally had a $300,000 loan for a $300,000 house, they had no equity in the house. Now they still have a $300,000 loan but they have a $400,000 house, so they have equity of $100,000, or 25 percent of the house value. With a much larger equity share in the house now, the borrowers can get a better rate when they refinance because the lender has better protection against default.

At least that was the original plan. In order for this to work, it is glaringly obvious that the market value of the home must always keep rising.[20] For a few years prior to 2005 it seemed home prices would always rise. (Measuring average home price values is complicated because each house is different; the Case-Shiller index is commonly used.[21]) In a given city there is only a certain amount of land available for housing, so a rising population does put upward pressure on prices. It would not be uncommon for people in the late 1990s and early 2000s to be extremely worried about the lack of affordable housing. One may have wondered, "how can so many people afford to pay these absurdly high housing prices?" The fact that it was so easy to get loans is a major part of the answer, but even that could not keep housing prices rising indefinitely. When the price of an asset keeps rising, and people come to expect it to continue rising, and those expectations cause more people to try to buy it, pushing the price up even further—it's called a bubble. Like a child blowing a soap bubble, it can keep expanding and expanding . . . until it reaches the moment it pops.

Economics is about trade-offs, so it is the nature of economics that sometimes when one problem gets worse another problem gets better. In this case the collapse of housing prices which lead to the financial crisis did help alleviate the housing affordability crisis.

Securitization

There's more to the story. Lenders were gradually realizing that they didn't need to care about whether their borrowers could repay their loans because of a new phenomenon: securitization.

Consider a traditional small mortgage lender that makes home loans to people in its own community (think of Jimmy Stewart's character in *It's a Wonderful Life*). The bank's risk is reduced by diversification (see page 109): since it makes loans to many people, the chances of them all defaulting on their loans is relatively small. However, that protection breaks down if one event effects all the borrowers. For example, if a natural disaster destroys all the homes in the town, or a collapse of the local economy causes everyone in town to lose their jobs, then the lender is sunk. Diversification across many households in town won't help if the whole town is in trouble.

So, one way to help reduce the risk is to hold a portfolio of loans across many towns widely separated geographically. Our small-town bank can't conveniently do this, but if its loans are combined with loans from other areas, they can be sold to investors who would like to hold a geographically diversified loan portfolio. Therefore, mortgage-backed securities were created, and they turned out to be very profitable for Wall Street investment bankers.[22]

Another advantage for the mortgage backed security came from the fact that the local bank could now potentially raise more funds for lending. Instead of being limited by the funds available from local depositors, the bank can now raise funds by selling its mortgages.

The process of turning loans into securities is called securitization. However, there are disadvantages with securitization. These became painfully obvious as the crisis hit, and they should have been clear a little earlier.

Since the borrowers are not paying the loans back to the original lenders, the original lenders don't need to care about whether the loan will be paid back.[23]

The borrower will send money to a loan servicer, and eventually the payment makes it to the holders of the security. The original lenders received their money back at the time they sold the loans. Granted, the securitizers weren't quite as dumb as this makes them sound. There were standards that the lenders had to meet before the loans could be sold on the secondary market, but these standards had become lax enough that they didn't prevent the problem. Also, the securitizers shared the expectation of ever-rising home prices.

Fannie Mae/Freddie Mac

The problem became massively worse because of Freddie Mac and Fannie Mae (hereafter called FM). There never should be any organization of the character of these two. Think of four kinds of organizations:

- Private profit/private risk, or pure capitalist: ordinary businesses in a market economy fit in this category. The owners make money if they can meet a need and sell their products; if not, their investment is at risk and they might have to shut down.
- Public profit/public risk, or pure socialist: factories and other organizations in a socialist economy such as the former USSR fit this category (you can't really call them businesses). The government reaps the profit when the organization is successful (although it is tricky to provide the organization's managers with an incentive to earn profit if the reason the society became socialist is because it doesn't like profits). However, if this type of organization fails, the price is paid by the government. Those that advocate government takeover of profitable businesses because they want the benefit of the profits to flow to society rather than the owners need to keep in mind that government ownership of failing businesses mean that the losses then hit society rather than private owners.
- Public profit/private risk: imagine that the government taxed 100 percent of the profits of a business. These organizations won't exist because nobody will invest in a business with no upside.
- Private profit/public risk: in truth many business owners aren't 100 percent in favor of a market economy. They like the part about keeping the profits that their business makes, but they lose a lot of sleep over the risk inherent in owning a business. So, in capitalist heaven the owners get to keep the profits from good times, but the government will pick up the losses in bad times. Capitalist heaven is taxpayer hell, and Fannie Mae and Freddie Mac were in this dreadful category.

Fannie Mae was created in 1938 as a government agency[24] (so it originally wasn't as bad as it became). It started with the noble goal of encouraging more housing. In 1968 Congress passed and President Johnson signed legislation turning it into a private firm to keep its numbers off the budget (so there was deception in its original privatization). Freddie Mac was created in 1970 so there were two of these entities doing basically the same thing. (Originally they had longer names indicating their function, but they later adopted the shorter version of their names as official.)

The two organizations were called government sponsored enterprises (GSE).[25] They bought mortgage loan securities; holding some and selling some (see Figure 8.3). They could sell bonds in the bond market. For any organization selling bonds, they will have to pay an interest rate that depends on the perceived risk of their bonds. They can't sell the bonds unless someone will voluntarily lend to them, and the lenders need to be compensated (with higher rates) for undesirable features like higher risk.

The U.S. government pays low interest rates for a particular type of debt, because its debt is very safe. The government owes a lot of money, but it is always able to pay off each particular bond when it becomes due because it will borrow money from new borrowers to pay off the old borrowers. This works for the government, but don't try it at home.

So, how should the debt of the government-sponsored entities FM be rated? Even though the government said they would not back the debt of the FMs, it seemed plausible to bond market lenders that the government wouldn't let them default (their expectations were correct, notwithstanding the government's incorrect disclaimer). Therefore, the debt of the FMs was sold as if it were nearly as safe as government debt, which allowed the FMs to

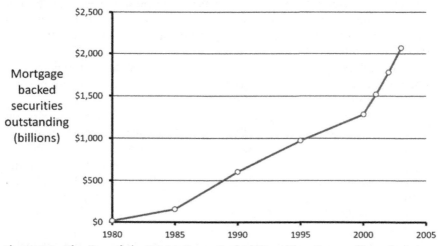

Figure 8.3 The Growth in FM Mortgage-Backed Securities. *Source*: Figure based on data obtained from Journal of Economic Perspectives, Spring 2005, p162

borrow money at a rate lower than a typical private business could. However, the rate on FM debt was slightly higher than on U.S. government debt, so FMs had no trouble borrowing funds: they offered debt that was seemingly as safe as government debt but with a higher rate.[26]

FMs raked in enormous profits. Despite being GSE's, the profit wasn't shared with the government, and FM executives raked in tremendous compensation packages Even though they were rolling in money, they somehow managed to lose track of the need for careful accounting standards, and they were involved in accounting scandals in the early 2000s even before the crisis hit.

Part of the money FM took in flowed into congressional campaign contributions to make sure that members of Congress were inclined to keep the racket going.

FM contributed to the crisis by encouraging even more mortgage securitization, drawing even more funds into that area. Drawing more funds into housing contributed to the continuing rise in prices, which created a vicious circle. Prudent people who refused to take on the risk of buying more houses than they could afford ended up paying the price, because the cost of their housing was driven up by the pressure from the reckless borrowers.

There were some who saw the possibility of the impending FM train wreck,[27] but Congressional leaders scoffed at their warnings.

The FMs were taken into receivership in September 2008; equivalent to the government taking over the affairs of someone too incompetent to manage their own. However, they continued to be black holes sucking in taxpayer money.[28]

It is controversial how much blame the FMs deserve. The reason it is very hard to answer that question is because economics is not a laboratory science. If it were, we could do an experiment where we create two copies of the world. In one world we would see what happens with FMs in existence; in the other half of the lab we would create a world where we would eliminate the FMs but keep all other conditions the same. Then we could see what difference was made by the existence of the FMs. We can't do that kind of experiment, but the private-profit-public-risk problems inherent with the FMs are so deeply engrained they need to be abolished even in the absence of lab data. (But this does not mean they should be vaporized tomorrow—there needs to be a gradual transition. Steadily lowering the amount of their loan limit provides a way of unwinding them.) President Obama has proposed gradually winding them down, but at the time of this writing their future remains unclear.[29]

Should we be concerned that eliminating FMs would make housing less affordable? Note the government already subsidizes housing in a substantial manner with the mortgage interest reduction to homeowners. Because this policy does not benefit renters it is debatable, although it does help renters become homeowners. In any case, any subsidy should be administered by a government agency, not a GSE like the FMs.[30]

The Bond Raters

It gets worse. Three firms helped the real estate price cauldron bubble by telling everyone that the growing pile of mortgage-backed securities was perfectly safe. Anyone is entitled to their opinion about the future, however, misguided it might turn out, but the opinion of three seers had a unique legal standing: the bond rating companies Moody's, Standard & Poor's, and Fitch's.[31] The bond rating companies perform what could be a useful function: they investigate the characteristics of bond borrowers and assign them a rating based on the risk of default. It would be massively useful to society if they truly provided insurance: that is, if a bond they rated safe had defaulted, they would pay the borrower. However, this would be exceedingly risky to the bond rating company, so it is not surprising they don't do that.

One might wish the rating system might work something like this: if a buyer is considering purchase of a particular bond, they would pay the rating company for their rating, if they wanted to. Alternatively, knowledgeable buyers might decide that they know enough about the bond already so they don't need to pay for the bond rater's opinion. If the system worked like this, note two crucial features: (1) the bond raters would have to make sure their opinion was worth paying for, and (2) it would be clear to the raters that they work for the bond buyers (lenders), not the bond sellers (borrowers). However, one problem with doing it this way is that a potential buyer might share information with other potential buyers, so the rater might have trouble making sure that everyone that uses their information pays a fair price for it.

In practice, this means the raters are paid by the borrowers. Here's the problem: the borrowers (bond sellers) have a strong interest in receiving a nice, safe rating for their bond (even if that means rating the bond as safer than it really is). In contrast, the potential lenders (bond buyers) have a strong interest in getting an accurate rating before they decide whether to buy it (they don't want the bond to be rated safer than it really is, but they also don't want the bond to be rated less safe than it really is). The risk to the bond raters is that they won't get as much business from a bond seller if they start giving their bonds risky ratings. It's not hard to see the problem if the raters are paid by volume rather than by accuracy: their incentives lead them to try to increase the number of bonds they rate.[32] Even this problem could be dealt with if bond buyers (lenders) were free to ignore the (possibly tainted) opinion of the raters. The problem is compounded by the special legal status that was given to the bond raters. A variety of institutional investors were only allowed to hold bonds if they held a minimum rating from one of the three official ratings agencies. This government policy turned the three into privileged businesses with a guaranteed market: no matter the quality of their opinions, bonds still had to be rated by them. (Remember the pig-trough principle: beware the organization with guaranteed funding (page 20).)

Sometimes the solution to a previous problem helps set the stage for the next problem. As seen on page 117, insured banks can become very reckless when their equity capital falls to zero. So, one way to help this problem is for bank regulators to set minimum capital standards. At first glance, it also makes sense to make the capital standard depend on risk, so that a bank making riskier loans has to hold more capital. The question is: who do you let decide in advance which loans are riskier? The unfortunate answer, as you might have guessed: the bond raters decided. When mortgage-backed securities were rated as low risk, banks were encouraged to hold more of those.

The 2010 Dodd-Frank law[33] made some changes affecting the bond rating companies, but as of this writing it is too early to tell how they will be implemented or how they will work.

Liar Loans

More factors entered the toxic mix.

Subprime loans were loans to riskier borrowers. Instead of carefully verifying borrower information (as was traditional), some loan originators simply accepted what the borrower claimed, or made up the numbers (these became known as no-documentation, or no-doc, or 'liar' loans). Responsible lenders would find it hard to compete if reckless lenders attracted most of the customers.

Low Interest Rates

Interest rates were very low during the bubble (see online graphs). The Federal Reserve was trying to keep the economy from falling into too deep of a slowdown after September 11, 2001. One of the effects of this effort was it encouraged more and more borrowing.

Accounting Rules

Often we know how to fix the last problem, but the solution for the last problem may exacerbate the next problem. One of the problems of the 1980s S&L crisis was lax accounting standards that allowed lending institutions to look better than they really were. To solve that problem, mark-to-market accounting rules were established that require securities held by banks to be valued at their current market values. This is partly a good thing, in that it prevents banks from maintaining fictitious balance sheets with assets listed as being worth more than they really are. However, in a thinly traded market, price may fall because of a few unrepresentative transactions. Lowering the value of the bank assets results in a lower value for its capital, so the strict capital standards require it to stop making loans until it can raise more capital.

Inconsistent Policies and the 2008 Crisis

As the crisis struck, inconsistent policies by the George W. Bush administration added to the problem.[34] In March 2008 the government arranged a mini-bailout of overleveraged investment bank Bear-Stearns.[35] If Bear-Stearns had gone bankrupt its shareholders would have received nothing and its creditors would have had to accept losses as the company's assets would not cover the value of their debt. Instead, the government arranged for shareholders to receive $10 dollars per share by being bought out.

The equity holders did lose a lot compared to where they had once been.

A partial bailout of a business like Bear-Stearns is an example of the "too big to fail" (TBTF) policy. There is a risk to the economy if a TBTF company fails, but the TBTF policy itself creates serious problems. Consider different savers, some looking for safety and some willing to tolerate risk. The safety-seekers avoid stocks and choose low-yielding insured bank deposits. The risk-seekers choose stock in a highly leveraged investment bank, and enjoy high returns for a few years. Then the investment bank fails but is bailed out by the government, and these investors get their money back.

The safety-seeking investors have to live with the unfairness of seeing the other investors protected from the consequences of the risk they took, while also earning the high returns from what would have been a riskier investment (absent the bailout). Adding insult to injury for the risk-averse investors, those poor saps will see their taxes used to bail out the reckless investors. It gets worse.

If people expect a big company will be bailed out if it fails, it finds it can start taking riskier investments while borrowing money more cheaply (because lenders see the bailout as reducing the risk of lending to the company.) The result is that TBTF can lead to more risk taking which can lead to more future bailouts.

For example, as investment bank Lehman brothers became increasingly distressed during the summer of 2008, its expectations grew that it would be bailed out. In September 2008 Lehman was denied a bailout and pushed into bankruptcy.

Whether or not this was the right decision, it was different than the decision made for Bear-Stearns, and it is hard to justify the reason for the difference. As the crisis peaked in September 2008, there was more inconsistency: AIG was bailed out, but Washington Mutual was allowed to fail and be acquired.

As the astronauts and ground crew desperately worked to bring the damaged Apollo 13 spacecraft home, they followed the motto "failure is not an option."[36] However, for government policy toward business, this is a wrong motto. Failure *must* be an option for a business. Otherwise you've recreated the pig-trough problem (page 20): an organization with guaranteed funding.

The "Too Big to Fail" Problem

Reducing the size of depository institutions (banks) would reduce the danger of "too big to fail"—the problem that happens when a large financial institution is bailed out because of a fear that its failure would have a contagion effect that ripples across other financial institutions. Even if the bailout is justified because of the fears, the negative effects of bailouts include encouraging recklessness and providing unfair competitive advantages to institutions that have been bailed out before and might be expected to be bailed out again. Immediately following a bailout, the government might avidly claim that it will never bail out another institution, but it is hard to make this denial credible if you have already bailed them out earlier.

To effectively limit the size of deposit institutions, there should be a limit on the total amount of deposits that will be insured in an institution. If a bank has deposits that total twice the level of the cap, then only half of the amount will be insured for each depositor.[37] This policy will provide a strong incentive for depositors to remove deposits from banks that become too large. The result will be a natural shrinkage of banks that are too large, until they are back at the point where 100 percent of their deposits are insured. The cap would need to be gradually lowered to provide an orderly transition. Ordinarily the government should not impose an arbitrary size limit on a business, but in this case it is government deposit insurance that gives the government a significant interest in avoiding too-big-to-fail institutions. Also, this does not mean we should return to the pre-depression days of 30,000 very small, very risky banks. Very small banks are riskier because of a less diverse loan portfolio. Ideally, we would avoid both very small and very large banks.

Interstate Banks

For a long time the size of banks was limited because banks were not allowed to operate in more than one state, and some states limited the number of branches a bank could have in its home state. However, there are advantages when banks can operate across state lines. A bank limited to one state holds a less diverse loan portfolio and is vulnerable if there is a downturn in the economy of that state. A more geographically diversified bank is better protected from local downturns. Banks with more branches can provide more services. For one thing, interstate travel was more complicated in the days before ATMs when it was very difficult to obtain cash while you were away from your home state. People had to carry around a lot of traveller's checks which were awkward to use.

Banks found ways of getting around the restriction by setting up holding companies that could purchase banks in other states and by opening out-of-state offices to process loans but weren't full bank branches. Direct deposit of paychecks, the ability to get cash from ATM machines, the ability to package loans together and sell as securities, and the ability to get credit from credit cards all served to make the physical location of bank branches less significant. In 1994 Congress finally allowed banks to operate nationwide.[38]

Separating Commercial and Investment Banking

Another limitation on bank size was the separation of commercial and investment banks created by the depression-era Glass-Steagall Act. This law was repealed in 1999.[39] By allowing banks the ability to engage in a greater range of activities it provides banks with the ability to diversify, reducing the risk of reliance on a narrower line of business. If profits from these activities can help cover the bank's deposits, even if its traditional lending activity is in a downturn, the result is more safety for the banks' depositors and the deposit insurance fund. However, if the bank is engaging in other activities that are riskier it is important to make sure that losses on those activities do not spread to the depositors and the deposit insurance fund. The basic principle is that the insured depositors need to be protected, but everyone else can invest in other assets or not as they wish. The deposit insurance regulators need to make sure that the bank's loans are only available to support its insured deposits and cannot be used to cover losses on other activities of the bank.

In summary: allowing interstate banking and the repeal of Glass-Steagall raise new issues for the banking system but the mortgage crisis could have happened even if both of these restrictions had remained in place.

The TARP Bailout

In October 2008 the government adopted the Troubled Asset Relief Program (TARP) policy, providing for financial sector bailouts to steer past the crisis. Nobody really liked this measure although it was adopted as a bipartisan policy, in the last months of the George W. Bush administration while Demo-crats controlled Congress.

The policy did avoid a catastrophic meltdown of the financial system. The problem is that we can never know how bad it might have been if policies had been different. By analogy, if the *Titanic* had managed to alter its course a second earlier and avoided the iceberg, it would be largely forgotten to his-tory. Nobody would say today, "I remember the *Titanic*—that's the ship that *almost* crashed into an iceberg."

PREVENTING FUTURE CRISES?

Congress attempted to solve the problem with the Dodd-Frank Wall Street Reform and Protection Act of 2010. However, by providing more discretion-ary power to regulators to deal with institutions they decide pose a systemic risk the result is even more uncertainty about future policy.[40] There's no guarantee that regulators that failed to crack down on excessive risk taken by financial firms before the crisis will know how to use increased discretionary power, particularly since regulators also missed the warning signs for the bra-zen massive fraud perpetrated by Bernie Madoff. It is too early to tell whether the Dodd-Frank law will be effective.

Any solution requires three different types of investors be treated differently:

1. Equity holders need to bear the risk. If they don't want to take on the risk, then they shouldn't buy equity.
2. Debt holders need to have their rights protected according to clearly defined-in-advance rules of bankruptcy.[41] If they can't get their money back, they at least need to know that they will be treated fairly in bank-ruptcy court.
3. Insured bank depositors need to be protected. Requiring insured banks to purchase private loan default insurance would provide a way of providing greater protection for the deposit insurance fund while also establishing a market for pricing loan default risk. (The loan default insurers would have a reason to care about the accuracy of their estimates of the probability of default, unlike the bond rating companies.)

Banks make their living by making loans, so normally they will only hold as many non-loan assets, or reserves, as the government requires them to do so (with the required reserve ratio). Suddenly the situation changed with the 2008 financial crisis. "Over-borrowed firms and households are reduc-ing their spending to reduce their debts just at the moment when banks are engaged in restoring their balance sheets by reducing their loans."[42] When lenders lack confidence that they will be paid back, the economy suffers from a shortage of credit.[43]

Prior to 2008 the Federal Reserve paid no interest on the reserve deposits that banks were required to hold with the Fed. Once they started paying interest one result was that bank reserves skyrocketed to way more than was required (see online graphs). If the Federal Reserve did not pay interest on reserves held over the minimum required amount it would provide more of an incentive for banks to increase lending rather than hoard excess reserves.

Eliminating the FMs, making it voluntary for a bond to be rated by the bond raters, replacing the risk-based bank capital standards with a plain minimum capital ratio, and reducing the size of the "too big to fail" institutions would also help reduce the risk. Even more importantly, providing for policies for greater macroeconomic stability would reduce uncertainty in the economy and reduce the risk of crises (see the next chapter).

NOTES

1. Nobody would willingly sell either gold or silver at a price below its official price, because people had the free coinage option, which was the equivalent of selling the metal to the mint at the official price.

2. Galbraith, *Money*, p100 and related pages cover this history.

3. A new political party, the greenback party, came into existence to press for the continued issuance of greenbacks. They elected 14 members of the House in 1878 (Galbraith, *Money*, p106).

4. Galbraith, *Money*, p113.

5. Hamlet, act I, scene 3, line 75.

6. The bank run in the movie happened during the depression. Krugman (2012, p59) apparently does not understand the flashback structure of the movie when he thinks the run is anachronistically set after World War II.

7. Kindleberger reviews a history of financial crises and the role of a lender of last resort.

8. Friedman, chapter 3.

9. see Taylor, p47.

10. Keynes had previously been involved at the Versailles conference after World War I, and issued a prescient warning about the damaging effects of the reparations the victors imposed on Germany. (*Economic Consequences of the Peace*).

11. Note that maintaining full employment does not mean that all jobs need to be preserved as they are. As pushbutton elevators became common, society no longer needed workers with the skill to operate an elevator control lever. These workers can be employed in more productive jobs, but the transition of workers from one job to another can be traumatic for the workers and costly for society.

12. Samuelson.

13. In 2012, Krugman (p59) wrote that the "system worked pretty well" up until the early 1980s. Back in 1994 Krugman did remember that inflation was driving many savings and loan associations toward bankruptcy in the 1970s. (Krugman 1994, p160–61).

14. Fellner, p15, p116; Dornbusch and Fischer, p571. Stiglitz (2010, p264) writes that it is a fallacy that the cost of reversing inflation is high, which is slightly odd because on this point he is agreeing with the rational expectations school although he criticizes them elsewhere in that same chapter.

15. Okun 1981, p302.

16. Ironically, a few years after the deposit rate ceilings were ended, interest rates declined so that the rate on deposits fell below the previous ceilings, so by then removing the ceilings made no difference.

17. Muolo and Padilla, p52.

18. The balance sheet also includes a small provision for some loans going bad. That provision is not shown here for simplicity. If the bad loan amount is smaller than expected, it fits within the loan loss provision and then there is no loss for the owner's equity. When the loan loss amount is larger than expected, the owner's equity takes the hit.

19. Stiglitz 2010, p124.

20. Stiglitz 2010, p86.

21. Shiller, p35.

22. Gasparino, p15.

23. Muolo and Padilla, p87; also Kirsten Grind describes the failure of Washington Mutual.

24. Shiller, p16.

25. Stiglitz (2010, p10) misleadingly describes the FMs as "two private companies that had started as government agencies," as if their activities weren't the government's fault. The government was not an innocent bystander as mortgage securities were created. Booth wrote in 1989 (long before the crisis): "The popularity and success of mortgage loan securitization largely is due to the credit enhancement provided by government agencies responsible for creating a secondary market for residential mortgages." Booth writes that another factor was the government's risk-based capital regulation, which encouraged banks to hold mortgage-backed securities instead of mortgages because banks had to hold more of their own capital to back up the mortgages.

26. Gasparino, p109.

27. Martin and Pozdena wrote about the taxpayer exposure to Fannie Mae risk way back in 1991, long before the crisis. See also Taylor, p152; Frame and White, *Journal of Economic Perspectives*, Spring 2005; Brooks, p41; Richards, p71, p76, p144, p156, p172.

28. See online notes for updates.

29. *Wall Street Journal* online, April 28, 2014.

30. See section 3.6 for a description of the proposed Universal Opportunity Loan.

31. Gasparino, p200–2.

32. Stiglitz 2010, p92.

33. Public law 111–203, sections 931 to 939H.

34. Stiglitz 2010, chapter 2.

35. John Geanakoplos writes about how too much leverage destabilizes the economy.

36. Kranz.

37. In general, if C is the cap on total deposit size and D is the actual level of deposits, then this proposal would have each depositor have a fraction equal to C/D of their deposits insured, if $D > C$. One hundred percent of deposits would be insured if $D < C$.

For example, if the limit is 100 billion:

Deposit Size (billions)	Fraction of deposits insured
300	0.333
200	0.500
175	0.571
150	0.667
125	0.800
100	1.000
less than 100	1.000

38. Riegle-Neal Interstate Banking and Efficiency Act of 1994 (Mishkin, p300).

39. Gramm-Leach-Bliley Financial Services Modernization Act of 1999 (Mishkin, p303).

40. Taylor, p153.

41. Taylor, p158.

42. Skidelski 2010, p22.

43. Akerlof and Shiller 2009, p17.

Chapter 9

Economic Stability and Financial Security

The great depression was a catastrophe as the unemployment rate exceeded 25 percent, and serious recessions since then have seen the unemployment rate exceed 10 percent (in 1982 and 2009). If we could find a way to create an abundant job economy many other problems will be much less severe. Concerns about corporate power will be lessened if workers know they could easily find new jobs if their current employer treats them shabbily. Legitimate fears about opening international trade would be lessened if workers knew that other jobs were available and were in fact begging for more workers. Concern about people being thrown into poverty would be lessened if a plethora of jobs was available. Concern about low wages for unskilled workers would be lessened if employers desperate for workers engaged in bidding wars to attract them. Fear of economic change, plant closings, and job losses would be less if workers losing their jobs knew that other employers were intensely recruiting them.[1]

Solving the unemployment problem is the essential as-yet unreached goal of studying economics. Some unemployment results from macroeconomic instability, so it is essential to continue to strive for macroeconomic stability. However, it is also important to focus on ways that microeconomic policy can help alleviate unemployment, because there does not seem to be any way that policy makers can guarantee complete macroeconomic stability. Microeconomic policies include those that would increase economic efficiency, such as fundamental tax and regulatory reform and reducing narrow interest influence on policy.

Economist Alan Blinder wrote in 1987 that the reason for the rapid economic growth in the mid-1980s was because the economy naturally grows fast as it rebounds from a steep recession (as in 1982).[2] He called this the "Joe Palooka" effect, after a toy with a weighted bottom that would spring back very fast if you punched its head. The Joe Palooka effect implies that economic policy isn't that important because the economy will bounce back from a recession anyway. However, that didn't happen following the 2008–2009 recession. Once the recession was officially over and the economy started growing again, the growth rate was very slow. There was no "Joe Palooka" bounce back from this serious recession. Policies do matter. Effective policies will encourage job creation; ineffective policies discourage job creation.

THE KEYNESIAN VIEW: SEVEN ISSUES

The Keynesian view calls for active government policy aimed at stabilizing the economy, and during the 1960s this view dominated macroeconomics and seemed to provide hope that the path to creating an abundant-job economy was understood. However, it turns out that the Keynesian view is not general enough. Here are seven specific issues.

How is the Money Spent?

Focusing on the aggregate level of spending tends to undervalue the importance of considering what the money is being spent on. During the depression Keynes at one point joked that having the treasury bury old bank notes would be better than doing nothing, because the effort people would make to try to dig them up would generate employment even if it would be wasteful.[3] True—but wasteful employment is still a problem. Keynes did add it would be better to build houses and the like. Krugman suggests the economy would get out of the slump if somehow everyone became afraid that Earth would be invaded by aliens, so the government spent a large amount of money on constructing alien defenses.[4] He is not exactly serious about the alien invasion part, but he is totally serious that the only thing that matters is the amount of the spending—it doesn't matter what the money is spent on. Part of the problem here comes from the way GDP is measured. A $1 government purchase is counted as adding $1 to GDP, regardless of what it is spent on. By contrast, when a business spends $1 to buy an input, that $1 does not count directly for GDP. It will only count for GDP if it becomes part of a product that is sold— and the value of the product that is sold is added to the GDP. This means that totally wasteful purchases by a business will not count in GDP, but totally wasteful purchases by the government will count. In reality, totally wasteful spending by either subtracts from national wealth, instead of adding to it. It would be better to not spend the money so those resources would be available to someone that can spend it more wisely.

If lack of spending causes unemployment, then the solution might be either lower taxes or more government spending, but Keynesian theory itself doesn't provide a way of indicating which it should be. If the government knows of some wise investment opportunities, then the government spending is good. Otherwise, cutting taxes is better than government spending because then the public in general will decide where the money will be spent.

Uncertainty of Future Discretionary Policy

A government that uses its discretion to try to find the best policy to promote stability will inevitably create uncertainty about future policy. Even if the current government is extremely wise it may be followed by governments that are less so. It is hard to imagine anyone would think Presidents Johnson, Nixon, Ford, Carter, Reagan, Bush, Clinton, Bush, and Obama *all* made wise economic decisions. The uncertainty about future policy itself imposes a cost (see page 141).

Multiplier Effects on Spending are Complicated

Kahn (1931) analyzed the multiplier effect, which explains why a fall in spending in one area spreads a ripple effect across the economy. When workers lose their jobs they spend less at stores, leading to employment reductions for stores and their suppliers and across the economy (including a fall in government employment as a result of less tax revenue).[5]

Another kind of multiplier exacerbates this effect. Because informal contacts often provide the means for teenagers to obtain their first jobs, the effect of increasing unemployment can be magnified as teenagers (particularly minorities) find it harder to make the contacts they need to become connected to jobs.[6]

However, the same multiplier concept does not work on the upside as well as it does on the downside.[7] The true effect of the increase in government spending cannot be determined unless you know the answers to a long list of questions (see online appendix myhome.spu.edu/ddowning/fos.html).

Supply Shocks

The Keynesian focus on demand-side fluctuations in the economy leaves it unable to provide a remedy for supply shocks, such as those associated with the inflation and unemployment of the 1970s.[8] The disruption in the availability of a crucial product can lead to higher prices for that product, creating ripple effects of higher prices on other products, and also fewer jobs as goods become less affordable. Two bursts of rising gasoline prices (in 1973 and 1979) wreaked havoc on the U.S. economy. It became clear that economic models also need to represent the supply side of the economy, in addition to the demand side included in Keynesian models.

Supply shocks cause wealth destruction. Some categories include physical wealth destruction (as by a hurricane); stranded capital wealth destruction (as when a factory becomes obsolete because of new technology or a change in preferences); and loan default wealth destruction.

Inflation Momentum

The painful lesson of the 1970s was that inflation develops momentum and is harder to stop than it is to start (see page 113). The implication is that it is best to prevent inflation before it starts. In 1979 the Federal Reserve under Paul Volcker announced a new course where they would tighten the money supply to wring inflation out of the economy. The policy was successful, and it worked faster than some had expected. The double-digit inflation of 1980 had fallen to 4 percent inflation by 1982. However, there was a severe cost: tightening up the money supply depressed spending, and drove unemployment up above 10 percent during the depth of the 1982 recession. That was the only time unemployment crossed above 10 percent between the Great Depression of the 1930s and the financial crisis/recession following 2008.

Inflation makes it harder for long-term credit markets to function well. If inflation is expected accurately, then nominal interest will increase by the amount of the inflation. For example, if lenders and borrowers agreed upon a 5 percent (real) interest rate in the case of no inflation, they would agree on a 15 percent interest rate when inflation is expected to be 10 percent over the course of the loan. However, this inflation adjustment creates a cash flow difficulty for the borrower. The no-inflation payment schedule calls for equal loan payments each period, but once the interest rate is adjusted for inflation the borrower who has to pay a constant nominal amount each period is no longer paying a constant real amount each period. The effect of inflation causing higher nominal interest rates means that the borrower ends up paying a larger real payment at the beginning of the loan (compared to what the payment would have been in the absence of inflation). Near the end of the loan, the borrower is paying a smaller real value than they would have without inflation, so in the end the present value works out to be the same as if there had been no inflation. However, the cash flow difficulty for the borrower is still there: inflation increases the real amount of the payment the borrower needs to come up with in the early stage of the loan.[9]

The main problem with inflation comes from uncertainty about future inflation. Unexpectedly high inflation hurts lenders, and unexpectedly low inflation hurts borrowers. (Borrowers will agree to pay high nominal interest rates if inflation is anticipated, but if subsequent inflation is lower than expected the borrowers end up paying high real interest rates.)

Inflation is a problem, but that does not mean that falling average prices (deflation) is good. The great depression was a time of deflation, and deflation generally causes more economic hardship than does inflation. Lenders can compensate for inflation by making borrowers pay higher interest rates, but borrowers cannot compensate for deflation by making lenders take negative interest rates (since lenders have the option of holding currency in their mattress, or some other form that pays a zero interest rate). Credit availability might dry up during a time of deflation.

Policy Popularity Asymmetry

If Keynesian economists tell policy makers, "Government deficits are good during times of deficient aggregate demand, but they are not good in times of high aggregate demand," the policy makers are likely to hear "Government deficits are good blah blah blah blah. . . ." Demand expansionary policies (spend more, cut taxes, print more money) are likely to be more popular than demand contractionary policies, so Keynesian policies in actuality may be biased toward more deficits than the theoretically symmetric theory would call for.

Government Borrowing

In the short run, when the government runs a deficit it means that it can spend more than it collects in taxes. However, in the long run you have to take into account the fact that borrowing money means that the total debt has increased (see the next section).

FUTURE EFFECT OF GOVERNMENT BORROWING: THE 6 OPTIONS

Keynes correctly argued that a government deficit during a time of recession would be better than following a fiscal contractionary policy that would exacerbate the economic slowdown. However, the simple Keynesian view does not consider the long-run effects of government borrowing. Keynes at one point expressed his view of long run issues by saying "in the long run we are all dead,"[10] but that attitude is a bit of a problem. Keynes meant (correctly) that we need to be concerned with alleviating short run downturns. It is bad to ignore those fluctuations just because they will naturally cure themselves if you wait a long time. However, focusing only on short run fluctuations is also a serious problem, because the long run consequences of economic policies today will be magnified by the passage of time. An annual growth rate of 3 percent will lead to a national income that is twice as large as an economy with an annual growth rate of 2 percent if you wait about one lifetime (71 years).

Should we worry about a problem even if it has no immediate bad effects, but it has potentially troublesome effects further in the future? That would describe the U.S. national debt. One argument that says we don't need to worry about the national debt comes from the "we-owe-it-to-ourselves" fallacy of government debt.[11] Instead, we should look at it this way. If the government debt has supported productive investment, then it has beneficial effects. If the debt supports current consumption, then it crowds out what otherwise would have been investment in productive capital, so it does make the nation poorer.

There are six possibilities for the future effects of government borrowing: default, monetize, rollover, tax rate increase, lower government spending, or economic growth. The actual result must be a combination of the following six possibilities.

Default

Default on the debt would be dishonest and would cause massive hardship for those that trusted the government, so this should not be done except in extreme emergency. Also note that nobody will lend to the government if they are expecting default.

Monetize

The Federal Reserve could buy the debt with newly created money, but if too much of this is done the result will be inflation.

Perpetual Rollover

Instead of using tax revenue to pay the interest, the government could continue borrowing each year to repay the previous interest. Because of compound interest, the debt amount keeps growing, even for a small initial amount of borrowing.

By pushing up interest rates, the result could be crowding out of productive investment and lower future living standards.

Higher Future Tax Rates

Suppose the government borrows X dollars, to be repaid n years in the future. In year 1, spending can be higher than taxes because of the borrowing.

In years 2 to $n-1$, taxes must be higher than spending because some revenue is needed to pay interest. In year n, taxes must be significantly higher than spending, because both the interest and the principal amount of the debt from year 1 must be repaid.

The expectation of higher tax rates in the future deters investment today, since investment decisions are based on expectations of future after-tax returns. As in the previous case, crowding out of productive investment lowers future living standards.[12]

Lower Future Government Spending

The government might cut back spending in the future to make funds available to pay back the debt, which could be a problem if vital government services are cut back because of the need to pay back the debt remaining from past government borrowing.

Higher Revenue from a Growing Economy

If the economy grows enough, higher revenue in the future can pay back the debt without an increase in the tax rates. This would be the best situation. It is most likely to happen if either (a) the debt finances valuable infrastructure or research investment that provides a valuable payoff to society in future years; or (b) the debt finances spending that puts otherwise unemployed people to work, thereby expanding national income. If the people had remained unemployed that year, then their potential contribution to national income for that year is lost forever.

Does government debt provide a burden for future generations? It depends on the reasons for borrowing the money and what it is spent on. If the borrowed money is used to finance projects with long-term benefits, than the borrowing is probably a good idea (it depends on how the cost compares to the benefits).

The other possibility is myopic (near-sighted) borrowing, where the borrowing finances current spending without providing an investment for the future. The same rule applies to a person: borrowing for a house likely is beneficial; borrowing for a party is less likely to be beneficial.

The U.S. government went heavily in debt during World War II. It would be very hard to attach a monetary value for the results of this spending. The ratio of U.S. government debt to GDP exceeded 1 right after World War II.[13] A ratio of 1 means that it would take 100 percent of all the goods and services produced in the country for one year to pay back the whole debt if it was to be paid back at once. It is important to look at the ratio of debt to GDP, rather than the level of the debt, to avoid the fallacy of Argument by Very

Big Numbers (which says that a debt of 14 trillion dollars is bad just because 14 trillion is a very big number).

It would help to have the U.S. government maintain its financial records in a way that would pass an introductory accounting class. This would require that current expenditures be accounted for separately from capital expenditures. (Note that state governments do this.)

THE STATUTORY DEBT CEILING

Congress sets tax rates, government spending, and government borrowing (through the debt ceiling). However, these three decisions can't be made independently. Once two of these decisions are made, there is no choice about the value for the third:

$$borrowing = spending - taxes$$

Having a statutory debt ceiling is harmful for democratic accountability, because it lets members of Congress take contradictory votes. Members can vote for increasing spending while still telling voters that they cast a (meaningless) vote against raising the debt ceiling.[14] It would be better if Congress is held accountable for its spending decisions and then the Treasury is allowed to borrow as much as needed to spend the money Congress authorized.

THE POLICY CREDIBILITY QUESTION

Policy decisions today affect expectations about the future. Here is a story about a subway system that requires passengers to use tokens to ride the subway. When the fare is increased, the system has a choice between selling the same tokens at the new higher price, or else going through the expensive process of creating new tokens and redesigning all of the turnstyles. The problem with keeping the same tokens is that riders will hoard the tokens when they can buy them before the price increase takes effect, and the system freezes if no tokens are available. So, the system usually has to announce that there is no point in hoarding the old tokens because when the fare increase happens new tokens will be used. If they are credible when they make this announcement, people won't hoard the tokens—and then the system realizes that once the day of the fare increase arises they may as well keep the same tokens and avoid all the costs of conversion.

The problem is: what happens the next time they announce a fare increase? They've now blown their credibility, so people will hoard the tokens regardless of whether the system announces that they will change the tokens, so they usually have to change the tokens to convince people that is what they will do.

The analogy for government borrowing is: if the government can credibly announce that it will not default or inflate its debt away in the future, people will be willing to lend to it at lower rates. However, once the government approaches the ultimate borrowing limit, then the possibility of inflating the debt away becomes irresistible. Once the credibility is ruined, then future government borrowing becomes more expensive, because potential lenders won't believe the government when it tells people to ignore what it did last time; instead, this time it really really means it when it says it will not inflate away the debt.

SMOOTHING OUT INSTABILITY IN NOMINAL GDP

Even Keynesian skeptics have to admit that bad government policy can destabilize the economy, so it is crucial to find the best government policies that will be the least destabilizing.

Any business faces three categories of uncertainty: (1) industry-specific demand fluctuations, (2) aggregate-demand-based output fluctuations, and (3) price level fluctuations. The first category is an unavoidable feature of any business, but the goal of macroeconomic policy should be to eliminate the last two sources of uncertainty. Failure to do so increases the risk of being in business, which can be expected to lead to a higher cost of capital to compensate for the higher risk. The result is less current investment and lower future living standards than would be the case if macroeconomic stability could be guaranteed.

Any policy based on discretionary action by monetary policy makers creates uncertainty. An omniscient benevolent policy maker could presumably achieve better results with a discretionary policy than could be achieved by following a rule, but in reality the difficulties of determining the correct policy make it inevitable that mistakes will be made. The problem becomes even worse if monetary policy makers are subject to sheer incompetence or deliberate political manipulation. Even if current monetary authorities follow a sound policy, there is no guarantee that such policy will continue when new people are in charge. Therefore, any discretion-based policy is incompatible with a guarantee of future stability of the economy.[15]

The question of determining the correct rule is difficult. No possibility can be expected to be perfect, but the goal should be to find the best feasible option.

A fixed price level rule (or fixed inflation target rule) would work well if perfectly flexible prices guarantee that full employment is always achieved, even in a society subject to aggregate demand shocks. A positive shock would tend to raise the price level, but this shock would be countered by a contractionary monetary policy to restore the average price level to its previous level. Such a policy could be accomplished with no cost to real output in the world of perfectly flexible prices. However, a fixed price level rule causes real instability if prices are not flexible, because a fall in aggregate demand leads to a fall in employment without immediately lowering prices. Then, following the fixed price rule would not provide the aggregate demand stimulus that the economy needs to return to full employment.

Furthermore, a fixed price rule (or inflation target rule) causes problems in the event of an unfavorable supply shock.[16] If there has been a fall in availability of a key resource, there would tend to be both a fall in real output and an increase in the price level. The fall in real output is an inevitable feature of the real supply shock, and it cannot be remedied by any aggregate-demand-based policy. However, the goal of macroeconomic policy should be to see that the supply shock does not trigger a further decline in real output and unemployment among other resources, such as labor. The fixed price rule would react to the rise in prices from the supply shock with a contractionary policy, which will exacerbate the negative effect on real output. This result depends on the assumption that prices are not flexible enough to keep the economy constantly at full employment. (Trying to increase output to its original pre-shock level by expansionary demand-side policy will not be possible; such an effort will lead to accelerating inflation.)

If the ratio of GDP to the money supply (called the *velocity* of money) remained constant, then a fixed money supply growth rule would be stabilizing.[17] However, the changing nature of money technology has increased the volatility of velocity in recent years (see online graphs).

What might be the best rule would be to establish a target for the growth of national income, or nominal GDP[18] (as suggested by Bennett McCallum).[19]

Figure 9.1 shows the actual nominal GDP compared to a trend curve—what the nominal GDP would have been if it had grown at a constant rate of about 7 percent per year (the actual average percent growth for nominal GDP. "Nominal" means that the value is measured using the actual current prices, without correcting for inflation. The real GDP is the measure that corrects for inflation). What is striking in the figure is the sizable gap between the trend and the actual as a result of the 2008 financial crisis, and the related recession and the slow recovery. Under the nominal GDP rule, that gap calls for pouring money into the economy to push more spending to get the GDP back to the trend. Ideally, if this policy had been followed all along, the gap from actual to trend would never have grown as big in the first place. Krugman

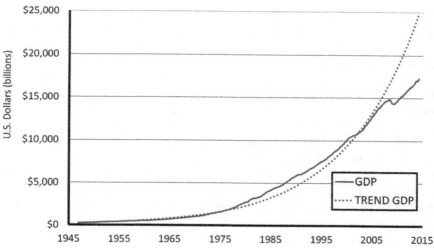

Figure 9.1 GDP Trend. *Source*: Figure based on data obtained from the Federal Reserve Bank of St. Louis

was right that a larger stimulus was needed to reduce the downturn in demand caused by the financial crisis.

We could match the trend of recent decades by setting the nominal GDP target at 7 percent growth per year, with the hope that there would be 3 percent real growth and 4 percent inflation. However, we might decide a better policy would set a target of 5 percent nominal GDP growth, with the hope there would be 3 percent real growth and 2 percent inflation. In a slump, this might mean −1 percent real growth and 6 percent inflation, but the hope would be that this policy would reduce the severity of slumps.

Pouring money into the economy does potentially create the risk of inflation. Even if inflation has not taken off yet, that does not mean that we can ignore the risk of future inflation (contrary to what Krugman says). If too much spending results, and the nominal GDP rises above the trend, then the rule provides a predictable framework to drain the right amount of liquidity out of the economy—not too much, not too little. "Predictable" is the key word here.

A debate in macroeconomics has been whether perfectly flexible wages and prices would keep the economy at full employment. If labor supply exceeds labor demand, then wages would fall until supply equals demand (if the wages are perfectly flexible). In reality wages are less flexible than prices, but even if wages were flexible it would not be a good thing if a fall in aggregate demand causes a fall in the wage and price level. A better policy response to a fall in aggregate demand would be a stimulus to aggregate demand to counteract the fall. In other words, Keynes was right that we should try to stabilize demand (aka spending, or nominal GDP). Keynesians went off track when they thought the best approach was government discretionary policy. What we need is a rule-based Keynesian policy.

Sad experience has shown that we cannot consistently stabilize real GDP, which is what we would need to do in order to achieve our real goal of stabilizing employment. However, if we could stabilize nominal GDP we could remove one of the major causes of instability in real GDP.

In the event of the fall in demand with non-flexible prices, the fall in nominal income will trigger an expansionary policy—which is just what is needed to push the economy back toward full employment. In the case of the adverse supply shock, the fixed nominal income rule provides a compromise: it avoids the contractionary policy inherent in the fixed price rule, and it avoids the futile effort to counteract the fall in output from the supply shock by a stimulus to aggregate demand.

Economists since Keynes have worried about the possibility that in times of very low interest rates expanding the money supply will not expand demand because people will simply hold on to the extra money (this situation is called a "liquidity trap").[20] However, in practice the expansion of the money supply does not happen alone. In recent years the government deficit has almost always exceeded the increase in the monetary base.[21] (The exception came during a brief time in the late 1990s when the U.S. government budget ran a surplus.) The combination deficit and monetary expansion means that there is a fiscal stimulus along with the monetary stimulus.[22]

The question of how to implement a fixed nominal income rule is difficult, but here is a proposal that relies on providing private traders with incentives to trade bonds with the Treasury and the Federal Reserve in a manner that automatically provides monetary expansion or contraction as necessary to push nominal income back to its target trajectory. In this proposal, the Treasury issues medium-term zero-coupon bonds whose maturity payment is proportional to the level of actual nominal national income at the time of maturity. The Federal Reserve buys or sells these bonds at a fixed rate, corresponding to the targeted level of nominal national income. If actual income lags below target, people will buy bonds on the secondary market and then sell them to the Federal Reserve, causing an expansion of the money supply—just what is needed to push the economy back to its nominal target. If actual income is above target, then people will buy the bonds from the Federal Reserve and sell them on the secondary market, draining money out of the economy and pushing nominal growth back to its target. Because of the arbitrage possibility, the prices of the bonds at the Fed and on the market will stay very close together, providing an automatic control to keep the economy along the nominal income target path. (In reality a small trading charge would be added for transactions with the Fed, so there would have to be small gap between the two prices before the arbitrage possibility sets in.)[23]

Recently the monetary base[24] has increased substantially because of the Federal Reserve's expansionary policy. Normally such an expansion would lead to increased bank lending and growth in the money supply, but recently banks have been holding a huge amount of excess reserves instead of making loans. This means there is a risk of a future surge in the money supply when bank's lending behavior returns to normal. At that point there will be a need to withdraw liquidity to prevent a burst of inflation. The fixed nominal GDP growth rule would provide a foundation for a credible, predictable way for accomplishing this liquidity withdrawal, and therefore would reduce uncertainty.

NOTES

1. However, guaranteed job availability does not mean that an individual worker is guaranteed to keep a particular job. Workers with a guarantee of never being fired would lose incentive to care about how they performed at their job.

2. Blinder, p98.

3. *General Theory*, p129.

4. Krugman 2012, p39.

5. Akerlof and Shiller, p15.

6. Downing 1987.

7. A naive Keynesian model sees an increase in total spending of

$$\frac{1}{1 - MPC(1-t)}$$

when \$1 of government spending is added to the economy. The size of the multiplier is determined by only two quantities: MPC is the marginal propensity to consume out of disposable income, and t is the marginal tax rate. If

$$MPC = \frac{4}{5} \text{ and } t = \frac{1}{4},$$

the multiplier is 2.5. However, this multiplier model is an example of a model that is missing so much reality that it is harmfully misleading, and it is unfortunate that this is the type of model introductory macroeconomics students sometimes encounter first.

8. Okun 1981, p321.

9. This problem could be solved by changing the way that loan payments are adjusted for inflation (see online appendix myhome.spu.edu/ddowning/fos.html).

10. Keynes, *Tract on Monetary Reform*, 1923.

11. See Krugman newspaper column, April 6, 2013.

12. The view that government borrowing will cause informed citizens to save money today because they expect higher taxes in the future is known as Ricardian equivalence after David Ricardo. It was advocated by Barro in 1974, and critiqued by Tobin (1980, chapter 3).

13. There is nothing particularly significant about the value 1 for this ratio. It depends on the time unit we use for GDP. If GDP was measured per week, rather than per year, than this ratio would have been about 52, instead of about 1.

14. The vote is meaningless as long as the debt ceiling increase passes anyway.

15. John Taylor proposes a rule (which has become known as the Taylor rule) which would also achieve a similar purpose. The Federal Reserve would have a predictable rule to set interest rates based on inflation and the gap between GDP and potential GDP (Taylor, p127).

16. Stiglitz 2010, p264.

17. Milton Friedman and the monetarists advocated a fixed money supply growth rate rule.

18. The national income is just about the same thing as the gross domestic product (GDP)—the total value of goods and services produced in an economy. There are only some slight technical differences between national income and GDP. Economists know that GDP is not an overall measure of how well a nation is flourishing. In 1972, James Tobin and William Nordhaus, proposed a "Measure of Economic Welfare" as a more comprehensive measure of how well the nation is doing. However, GDP is relatively easy to measure, compared to a more comprehensive measure, and it does appear that working to stabilize GDP will have the goal of stabilizing employment (which is the goal of this whole discussion).

19. See McCallum; also see Dueker.

20. Tobin 1980, p5.

21. See online table. The monetary base consists of the part of the money supply that is directly a liability of the Federal Reserve, consisting of currency in circulation and reserve deposits of banks at the Fed. The rest of the money supply is created when banks make loans.

22. Even if the formal mechanism is different, the reality is that expansion of the money supply in times of government fiscal deficits is equivalent to having the government print the money and then immediately spend it. In reality new money is put into circulation by having the Federal Reserve buy a government bond from a member of the public. When the Treasury department is simultaneously selling a government bond to the public to finance its spending, the result is that the two bond transactions with the public cancel out, and the result is the same as if the Federal Reserve prints the money and then hands it to the Treasury to spend.

23. See Eagle, Koenig, Sumner, and Woolsey for further discussion of nominal income targeting and alternative ways of implementing this policy.

24. The monetary base equals currency in circulation plus bank reserves.

Chapter 10

Taxes

How should the tax system work?

For some issues, there are trade-offs involved: trying to achieve more of one desirable goal means sacrificing some of another desirable goal. For other issues, it is a matter of opinion: different people will disagree over how the tax system should work, and the best that can be hoped for is that the actual system will end up as a compromise between these divergent opinions. For other issues, there is a smart way and a stupid way to design the tax system.

It should be regarded as a national scandal that ordinary people feel the need to hire professional help to calculate their tax liability. A simple, clearer tax system would provide widespread benefits.

One billionaire claimed that tax rates should be raised for high-income taxpayers because he ended up paying a lower tax rate than people that worked for him.[1] The problem with this reasoning is that the billionaire already faces a higher published tax rate than do the workers, but is somehow able to avoid paying that rate. If we give the billionaire the benefit of the doubt by assuming that he is not a tax cheater, this story shows the need for fundamental tax reform that reduces the number of perfectly legal ways to avoid taxes.[2]

TAX SYSTEM: GOALS

1. The tax system should raise enough revenue for government services.
2. The tax system should be clear (even if it can't be simple, it should be as comprehensible as possible).
3. The tax system should be fair: two taxpayers in the same circumstances should pay the same amount of taxes (called *horizontal equity*).

4. The tax system should be progressive: a taxpayer with higher income should pay a greater fraction of income in taxes than a taxpayer with less income (called *vertical equity*). However, there is considerable difference of opinion about how progressive the tax system should be.[3] For what it's worth, my opinion is that the combined[4] marginal tax rate for the highest income taxpayers should be 50 percent—no more and no less.
5. The tax system should provide incentives to work and undertake productive investment.
6. Taxes on certain items should be applied to mitigate damage caused by that item, or applied to specific services related to the use of that item (for example, a tax on gasoline should be applied to road construction, health care for traffic accident victims, and mitigation of environmental damage caused by vehicle emissions).
7. The tax system should be stable, without being changed too often. Changes in the tax code are costly and provide a burden for all taxpayers. Increasing uncertainty about the future tax code adds to the risk of investment.

WHAT TO TAX?

Per-person Tax

A per-person lump sum tax has the advantage that it won't have any effect on incentives to work, since you have to pay the same tax no matter what you do. However, making everyone pay the same tax is highly unfair to people with low incomes, so this idea has to be ruled out.

Tax Income or Consumption?

Taxes need to be based on some measure of economic activity. Figure 10.1 shows a simple diagram of the economy where people buy products from businesses, and businesses pay income to people. Think of the money as flowing like water through a pipe. (There will also be a flow of goods and services that runs in the opposite direction.) We set up a meter somewhere along the pipe to determine the rate of flow, which determines what will be taxed. We could set up our meter in the income stream and tax income (Figure 10.1) or we could set up our meter in the consumption stream and tax consumption (Figure 10.2). In the simplest model it doesn't matter which we do.

Figure 10.3 shows a more realistic model that includes savings. Now it makes a difference whether income or consumption is taxed. Taxing consumption has the advantage that it provides a strong incentive for saving. Because people won't be taxed on money they save, there is an incentive to save more which creates the possibility of increasing national wealth and

Figure 10.1 Income Tax

Figure 10.2 Consumption Tax

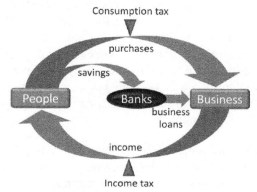

Figure 10.3 Income Tax, Consumption Tax, and Savings

Figure 10.4   Income Tax with Retailers and Producers

productivity. (People would have to pay tax when they withdraw their savings at a later date to spend it.)

However, a consumption tax does have one big disadvantage. Higher income people tend to save a higher portion of their income than do low-income people, so a consumption tax hits lower income people harder than high-income people.

There are three more problems with a consumption or sales tax:

1. A problem with a sales tax is that it is difficult to apply for large purchases such as a house or a car. With an income tax, your income is more likely to be spread out evenly across the years, so your tax payments will be spread out more evenly across years. If a sales tax applies to houses and cars, you will have a huge tax bill in the year you buy a house or a car, which will make it more of a burden than would be the case when taxes are spread out more evenly across years. Also, government revenue could be more volatile since spending on very big items could be more volatile because people might postpone those purchases.
2. There is a problem with local sales taxes, since the jurisdiction of the sale may not match the jurisdiction where the buyer lives. Many people live in metropolitan areas consisting of more than one town, and commonly buy products in a neighboring town. Also, these days people often buy products on the internet where the seller likely is from a different state.
3. There is a problem because the sales tax is more opaque. Most people won't add up the amount of sales tax they pay during a year and so will be unaware of the total amount.

These considerations suggest that an income tax is preferable to a consumption tax. The disadvantage of an income tax is that it does not provide as much incentive to save as does a consumption tax, but this can be taken care of by providing a deduction for savings (as with Individual Retirement

Accounts (IRAs)). This tax provides the benefit of providing an incentive to save, but the deduction amount can be limited so it can make sure that high-income taxpayers pay their fair share even if they save a lot.

Most individuals are involved in more frequent spending transactions than they are paycheck transactions (they may be paid only once or twice a month). This means that monitoring/enforcement costs of an income tax likely are less than with a consumption tax. Needless bureaucratic duplication could be eliminated by not having *both* a consumption and an income tax (as many states do). Each state and locality should be able to set its own tax rate, but much needless administrative redundancy could be eliminated if state and local taxes were collected on the same tax base as the federal income tax.

Much of local revenue comes from property taxes that would be best eliminated in most cases. In particular, if a local government collects income tax from someone residing at a particular address, then there is no need for them to also collect property tax for that address. There are also two serious problems with property taxes: (1) they violate the principle of progressivity/ability to pay, since a person's property tax liability does not go down when their income (and thus ability to pay) goes down; and (2) property taxes are not based on an objective tax base, but instead on inherently subjective estimates of property value (the only way to determine the true value of a property is to put it up for sale and see what it will sell for).

Property taxes are needed for any address for which the local government does not collect income taxes. For example, if a taxpayer has a vacation home, they need to pay a property tax on their vacation home (since their income tax payments would go to the local government where they are residents). Commercial properties need to pay property taxes at each of their locations. For example, a nationwide chain of stores needs to pay local taxes for each of their locations, in order to make sure that the local government receives revenue needed to provide services for that location.

Although there are advantages with having small towns that have governments that are close to local voters, it is a problem if a metropolitan area contains a lot of small towns, particularly if high-income individuals tend to live together and find they can provide reasonable local government services at a reasonably low tax rate (because the amount of income is so high). That approach leaves other small cities in the same metropolitan area with a higher concentration of lower income people, which makes it harder to raise enough revenue to pay for local government services.

Intermediate Goods and Value-added

Consumers (people) buy final products from businesses, but businesses also buy lots of products from other businesses.[5] For example, a peanut butter company buys peanuts from a peanut farmer. In Figure 10.4, people buy everything from retailers, and the retailers buy their products from producers.

If your goal is to tax consumption, then tax the flow of spending from consumers to retail stores. This way you will tax all of the flow of economic activity. Note that you don't tax the flow of money from retailers to producers, since this would double-tax the spending that you have already taxed by taxing the receipts of the retailers.

If your goal is to tax income, then you need to tax both streams of income that flow to people: the amount that the retailer pays to its workers and owners, and the amount the producers pay to their workers and owners. Taxing both of these streams will allow you to tax the full income stream.

Taxing Business Income

Measuring and taxing the income of workers is relatively straightforward, since you can measure the amount of their paychecks. Taxing the income of business owners is more complicated.

Consider a one-person business, such as a very small farm, or an espresso stand, or a one-person artist studio, or a garden service, or a taxi driver.

Suppose that our one-person business sells directly to the public, so is very similar to the retailers we saw earlier (see Figure 10.4). It should be clear that you should not tax the gross receipts (the total money coming in) since some of that money is used to buy the intermediate goods needed to run the business (seed and fertilizer for the farm; coffee beans for the espresso stand; canvas and paint for the artist; rakes and hoes for the garden service; and a car and gas for the taxi driver).

The *income* for the business owner is equal to *revenue minus expenses.* There is no sensible way to tax business income without providing for subtraction of business expenses. However, once you allow someone to subtract something from their revenue before they have to pay tax, there is a risk that unscrupulous business people will try to subtract some of their consumption spending that is masquerading as business expenses.

The same problem arises with a consumption tax. A consumption tax needs to be based on value-added, not gross receipts of a business. In Figure 10.4, it would be incorrect to tax both the gross receipts of the retailer and the gross receipts of the producers that sell them the good. (The word "incorrect" here means that the flow of economic activity is being measured in a misleading, incorrect fashion, and a tax system based on an incorrect measure will inevitably be arbitrary and unfair—some economic activity will be taxed at a different rate than others for no sensible reason). If you did try to tax the gross receipts of both retailers and producers, then you have created an incentive for a retailer to merge with its suppliers to become one company. This could have detrimental effects by increasing the concentration of economic power.

Since a value-added consumption tax would let the business owner subtract the amount they buy from other businesses, the same issue arises as with an income tax.

There is no way to avoid some complexity in the tax code, since there need to be rules about what business expenses can be deducted and what cannot. (For example, the 1986 tax reform law ended the business expense deduction for business education cruises—it seems clear that spending a week on a cruise ship should not count as a business expense even if you spend an hour each morning at a seminar learning more about business.)[6]

What if someone claims as a business expense an item that is really part of their consumption (such as a business meal, entertainment, etc.)? What if someone takes a trip to the location of an essential business meeting (so there is no question that it is a legitimate business expense) but then they also do some fun non-business things as part of the same trip?

Capital Investment

If your taxi company buys gas, that gas is consumed—and the expense of the gas is (and should be) recorded for the same month in which you record the revenue earned by providing taxi rides using that gas. However, if you buy a taxi, that taxi is not used up this month. It is a durable capital good that will last.

A basic principle of accounting says that you need to try to match expenses and revenue for different time periods. If your taxi lasts eight years, then it makes sense to count one-eighth of the cost as a business expense each year. If you counted the entire expense in the year you bought the taxi, your income for that year would look terrible (worse than it really is), whereas your income for the next seven years would look better than it really is (because you're not recognizing the expense of the taxi in those years). If you're extremely accounting-naive, you will be overly depressed in the first year but then overly happy in the following seven years. For our purposes, the more important fact is that you will be underpaying your taxes in the first year (when you are overstating your expense for the taxi). True, you will be overpaying taxes in later years, but delaying paying a tax is effectively the same as reducing the amount of tax you have to pay.

The tax code needs to make some provision for how to account for the expense of capital assets. There is no obviously right way to do this. In theory, every year you should value the taxi (or any other capital asset) at what you could sell it for at that moment, and then record the decrease in the value of the asset over the year as an expense. However, if you don't actually sell the asset, there is no way to know for sure what it would sell for.

If the tax depreciation amounts exceed the real depreciation (so for tax purposes the value of the capital asset is falling faster than it really is), the advantage is that there is a greater incentive for capital investment. However, there is a risk of encouraging tax shelter activity. If you're a high-income professional, one trick to reduce taxes would be to invest in certain assets (such as real estate) that allow for faster depreciation for tax purposes. If the depreciation amount is large enough, your real estate investment business runs a loss, which you used to be able to subtract from your professional income to lower your taxes. However, the trick to run a tax shelter is that you only want your investment business to make losses for tax purposes—you don't want it to make real losses. If the value of your asset actually goes up (as real estate might, regardless of what the tax code thinks) then you can later sell your asset for a profit and pay taxes at the capital gains rate, which has the effect of both delaying and lowering the amount of tax you have to pay. The 1986 tax reform act cracked down on this type of shelter by preventing people from deducting "passive losses" (as from the real estate investment business) from their active income (as from their professional job).[7]

INCENTIVES

When a tax is imposed on the sale of a product it usually reduces the quantity of that product that is sold. This is usually an unintended consequence, rather than being the purpose of the tax. For example, when a state imposes a sales tax on the sale of books, they are not deliberately trying to discourage people from reading—that is just an unintended consequence. In 1990 the government attempted to tax rich people by taxing boats, but the result was that rich people could buy things other than boats, and the middle class workers in the boating industry were the ones who were hurt the most.[8]

There are exceptions; for example, the cigarette tax is deliberately designed to discourage people from smoking. A tax can't be effective at both raising lots of revenue and significantly reducing consumption. If smokers are determined to smoke no matter what the price[9] then the cigarette tax will raise a lot of revenue but it will have little effect in discouraging smoking. On the other hand, if smokers are sensitive to the price, the higher price after the tax will be successful at causing a lot them to quit smoking, but the tax will not raise very much revenue.

TERRITORIAL TAX SYSTEM

In one *Monty Python* episode, they came up with a tax system that would be extremely popular at home: tax all foreigners living abroad. Just in case you didn't get the joke, the point is that a government can't very well tax income earned in other countries. The U.S. tax system recognizes this fact, but unfortunately it also recognizes one opportunity for collecting taxes: if a U.S. company earns income abroad, it is taxed if it returns the income to the U.S. (minus a credit for taxes paid on the income in the country in which it is generated, which is at a lower rate).[10] The resulting perverse incentive should be obvious: if the company pays tax on foreign-earned income returned to the U.S., but not on foreign-earned income not returned to the U.S., it can simply choose to leave its foreign-earned income overseas. The result is less money to invest and create jobs in the U.S.

The solution adopted by most countries is a territorial tax system, meaning that income is taxed by the country in which it is earned.

The online appendix has data on the actual tax distribution.

THE PROBLEM OF THE CORPORATE INCOME TAX

There are two general views about the taxation of corporations. The conduit approach views a corporation as nothing more than a mechanism to distribute income to its owners. In this view, there is no economic point in taxing income at the corporate level, as long as the income of the owners is taxed. The government can no more tax corporations themselves than it could tax domestic cats, since the only way to tax cats would be to levy a tax that hit the cat owners.

Another view is that corporations act as independent entities. Many people have a legitimate concern about corporations amassing too much power. The current tax code contributes to this concern by giving corporations an incentive to accumulate assets on their own, rather than distribute profits as dividends. These concerns could be lessened by making sure that the tax code favors corporate dividend payout, rather than retention of earnings.

The corporate income tax has no place in the conduit view. Redesigning the tax code to encourage dividend payment would help reduce the concerns of those supporters of the independent entity view that corporations are too powerful.

One major problem with the corporate income tax is that the incidence is difficult to determine.[11] It is difficult to design good tax policy when the incidence is unclear. The corporate tax cannot actually be "felt" by an inanimate object, so the incidence of the tax falls on owners (in the form of lower profits), or on consumers (in the form of higher prices), or on employees (in the form of lower wages).[12]

Superficially, the corporate tax has appeal on egalitarian grounds, but the case for this is weak if the true incidence of the tax is difficult to determine.

There is also a problem because different types of income are taxed at different rates. Estimates indicate that the tax on dividend income can be as high as 60.1 percent, while the tax on corporate retained earnings can be as high as 40.1 percent.[13] The goal of income tax policy should be to include all income in the tax base, and tax it all with the same rate schedule to avoid distortions that favor one source of income over another. Specifically, income earned in the corporate sector should be taxed no more and no less than other income. Too little capital will flow to the corporate sector if corporate income is taxed at a higher rate.[14] Ending the tax discrepancy could add $52 billion each year to national income.[15]

Taxing dividend income at higher rates than other income creates a perverse incentive for companies to avoid paying dividends. This can make it easier for Enron-style accounting fraud to take place, since reported earnings can be manipulated but dividends cannot. The dividend avoidance problem becomes exacerbated if corporate executives are motivated by stock options, which have value when stock prices rise but have no value when dividends are paid.[16]

If all corporate profits were paid as dividends, and all dividends were taxed as income, there would be no need for a corporate tax. In reality, corporations still should be able to raise funds from retained earnings, but the tax code should not be biased in favor of this. The tax distortion contributes to the problem of corporations growing big for bigness' sake, whether or not being bigger is more efficient. Corporations that accumulate cash can make future investment decisions or plan wasteful corporate takeovers without being tested in the market. Society's investment decisions may become distorted if corporations that already have accumulated funds are favored over other companies that need to raise funds in the financial markets. (This effect can be called "survival of the fattest."[17])

Top corporate managers are a much smaller group of people than corporate shareholders. If they are able to use corporate assets for their own purposes then society is less egalitarian, since a small group of people controls a large amount of assets.

Another concern is that the current tax system encourages corporations to use debt finance, since interest payments are deductible but dividends are not. This can increase the risk of bankruptcy.[18]

The corporate tax could be eliminated as long as all income earned in the corporate sector is taxed. This could be achieved if dividend income is taxed at the individual level, and if capital gains on publicly traded stocks are taxed annually, rather than on realization.[19]

Alternatively, the corporate income tax could be completely replaced with a much simpler tax on market value.[20] For example, if a company has a future income stream X, its market value would be X/r (r is the interest rate). If income is to be taxed at rate t, then revenue from the tax should equal tX. Let s be the tax rate on market value. Then

$$\frac{sX}{r} = tX$$

$$S = rt$$

The tax would be paid quarterly but the tax liability should be calculated daily, based on the closing price at the end of the day. There are roughly 250 working days per year (not counting weekends and holidays), so set the daily tax rate at

$$s_{daily} = \frac{rt}{250}$$

If $t = .25$ and $r = .05$ then the daily market value tax rate would be 0.000050.

If the company pays a dividend of [*DIV*], then deduct the amount $t \times$ [*DIV*] from the amount owed, to recognize that the dividend income is taxable income to the recipient. This system would make sure that all income earned by the corporation is taxed, while also dramatically reducing the administrative and compliance cost compared to the current corporate income tax.[21]

Corporations that are not publicly traded could choose to be taxed as above on a market value they state (with the risk that they could be bought out if they set their value too low) or as the equivalent of a sole proprietorship (so they would have to go through the complications of deducting business expenses as described earlier).

TAXES AND BENEFITS

Should one person be taxed in order to pay benefits to another person? It depends.

Government benefits may be needed to provide opportunity—as when the benefits support children whose parents are unable to support them.

Government benefits may be needed to provide security—as when the benefits support the aged or disabled who are unable to work.

However, if the taxes required to fund these benefits are too high, the freedom of the taxpayers is infringed upon. People must make a value judgment as to how high taxes can be before infringing on freedom. This is a matter of opinion so different people will differ. Clearly, though, the benefit payments cannot be ever-increasing. If they were, the tax rates would be required to be ever-increasing, and will sooner or later hit the point where they undoubtedly are curtailing freedom. Therefore, government benefit entitlement programs need to be reformed so they will be sustainable—that is, so they are not ever-increasing. More in the next chapter.

NOTES

1. Noah, p180.

2. Congress already set up a way to deal with the problem of high-income taxpayers not paying enough: the Alternative Minimum Tax (AMT). The mere existence of the AMT means that Congress admits the regular tax code is such a miserable wreckage that it cannot be trusted to work properly, so a totally separate alternative duplicate system is needed. The AMT should be abolished as part of comprehensive tax reform.

3. Everyone agrees that you shouldn't design the tax code in this stupid way: have everyone with income under 40,000 pay 10 percent of their income; while everyone with income over 40,000 pays 30 percent. In this case a person would see their tax bill jump at the moment their income reached 40,000. Instead, the actual tax system is designed something like this: everyone with income under 40,000 pays 10 percent of their income; everyone with income over 40,000 pays 10 percent of 40,000 (4000) plus they pay 30 percent of the amount over 40,000. For someone with income over 40,000 the 30 percent is called their *marginal tax rate*—defined to be the tax on the next additional dollar of income.

4. The combined rate is the sum of federal, state, and local taxes, including general sales and property taxes but excluding taxes that are imposed on specific goods for a specific purpose, such as gasoline or cigarettes.

5. These products are *intermediate goods.*

6. Title 26, United States Code, section 274.

7. Title 26, United States Code, section 58.

8. *New York Times*, online, February 7, 1992.

9. the term for this is *inelastic demand.*

10. Bartlett, p151.

11. The study of the incidence of a tax is the study of who really feels the effect of the tax. This is not determined by who writes the check to the government—for example, you feel the incidence of the income tax even though your employer writes the tax withholding check to the government.

12. See Harberger 1962; Stiglitz 1976.

13. CEA, p202.

14. CEA, p175.

15. CEA, p115.

16. Colvin 2003.

17. McLure 1979, p25. Galbraith also writes about this problem (*New Industrial State*, p39).

18. CEA, p203.

19. A proposal for replacing the corporate tax with a tax on corporate stock gains was discussed in the 1937 book, *Facing the Tax Problem*; Shoup 1937, p477.

20. Johnson; Bartlett, p160.

21. See online appendix myhome.spu.edu/ddowning/fos.html for an example.

Chapter 11

Government Spending

Many of the most important decisions the government makes relate to spending public money.

TRENDS

Trend graphs illustrate how the level of government spending and its components have changed over time, and pie charts illustrate how spending at a particular time is divided up. Budget data needs to be viewed as a hierarchy, so you can sometimes look at the very broad overall view, and other times drill down to see the detail associated with particular categories. See the web page for software that can generate tables and graphs of U.S. government spending from 1962 to 2013. It helps to look at both expenditures in current dollars and in constant (inflation-adjusted) dollars, and it is useful to look at per-capita spending to see how spending growth compares to population growth.

The Department of Health and Human Services accounts for the largest share of government spending in 2013. The largest share of that department's spending is for Medicare and Medicaid. The next largest categories are Social Security, Department of Defense, and Department of the Treasury (which spends a large amount on interest on the national debt).

SOCIAL SECURITY

The traditional social security system relies on collecting payroll taxes from current workers to raise funds to pay benefits to current retirees. Do you come out ahead with this system? It depends on how the total of payroll taxes you paid compares to the total benefits you receive.

The first beneficiaries had not paid any social security taxes. However, people just reaching retirement age now have been paying social security taxes during their working lives, so they justifiably expect to receive the benefits.

Changing demographics will force changes in the operation of Social Security and the related medicare program. The retirement-age population has increased significantly, even before the wave of baby-boom retirements started arriving.[1] In 2011 the earliest boomers (born in 1946) turned 65, and the last boomers born in 1964 will turn 67 in 2031. See the online graphs showing the animation of the age distribution of the U.S. population from 1930 to 2010.

The Nature of Savings

For an individual, wealth can be held either as something tangible, or as a promise to pay made by someone else. As long as the person making the promise is trustworthy, the wealth-holder doesn't care which it is. However, from society's point of view, it makes a big difference. The pure financial assets held by some people are cancelled out by the pure financial liabilities held by other people, so from society's point of view the only wealth available is actual tangible wealth.[2]

Consider some different ways to hold wealth:

- Own a house that you live in (so you receive the services of the house), or own a house that you rent out (so you receive rental income). You directly own part of the tangible wealth of society.
- Own stock in a company that owns tangible assets; you are indirectly owning a share of those assets that add to the wealth of society.
- Own bank deposits in a bank that lends money to people that own houses or to businesses that own tangible assets; you are indirectly owning a share of those assets.
- Lend money to someone that is a myopic borrower; that is, they promise to repay you out of their future income, but do not use the loan funds to purchase any tangible assets that would add to wealth today.
- Pay social security taxes today, and then expect to receive social security benefits in the future that will be paid for by taxing the future income of future workers. You will view the social security promise as similar as if you had lent out the money, but this is equivalent to myopic lending because the promise to pay comes out of future income rather than out of any tangible asset that adds to the wealth of society.

Martin Feldstein (1974) pointed out the effect of social security on reducing national savings. A similar issue happens with private pensions. Some pensions are defined benefit plans, when your employer makes a promise to pay you in the future. By contrast, in a defined contribution plan your employer contributes an amount that is used to build up savings for you to use in retirement.

An argument for defined benefit plans is that they shift the investment risk to the employer rather than the worker. However, this safety for the worker is illusory.[3] If the company goes bankrupt you can lose, and if the company can't predict future investment returns perfectly it can underfund the pension and you're also in trouble.[4]

Another problem with defined benefit pensions is that the benefits depend on arbitrarily chosen service times, so workers are at risk if they are forced to leave work before completing the required number of years.

The problem is compounded for public workers. Current elected officials can promise future pension benefits that will be paid for when new officials have been elected. The new officials will have to figure out how to pay the pensions if they have been (surprisingly?) underfunded by the previous elected officials. If current trends continue, vital government services will have to be cut back as an increasing share of state and local government revenue flows to defined-benefit pensions for retired public employees.

Another problem with the social security system is that it discriminates against population groups with shorter average lifespans. If someone dies in the same year they reach retirement age, they will have paid social security taxes their entire working career but will not receive any retirement benefits. If, on the other hand, they had been part of a savings program and had been accumulating wealth during their working years, then at least that wealth could be passed on to their heirs.

Sustainable Social Security Constitutional Amendment

Because social security involves a long-term promise, it should be established by constitutional amendment, providing social security benefits with long-term protection from the whims of future Congresses. The amendment should establish a sustainable path for social security, with a fixed amount set for the fraction of the population receiving benefits (so the retirement age automatically rises as more people live to greater ages), and a fixed amount for the fraction of national income that is paid as social security benefits. These amounts need to be fixed both to protect future beneficiaries from future cuts, and to protect society from unsustainable growth in the expenses.

As average lifespans increase, it becomes clear that the retirement age needs to increase. Current law does in fact provide for a gradual increase in the retirement age. For workers in physically demanding jobs, there will need to be a normal practice of transitioning to less physical jobs as they get older, and a practice of phasing in retirement would benefit many workers (so instead of transitioning one day from 40 hours worked per week to 0 hours, transition to work half-time for a few years before transitioning to full retirement).

Entitlement programs in general and social security in particular cannot keep growing as a percentage of national income. The question will be if the growth will stop as a result of a careful plan or a desperate crisis. The inexorable crisis will come when tax rates reach the maximum level the voters will tolerate, and further tax rate increases deter work effort and reduce revenue. Before that happens, most likely the government will try to keep borrowing to maintain entitlement spending, so the crisis will initially hit when the government strikes a hard borrowing limit when there is a dearth of lenders.

NOTES

1. See Kotlikoff and Burns.

2. Tobin 1998, p2–3. A nation can also hold wealth in the form of claims on other nations. If we consider "society" to mean the whole world, then all of these claims will net to zero.

3. For example, Noah (p54) falls for the illusion that the promise to pay a pension from one company (your employer) is safer than holding a diverse portfolio.

4. Kelly (p77) complains about the switch from defined benefit to defined contribution pensions, but then complains that workers don't share the benefit of pension fund gains—which is precisely the argument in switching to defined contribution pensions.

Chapter 12

Power

Often people feel powerless. Fortunately, consumers are not as powerless as they think. As a group, people (acting as consumers) are all-powerful in a market economy. The fate of almost any business is in their hands.[1] Individually, people don't have power in a market, but sometimes too much power is a real problem.

MONOPOLIES

If a group of sellers are taken over by a monopoly (or they form a cartel to act like a monopoly), they will, not surprisingly, try to increase their profits by increasing prices. In some cases the ordinary people might have no power to resist.

As expected, the monopolist increases profit by increasing price, but this doesn't mean the monopolist can keep raising the price as much as it feels like. At some point the price increases will cause such a large decline in quantity sold that revenue increases less than cost increases, so then it's time to stop raising the price.

Another problem is that a monopoly faces less pressure to be efficient than does a firm with competition. This is a version of the "pig-trough" problem—see page 20.

How to Stay a Monopolist

The very action that raises the monopolists' profit sows the seed for the potential destruction of those profits. Higher profit for the monopolist inherently means a larger margin between the sale price and the production cost.

163

That gap creates a profit incentive for somebody else to come in and sell the product. (For a cartel, each member has an incentive to increase its own production, but if they all do so then the cartel disintegrates.)

In order for the monopolist to continue earning monopoly level profits, it needs to somehow prevent other people from selling the product. Here's one way to do that: invent something, then either patent it or keep it secret. Monopolists are not all bad: for inventors, their ability to profit by monopolizing their invention provides an incentive to create more inventions. Protection of patents is one function of government explicitly written into the constitution (although patent protection is only temporary). That's why any analysis of economic power based on a current snapshot (rather than a feature-length movie) will be misleading. In 1975 people might have worried about the economic power of IBM, but they would not have dreamed about the eventual economic power of a startup company operating out of an apartment (Microsoft). In 1998 the people worried about Microsoft's economic power were not expecting the rise of the new companies (such as Google, Amazon, and Facebook) or the return to prominence of Apple. In 2010 Apple reached a pinnacle with the iPad (and the previously released iPod and iPhone), but it will only continue its dominance if it continually innovates. Otherwise it will be replaced at the top by new innovative companies (some of these are currently operating in obscure apartments, and others will be founded by dreamers who are still in elementary school today).

Another way a monopolist can prevent others from encroaching on its market is to own a unique resource. If your network paid a king's ransom for the rights to broadcast the Olympics, then other networks cannot enter your monopoly market. If you inherited a unique beachfront resort, other people can't sell the same product because they don't own the unique resort. Other people can sell products that may be reasonable substitutes, so with a monopoly the crucial question is what products are possible substitutes, and are they very close substitutes?

If you have to pay a lot to obtain the unique resource (as with the Olympics broadcast rights) that expense will reduce your profits. A big benefit will go to the owner who is able to sell you that resource. If you inherited valuable land, you can run a profitable business based on that land. However, in this case you are making money as a lucky landowner rather than as a savvy businessperson.

Consider a renaissance town where the clockmakers form a guild in an attempt to increase profits, like a monopolist. Fewer people buy clocks because of the higher prices. Clockmaking becomes highly profitable, but because it requires considerable skill they don't need to worry about other people rushing into the clockmaking business. What if the stable-sweepers try the same tactic? Initially the stable owners will tend to hire fewer stable-sweepers, but then they will find it is not hard to find plenty of people with the (minimal) skills needed to be stable-sweepers, so they can ignore the guild and hire those willing to work for lower wages. Unlike with the case of the clockmakers, the stable-sweeper guild isn't protected by a skill barrier, so the only way it can survive is if it can find some other way of preventing non-guild members from taking stable-sweeping jobs. The higher wages for the guild stable-sweepers is good for them, but not everyone who wants these jobs will be able to get them so the guild will need some screening mechanism to determine who gets the jobs and who doesn't.

When You don't Need to Worry about Monopolies

In some situations a monopoly will be less of a problem:

1. If the monopoly attained its position by inventing something, and then obtaining a patent, then its monopoly profits are a reward for its innovation.
2. If there are no barriers to entry. When a monopoly firm makes profits, it attracts other firms into that industry. If there is some barrier preventing them from entering this industry the monopoly will continue to earn profits. If there are no barriers to entry, its monopoly status (and its profits) will soon come to an end (as discussed on page 164).
3. If the product has close substitutes (meaning other products with very similar characteristics are available nearby). Coca Cola has a monopoly on selling Coke, but the competition from Pepsi prevents them from having much monopoly power. A gasoline station in a small town that is 50 miles from the nearest other gas station can act like a monopolist, but if the nearest other gas station is two miles away it won't have monopoly power.
4. If the product is a luxury that you can easily live without.
5. If it is a regulated natural monopoly. Certain products require delivery by pipes or wires connected to each house—electric power, water, natural gas, cable tv, landline phone service. It is inefficient for society to have multiple sellers in this business. Garbage collection provides another example. The government often regulates the price that these companies can charge to keep them from exploiting their monopoly position. The regulators can't set the price too low, because then the company will be unable to make enough profit to invest in the business. The term for this type of industry is *natural monopoly*. Since natural monopolies require connections along public infrastructure it is reasonable for the government to regulate the price charged as a condition of access to the public infrastructure.

ANTITRUST POLICY

"Antimonopoly" would be a better term for this type of policy aimed at preventing monopolies. Section 1 of the Sherman act prohibits both cartels and informal price-fixing behavior. This prohibition helps ordinary people because they don't have to worry about the sellers getting together and restricting the supply in order to drive the price up.[2]

The problem with antitrust policy is that not all monopoly behavior fits the clear-cut Section 1 prohibition against cartels. Sometimes a company acquires a monopoly in a "good" way, as when it invents something and obtains a patent. In this case not only does the government allow the monopoly, it will defend the patent holder's monopoly right. The purpose of awarding patents is to encourage invention, which is important because, among other reasons, inventions can improve productivity which improves real wages. In cases of natural monopoly it is most efficient to have only one company (see page 165).

Section 2 of the Sherman Act makes the act of monopolizing illegal, but the problem with this part of the law is that it is too vague. It does make sense to make it illegal to acquire a monopoly in a bad way (as when Standard Oil bought up many of its rivals before 1911), but it is harmful if someone is found guilty of monopolization after building up their monopoly in a good way. For example, the aluminum pioneer Alcoa was found guilty in 1945 and ordered broken up because it dominated the industry. The decision of the court in this case indicates that their main crime was being too efficient:[3]

It was not inevitable that it (Alcoa) should always
anticipate increases in the demand for ingot and be
prepared to supply them. Nothing compelled it to keep
doubling and redoubling its capacity before others
entered the field.

It insists that it never excluded competitors,
but we can think of no more effective exclusion
than progressively to embrace each new opportunity
as it opened, and to face every newcomer with
new capacity already geared into a great organization,
having the advantage of experience, trade connections,
and the elite of personnel.

If the logic of that case had been consistently followed in other cases, it would mean that one defense against a charge of being a monopoly would be to create a lousy organization filled with inexperienced incompetent personnel.

In 1969 IBM was accused of antitrust violations because of its dominance of the computer industry. The case dragged on until 1982, when it was finally dropped. Whether or not IBM deserved to be found guilty of monopolizing in 1969, the market for computers was totally different by 1982. Rapid technological change makes it very hard to develop a sensible antitrust policy. Another technology company that faced a major antitrust case was Microsoft, which was found guilty in 2001 for its dominance in operating system software. Note that Microsoft did not even exist when the IBM case was first filed in 1969. There could not be a market for microcomputer software before the development of the microprocessor. The trial court judge ordered Microsoft broken up, but that remedy was overturned on appeal so it ended up that Microsoft was only lightly punished despite the guilty verdict. A decade later Microsoft's position looked far less dominant when compared to a resurgent Apple and newcomers like Google and Facebook.

It would be best to repeal Sherman Act Section 2, because the prohibition on monopolizing is too vague. As time goes by and some companies are observed engaging in abusive behaviors that promote monopolization, the Federal Trade commission could recommend that Congress pass laws banning specific behaviors. For example, at one time one of Microsoft's tricks was to tell computer makers that they could have the operating system software for a lower price if they signed a contract where they agreed to pay Microsoft that amount every time they sold a computer, whether or not they actually included Microsoft software on the computer. This provision effectively locked the hardware makers into installing Microsoft software on their computers, because they had to pay Microsoft a fee for each computer they produced even if they put someone else's software on the machine. (If they did decide to put some other software on the machine, they would have to pay that company too—so they would have to pay double for that machine.) You can make a good case that this is an abusive practice that would be good to ban. Microsoft agreed to stop doing this practice in a consent decree they signed with the Justice department. We would be better off with a law banning this specific practice, rather than a very vague law which leaves it questionable whether this practice is legal or not. As technology changes very rapidly it is simply not possible to come up with a good general rule that can anticipate every type of abusive practice that might occur in the future. Also, it is essential to remember the constitutional prohibition of *ex post facto*—prosecuting someone for an act that is now illegal but was legal at the time they did it. It is wrong to prosecute someone for an act which is later found to have violated a very vague law.

Currently there is an anti-trust case involving Apple's pricing of e-books with the same problem: prosecutors make up the rules about what they think should be legal and then file the charges.

LEGAL RIGHTS FOR CORPORATIONS

Some people argue that the problem comes from the very existence of corporations. In particular, corporations are legally treated as a "person," and since they're not really people this seems bad. However, this concern is misplaced. The legal status of a corporation simply means that it is able to own property and sign contracts. If there were no corporations, then the world would be much less egalitarian, because only rich people could afford to own productive assets. (For an example, consider the world of professional sports teams. With rare exceptions, leagues require that their teams be owned by a person or partnership, rather than a corporation. The result is that only very rich people are eligible to become sports team owners.[4])

Imagine that all businesses could only be owned by the rich. The rich would get even richer, because there would be no way for ordinary people to share in those profits (by becoming shareholders).

Also, it is important to note that non-profit organizations are legally corporations. This means they are able to have a checking account in the organization's name and thereby can directly receive donations and pay their workers. (If corporate status did not exist a non-profit organization would have to collect donations in a personal checking account.)

WHY DO CAPITAL OWNERS CONTROL CORPORATIONS?

Why do shareholders have control of a corporation?

An entrepreneur needs to attract workers and capital investors by offering them compensation. Investors need to sacrifice funds today in return for profit in the future. One way to do this is to promise a specific rate of return, by issuing debt. The interest payment to lenders is fixed, as is the wage payment to workers. (The business could go bankrupt or lay off workers, so these payments are not absolutely fixed, but interest and wage payments are less variable than profit.) Workers benefit when greater capital investment adds to their productivity, so they have an incentive to make sure the business can attract capital.

However, it is not possible for all suppliers of productive factors to receive fixed returns. Since there is uncertainty about the future profit of the enterprise, somebody has to put up with an uncertain future return. It is usually not feasible for all capital suppliers to have a fixed promised return. The debt holders view their return as almost fixed—the only way they won't get their promised percentage is in case of bankruptcy. One reason it is very hard to finance a company entirely with debt is that the risk of default (which is low for reasonable debt levels) suddenly starts to skyrocket at very high debt levels.[5] Therefore, there generally have to be some capital suppliers that take on the risk of an uncertain return. In order to convince somebody to supply capital to the company in return for a claim on future uncertain profits, they have to be offered a share of control. Since shareholders bear the risk of receiving nothing, they have to be promised the possibility that they can receive more than bondholders if the company is successful—otherwise, there is no point in taking the risk.[6] (A mission-driven nonprofit or social venture company has more flexibility when it can convince donors who support its mission to provide some of its funding without expecting a monetary return.)

A rather naive objection[7] is that people who buy shares don't contribute anything to the enterprise because the money they spend goes to existing shareholders, instead of the company itself (unless they buy stock during an IPO or other public offering). Since the initial share purchasers would be much less willing to buy the shares if they knew there was not a market to sell their shares, the reality is that the ability to sell the shares to others is as essential as the process of the company initially selling shares to the public. With the stock market, the risk already exists (it is inevitable that there will be risk when assets are used for future production) and the stock market allows that risk to be transferred to those that voluntarily want to hold it (and it also makes it possible to reduce risk by diversification—but diversification does not eliminate risk, particularly if the entire economy suffers a downturn).

Managers of publicly traded corporations should not object to rules that clarify the ability of their shareholders to run the company. The managers have to remember that when they sold stock to the public, they did not promise the shareholders that they would get any money back—only that they would have control of the corporation.

However, it is important that the rules for publicly traded corporations not be too burdensome. If they can borrow enough funds to buy out their shareholders, then publicly traded corporations can "go private"—so that they remain corporations, but their shares are no longer traded by the public and so there are less restrictions on the type of information they have to make available. A big advantage of publicly traded corporations is that profits can be shared widely so it is important not to design rules that create a disincentive for corporations to go public.[8]

When a corporation sells shares to the public, it is important for the managers to work on earning profits for the company (rather than taking the shareholder's money and spending it on their own consumption). This need to deter stock swindles is the reason for the legal requirement for publicly traded corporations to maximize profit. Other types of organizations, such as nonprofits, sole proprietorships, partnerships, and closely held non-publicly traded corporations have more flexibility to pursue goals other than profit maximization if the owners desire.

One concern is that shareholders of publicly traded corporations have too much of a short-term focus.[9] This may well be true too often, but if you were sure that this was a problem there would be an incentive to purchase the stock of companies that undertake sound long-term investments, but are undervalued because of the stock market's short-term focus. In reality this is very difficult because of uncertainty, and it is difficult to distinguish an aversion to risk from an actual short-term bias. One step to help with this problem would be to require more of CEO pay to be in the form of stock that must be held for a longer term (see the next section).

Worker ownership is good, both to spread capital ownership to a wider group and to provide workers with an incentive to care about the future of the company. Employee stock ownership programs (ESOP) should be encouraged. However, true worker ownership cannot be mandated, since true owners have the right to sell their ownership share, so worker owners can decide whether or not they will retain their ownership shares. Encouraging worker ownership of restricted shares (that cannot be sold while the worker is with the company) would be beneficial.

The problem with paying capital a fixed return and workers the remaining revenue[10] is that a policy that pays workers well in profitable time ends up paying workers nothing in bad times. That illustrates the basic flaw with the concern that shareholders are flooded with wealth at the expense of the workers—in times when the wealth doesn't flood in, it is better for the losses to hit the shareholders rather than the workers.

THE CORPORATE GOVERNANCE AND CEO PAY PROBLEM

When a company sells shares to the public, it is taking money in exchange for nothing more than a promise to be governed by those who've contributed. (This is very different from when a company borrows money, where the promise is to repay the money with a certain rate of interest.) However, there needs to be an effective way for the shareholder owners to control their hired hands (the executives). Corporate executives should be compensated for their work, and those with special talent deserve special compensation. How can we distinguish deserved compensation for special effort from undeserved skimming of the shareholders' property? Distinguish two aspects of the CEO pay problem: pay-for-performance, and pay-despite-performance. Pay-despite-performance is a particularly serious problem: CEOs that have done the equivalent of looting their companies at the expense of the shareholders. The problem is that CEOs can often set their own pay.[11] However, even lavish CEO pay may not be a very noticeable fraction of the expenditures for a very large company, so the company profit might not increase much even if the CEO pay problem can be fixed.

One way that does not work well is to reward managers with stock options, which provide the opportunity to buy stock at a particular price. Compensating CEOs with stock options also creates a measurement problem. If a CEO has been granted stock options over a five year period, and cashes them in during year 5, it is incorrect to look at the total compensation in year 5 as if it were payment for that single year. In reality it is part of the pay for the last five years so it needs to be averaged out.[12] The positive incentive from stock options is that the managers will benefit from an increase in the share price (aligning their interests with the shareholders in that regard). However, there have been cases of the date of the options being manipulated to make the increase in stock price appear greater than it is. The main problem with stock options happens if the current stock price is at or below the option price. In that case the options are worthless, and the option-holding manager has nothing further to lose if the stock price falls even further. It's a bad idea to have decisions related to risk made by those that have nothing more to lose, because they have every incentive to take on extra risk in the hopes they will pay off (and with no fear of further losses if they don't). The situation is similar to a football team facing fourth down with a long ways to go. Normally, the team will make the obvious choice and punt (which is less risky), but if it is late in the game when the team is behind then they will go for the first down because they have nothing more to lose.[13]

A better solution is to compensate corporate executives with shares of stock in their own company. These shares should be restricted so that they cannot be sold before a predetermined date.

An inefficiently run, publicly traded company will see its share price decline providing an incentive for someone to take over the firm and install better management. Although unpopular, corporate takeovers provide a crucial function by preventing incumbent corporate managers from becoming fat and lazy. For example, somebody would take over Dilbert's stupid company (if it were real) and fire its inept management.[14]

However, this does not mean that takeovers should be encouraged. A problem with current tax policy that discourages payment of dividends is that it encourages firms to build up cash hoards that may lead them to attempt takeovers. Ideally, public policy would be neutral toward takeovers—neither encourage them nor discourage them, so that they would only be likely to happen in cases where they really did make economic sense.

NARROW-INTEREST PROVISIONS IN TAX LAW

The Tax Reform Act of 1986 contained, among other provisions designed to close tax shelters, a requirement that donors to university athletic departments could not take a charitable deduction if they were furnished the right to purchase seating at that stadium. However, there was an odd exception written into the law: the limit on charitable contribution would not apply if one donated to an institution that is "located in a State capital pursuant to a statewide election in September 1981" (Tax Reform Act of 1986, Public Law 99–514, section 1608, subsection (b), paragraph (1), subparagraph (B), page 2771).[15]

Although we do need to be thankful for the benefits we receive by living in a representative democracy where the government is responsive to the people and officeholders are held accountable in elections, the scandal of narrow interest legislation requires us to make an effort to restructure the government to reduce the chances of this type of legislation becoming law.

The basic flaw of section 1608 above is that it imposes a small cost on a large number of people while providing a large benefit on a very small group of people. All taxpayers will have to pay the cost of higher rates to make up for the revenue lost by section 1608, while the donors to the favored institution receive the benefit of the charitable deduction. The scandal in this case is magnified by the camouflaged language of the law. We can try to do some detective work to find out what institution this provision applies to, but then we will be puzzled when we find that there were no elections in September 1981 to establish a state university in a state capital. What's going on?

The section was intended to apply to a large state university, due to the influence of a leader of the House. However, in this case taxpayers were saved by an accidental typographical error. (How often have you made a typographical error on page 2771 of a document you are typing?) The provision intended to say 1891 instead of 1981, but as a result of the mistake section 1608 ends up applying to no institutions at all. Plenty of other such camouflaged sections did become part of this (and subsequent) laws.

Blinder [1987, p29] suggests this test for any economic policy proposal: "Does this change improve the efficiency of the market system; that is, does it give us *more* rather than *less*? If the answer is no, we should then ask: Does the proposed policy redistribute income from richer people to poorer ones? If the answer is again no, the proposal promotes neither efficiency nor equality and should be rejected unless it clearly serves some other vital national goal. Many policies that fleece the public to feed the special interests could be avoided by applying this simple test." Blinder [1987, p3] also suggests why this test is not applied: "the disuse and misuse of economics in policy making is not just a run of bad luck, bad judgment, or human errors. Rather, the problem is systematic. Economic policy is made by politicians, not by economists—which is just as it should be in a democracy. But politicians do not accept and reject economists' advice at random. They choose the solutions that they perceive to be politically correct. Unfortunately, there seems to be a systematic tendency for good economics to make bad politics."

A government with the power to provide benefits to the less well-off runs the risk of falling under the influence of the better-off and instead rigging the system to provide more benefits to them (see the paradox of government power on page 46).

Those narrow interests that try to get the government to twist the laws in their favor benefit when the public is distracted by the competition between Democrats and Republicans. If you're the beneficiary of a narrow-interest policy, you hope that lots of contentious issues will continue to arise between the parties so the public pays attention to those without ever focusing on the problem of narrow-interest policies.

NOTES

1. See page 19.

2. It is hard for a cartel group to stick together, since each member of the cartel has a temptation to increase its production and slightly undercut the price of the other cartel members. Making cartels illegal helps by preventing the group from developing formal arrangements to hold them together.

3. *United States v. Alcoa*, 1945.

4. The Green Bay Packers are an exception in being a corporation owned by shareholders, as a legacy of when the team was formed long ago.

5. Stiglitz 2010, p246; see also online animation.

6. Gregg (p113–17) discusses the situation in Germany and other countries where employees are required to have seats on the board of a corporation.

7. Kelly, p2.

8. Some people become confused by the terminology. Sometimes a publicly traded company is called a public company, but a "public company" is in fact a private company—that is, it has private ownership, not government ownership. The term "publicly-traded company" should be used for these companies.

9. Savitz, p245, p233.

10. as in Kelly, p167.

11. Picketty, p24; Stiglitz 2010, p152, p247.

12. Reynolds, p123.

13. For another example of this problem, see page 117.

14. see Scott Adams' *Dilbert* comic strip.

15. The bipartisan Tax Reform Act of 1986 did achieve an improvement in the tax system by lowering rates but also reducing tax avoidance (loopholes). It was passed by a Democratic House, a Republican Senate, and was signed by President Reagan. See Blinder, chapter 6.

Chapter 13

Government Structure

Tensions, Trade-offs, and Problems

What should be the structure of a democratic government?

EXTREMES: ELECTED RULER OR VOTE-ON-EVERYTHING

There are several choices for the structure of the government.

One extreme is to have an elected ruler; the other extreme is for the public to vote on everything.

An elected ruler can make all the laws, but the problems are insurmountable: society can't know in advance who (if anyone) can be trusted with absolute power. How would a ruler be held accountable? Even an elected legislature with absolute power creates the danger of freedoms being curtailed.

Severe problems are also inherent in the vote-on-everything plan. People don't have expertise on all the issues, and most people would rather spend time on something else rather than developing expertise on public policy.

The solution must be for the people to elect representatives. Many questions still remain: how many representatives? with what responsibilities? for how long of a term?

TENSIONS AND TRADE-OFFS

Part of the problem is that there are several areas in which two desirable properties of government contradict each other, so society has to make difficult choices.

Expertise Government Versus Representative Government

Should government give the people what they want (purely representative government), or should the government do what it thinks is best for the people (expertise government)?[1] The problem with purely representative government is that the people may not know what policy is best. Also, there is the voter's version of the John Kennedy question: do you vote for someone with expertise who will make decisions for the benefit of the whole society, or do you vote for someone who will benefit your group at the expense of others? The problem with pure expertise government is that there is no good way to determine which experts should have the power, and how to hold them accountable. How can you distinguish a case where the experts follow an unpopular policy that is really good for the people in the long run, versus a case where the experts follow an unpopular policy that is good for the experts themselves and less good for the people?

Most people would likely vote for experts that could deliver a stable high-employment economy, except for the fact that it is difficult or impossible to know in advance who would be the true expert that could best achieve this goal. Instead, there might be a risk that voters might support candidates promising policies with short-term benefit but long-term risk. For example, expansionary monetary policy might be popular in the short run but cause inflation in the long-run. The Federal Reserve board is set up in a semi-independent fashion in the hope that they will act as experts in determining how much money there will be, without being directly accountable to the voters.

Separation of Powers Versus Accountability

Should election winners be able to implement their desired policies, or should power be separated to provide checks and balances? The Constitution framers established the principle of separation of powers (an idea developed by the French philosopher Montesquieu). In particular, in the U.S. in recent years it has been common for the majority in one or both houses of Congress to belong to the party not holding the Presidency: 1947–1948, 1955–1960, 1969–1976, 1981–1992, 1994–2000, 2001–2002, 2007–2008, and 2011–2016. Split control of the government is very helpful in preventing extremists from implementing their policies, but it becomes complicated for voters to know who to blame or credit for the results.[2]

Some type of divided government is possible whenever voters vote on more than one office in the national government. U.S. voters vote on four national offices: president, two senators, and one representative. The only way to prevent divided government would be to adopt a parliamentary system with voting by district (so that a voter's vote for their local member also determines their vote for prime minister) or a national proportional system where one vote for a political party determines the percentage of parliamentary members for that party.

Majority Rule Versus Protect the Rights of All

We need to prevent a minority from tyrannizing the majority. Through most of human history, this has been the big problem: a powerful minority holding power that they used to control the rest of the population. A democratic government effectively ends this problem (but the powerful can still bend the rules in their favor).

However, there is a harder problem. We need to prevent the majority from tyrannizing a minority. It is harder to prevent this in a democratic government, because a democratic government is more likely to go along with what the majority wants. There needs to be somebody with the authority to overrule the democratic majority when necessary to protect essential rights, but who can be trusted with such extreme power, and how will they be held accountable if they are not to be accountable to the majority? Elected officials need to know they are under the law—for example, someone needs to have the authority to tell them they can't change the constitution to extend their terms in office. Much of the debate over ratification of the constitution concerned the fear that the proposed national government would infringe on freedoms.[3]

The constitution established the Supreme Court with the power to protect rights. The Court is indirectly accountable to the people because their members are appointed and confirmed by elected officials, but once in office the members are independent. The court cannot simply make decisions but it needs to write clear opinions stating the reasons for its decisions. This may be the best way of solving the difficult problem of protecting rights. This issue is complicated because courts do need to make decisions about how to apply rights that were written in the 1700s to the world of today. For example, the Bill of Rights guarantees the right to a free press, which reasonably needs to be extended to broadcasters even if it was written at a time when the press only referred to the printed press. However, the problem with the view that the rights listed in the constitution naturally change with time is that it is risky to trust anyone with the power to decide how those rights change. Courts shouldn't be able to change the constitution on their own, since their job is to interpret the law rather than rewrite it.

Stability Versus Adaptability

Basic laws, including the tax code, should not change very often. On the other hand, laws should adapt to changing circumstances.

The foundation of laws, the constitution, should be hard to change, so that the people can receive long-term promises from the government. On the other hand, sometimes the constitution needs to be changed, and there is a problem if it is too difficult to change. What if one group has the power to block any change that might be highly beneficial to everyone else in the nation?

Expedited Action Versus Contemplative Action

A bicameral legislature means that the process of making laws is slow and cumbersome. This has an advantage in that it generally will increase the amount of scrutiny and attention a bill receives before it can become a law, but it can be frustrating because of the difficulty of getting things done.

Ability to Make Long-Term Decisions Versus Frequent Accountability

Some government decisions require policy makers to focus on long-term consequences. If policy makers frequently need to campaign for re election, it becomes hard for them to support policies that provide long-term benefits but have short-term costs. However, if policy makers are secure in their positions for long terms, it becomes harder to hold them accountable.

Neutral Lawmakers Versus Live-under-the-Law Lawmakers

Should the legislature have part-time members that return to other jobs after the session is over so they live under the laws they make? Or should the legislature contain full-time members who make laws impartially, without considering how it would affect their own professions? If lawmakers are full-time, there is a risk they lose touch with what it is like to make a living. If lawmakers are part-time, there is a risk they will make laws for the benefit of their own professions. With the U.S. Congress, it would make sense for the Senate to be full-time and the House to be part-time.

Incentive for Compromise Versus Ability to get Things Done

Should the legislative majority go ahead and do what it wants (since the people voted them into the majority) or should it try to reach compromises with the legislative minority so major decisions are made on more of a consensus basis?

Flexibility Versus Enumerated Powers

Should Congress have the power to pass whatever laws it wants? Or does the constitution set binding limits? Should these limits be enforced by the unelected Supreme Court? What is the point of listing specific powers if the "necessary and proper" clause (Article I, section 8, last paragraph) effectively gives Congress the power to do what it wants?

Uniformity Versus Federalism

There is value in having some laws uniform across the country. There is also value in a federal system where different states can do things differently. At the constitutional convention there was great fear that the national government would trample liberties and override local interests. These understandable concerns lead to a resulting government that seems to lean slightly too far in the direction of representing local interests, not the national interest.

Any nation as large as the U.S. needs to have some kind of federal system. No central government can make all decisions for such a spacious area. Smaller governmental subdivisions are essential. The states would have to have been created (if it had not in fact been the reverse: the states were created first and then they got together to create the national government). However, the complication with a federal system is: how do you clearly decide what level of government is responsible for what?

Here is one approach that probably should be avoided: joint administration of programs. A program should clearly be either a federal program, or a state program, or a local program, so it is clear what level of government should be held accountable.

The big advantage of having more decisions made by state governments is that different states can do things differently. When there is vehement disagreement over a policy issue, it can help if different states can adopt different policies. For hopelessly divisive social issues, probably the best that can be expected will be to let different states make different decisions. People can move to states where the policies are more amenable to their beliefs, if it is that important to them. Or, if it is not feasible to move, perhaps they can sleep more easily knowing that some states follow policies more to their liking than does their home state. This approach doesn't work in the case of something exceedingly evil such as slavery, which had to be eradicated nationwide even if the cost of doing so was enormous.

THE U.S. CONSTITUTION: PROBLEMS

The U.S. Constitution is an amazing achievement. That a single document has governed the U.S. for more than two centuries provides a testimony to the tremendous vision of the framers who put it together. However, we shouldn't support the constitution because of a belief that the framers had timeless infallible wisdom. We need to support the constitution for this basic reason: not everybody can have the government structure designed to their personal tastes, but somehow there has to be agreement on what the structure of the government will be, and the constitution is the agreed-upon framework for this country. Still, there are a few problems. Some of the problems are only apparent after a couple centuries of experience. (The framers had a limited historical record of representative government they could look back on as models, they had limited time, and they were very concerned about whether they would ever actually come up with a final document.) There are also a couple problems that should have been apparent to the founders.

Narrow Interest Influence Problem

It should be hard to buy influence in Congress and persuade it to pass narrow-interest legislation.[4] Alleviating this problem should be top priority for improving the economic well-being for the most people.

Problem: National Policy Made by Locally Accountable Representatives

Congress votes on laws determining national policy, but members of Congress are only accountable to local constituencies. This problem is related to the narrow-interest influence problem.

A member of Congress who provides federal benefits for local constituents only has to face voters from those who receive the benefits. It is true that narrow interest provisions can only pass Congress if they receive a majority of votes, so a member might be at risk if local voters realize that their representative is voting to support benefits that go to other districts. Why would a member from one district vote for a provision that benefits residents of another district, but harms their own constituents? They're more likely to do this when the narrow interest provision is not brought to a separate roll call vote, but instead is tucked into a much larger bill—making their handiwork easier to hide. A narrow interest provision is more likely to be enacted if it provides a big benefit for one group of people, and imposes a small cost on a lot of people. The people who are harmed are less likely to mobilize to campaign against a provision, compared to the efforts made by those who will benefit.

A long-time Speaker of the House once wrote a book called *All Politics is Local*,[5] except that is definitely not the case. Some political issues are national issues, and it is part of the problem when members of Congress think all issues are local.

Committee Chair Problem

A core problem with Congress has been that committee chairs that control committee agendas have to be accountable to their local constituents. When faced with a policy choice between the national interest and the local interest, the need for political survival dictates the choice.

Prior to 1975 congressional committee chairs had enormous power over the fate of bills under their jurisdiction.[6] Congress ran efficiently, but lack of accountability was a serious problem. Committee chairs were decided on the basis of seniority, which worked for the benefit of members in safe districts or states who had little worry about being accountable to the public. Voters have little ability to vote a congressional committee chair out of office (unless they happen to live in the same district, in which case the pork barrel benefits they receive might make them reluctant to do so). You could vote against the party of that committee chair, but two problems are (1) you might prefer the general policies of that person's party—so you shouldn't have to vote against your general preferences just because you are trying to get rid of a pork-barreller-chair; and (2) if you do vote against the pork–bareller's party, and your vote is successful in contributing to the other party taking over the majority, you will find that this committee will have a new chair from the new majority party who may well also be a pork-bareller (just from a different state).

Narrow interests can pay particular attention to the reelection campaigns of committee chairs to help increase the chance they will get favorable treatment in that committee.

Since 1975 committee chairs are not automatically determined by seniority, so their power is limited by the need to win support of other members. However, the key problem remains: national policy is made by officials who are elected by local constituencies.

Gerrymandering Problem

There should be no political manipulation (gerrymandering) of House district boundaries.

Suppose you're trying to gerrymander a 10-district swing state with two million total voters, with one million voters favoring each party. Create three districts each containing 200,000 voters of the other party. For the remaining seven districts, each district will contain 1,000,000/7=142,857 voters from your party and 400,000/7= 57,143 voters of the other party. You have rigged a state where you have 50 percent of the votes into a state where you will win 70 percent of the representatives. There is a bit of a risk to you in doing this: you have created three districts that will be absolutely safe for the other party, but the seven districts you have created for your party will be a bit more competitive. Still, under the current system, that is a risk well worth taking.

Geographic Representation Problem

Gerrymandering is just one aspect of the broader geographic representation problem. Even if district boundaries are drawn in a neutral manner, without deliberately attempting to provide an advantage to one side or the other, the number of representatives won by a political party may only be loosely connected to the number of votes its candidates received in the election. A party will be underrepresented if its voters are either too geographically dispersed, or are too geographically compact.

To illustrate some possibilities, here is an example with 100 districts with 1,000 voters in each district. Of the 100,000 total voters, 40,000 will vote for candidates of party X.[7]

possibility A: party X voters uniformly distributed geographically:

	Number of Districts	X Voters in each District	Total X Voters
	100	400	40,000
Total	100	–	40,000

number of districts won by party X: zero

possibility B: party X voters very concentrated geographically:

	Number of Districts	X Voters in each District	Total X Voters
	40	1,000	40,000
	60	0	0
Total	100	–	40,000

number of districts won by party X: 40

possibility C: party X voters distributed to maximize the number of districts won by party X:

	Number of Districts	X Voters in each District	Total X Voters
	79	501	39,579
	1	421	421
	20	0	0
Total	100	–	40,000

number of districts won by party X: 79

possibility *D*: party *X* voters distributed to win bare majority of seats

	Number of Districts	X Voters in each District	Total X Voters
	51	784	39,984
	1	16	16
	48	0	0
Total	100	–	40,000

number of districts won by party *X*: 51

In possibility *B*, the number of representatives won by party *X* matches its share of the total vote (40 percent). In possibility *A*, the party *X* voters are so dispersed geographically that they win zero seats. In possibility *C*, the party *X* voters happen to be arranged so that they win a lot of districts with a squeak-by majority of 501 out of 1,000. They win the vast majority (79 percent) of the seats even though they have only 40 percent of the total voters. You could justifiably argue that the chances of possibility *C* are small, but there are many other possibilities (such as possibility *D*) which involve party *X* winning a majority of seats even though it receives only a small minority of the vote.

Constituent Service Problem

When people need help dealing with the federal government bureaucracy, they can turn to their representative in the House of Representatives. This feature of the government is very helpful in reducing the chances of individual citizens being bulldozed by bureaucrats. However, there is one problem here. When deciding whether to vote for an incumbent or a challenger, they both can campaign on public policy questions, but the incumbent can campaign on a record of constituent service that a challenger can never have. In order for representatives to be accountable to voters, they need to face credible challengers in elections. Structures that make it harder for challengers should be reconsidered. Incumbents have been so successful at finding ways to entrench themselves that the partisan control of the House changed only three times since 1954 (1994, 2006, and 2010). During that time the presidency switched parties seven times (1960, 1968, 1976, 1980, 1992, 2000, and 2008).

Congressional Compensation Problem

It is unseemly to watch someone with the power to set their own compensation, as do members of Congress. There is a risk that members of Congress

may try to raise their pay to excessive levels, but there is also a risk of dema-
gogues opposing increases in congressional pay when it is truly needed. If
congressional pay is inadequate, then only those already rich can afford to
serve in Congress, with severe detrimental effects on democracy.

What's needed is a constitutional rule providing for the automatic setting
of congressional pay, which should be indexed to the growth in real income in
the country. When the country prospers, members of Congress should prosper
(with the reverse also being true).

Members of Congress should also receive compensation for one unique
burden of their job: the need to maintain two residences. Each member needs
a home in their home state, and they also need a home in Washington D.C.
Instead of expecting members to pay for a second home from their salary
(which puts pressure on members to increase the salary, while also pressur-
ing them to enact tax breaks that benefit owners of second homes), it would
be better for each member to receive a housing allowance when they are first
elected. The housing allowance should equal the median price of a house in
the Washington D.C. area, which the member can use to buy a house. If the
member buys a house that costs the same as the allowance, then the member
owns the house as long as they are a member, and then the house reverts
to the government to auction off when the member leaves Congress. (If a
member buys a house worth twice as much as the allowance, then they will
own 50 percent of the house and will get 50 percent of the proceeds when the
house is sold after they leave Congress. Members only get the allowance to
buy a house, not for spending on anything else. Members from Virginia or
Maryland who don't need a second home can choose to skip the allowance
entirely.)

District of Columbia Problem

One of the strangest ironies of the U.S. government is that one can live in the
shadow of the capital and not be represented in Congress.

Bozo Candidate Problem

On occasion a member of Congress or congressional candidate is caught in a
personal scandal or says something very stupid. You are caught in a dilemma
if the candidate with the personal flaw is the one whose policy views you
generally agree with. Do you vote for the flawed candidate, or do you vote
against your policy views?

A three-quarter majority of party members in Congress should be able to
expel such a candidate from their party. Since parties need broad support it
normally would be against their interests to expel one of their own candidates,

but in extreme cases the party members should be able to disassociate themselves from a totally discredited candidate. Expelling a candidate needs to
be done at least seven weeks before the election so there is time to name a
replacement candidate, and so the voters have a chance to get to know that
candidate.[8]

Supreme Court Lifetime Tenure Problem

In a democracy nobody with ultimate power should have lifetime tenure.
Supreme Court justices should have 18-year terms, with one expiring every
two years. In addition to solving the lifetime tenure problem, this term limit
will solve the arbitrary-appointment-timing problem (for example, Nixon
made four court appointments in his first term, while Carter made none);
and it will also eliminate the possibility of justices trying to time resigna-
tions in hopes of having a congenial president appoint their successor. Also,
the number of justices should be constitutionally fixed at 9, to eliminate any
future president from trying to follow Franklin Roosevelt's attempt to pack
the court. (Since federal district and appeals court judges can be overruled by
the Supreme Court, there's not a problem with them having lifetime tenure.)

There is no way around the inherent problem that there needs to be an
authority that can protect the rights of minorities that is not accountable
directly to the majority. There does not seem to be a better way of doing this
other than having an independent court whose members are appointed and
confirmed by elected officials.

Emergency Reconstruction Problem

The Constitution urgently needs to be amended to provide a clear procedure for dealing with a crisis in which most of the government leaders are
destroyed. Most likely the best choice would be to provide a system for governors or state legislators to elect temporary leaders until new elections can
be held. Since governors and state legislators are geographically dispersed
it would be extremely unlikely for them all to be lost in a single event. This
procedure is one we all hope will never be used, but it is better to have it in
place to avoid the devastating crisis that would arise in such a situation if
there was no clear procedure about what to do.

The Lame Duck Problem

The lame duck problem arose partly by accident and partly by inattentive-
ness on the part of the constitution framers. The constitution specified that
Congress would convene annually in early December, but the framers of the

constitution had no way to know when the constitution would be ratified, and therefore when it would first take effect.[9] By the historical accident of final ratification timing and eighteenth-century travel time, March 4 ended up being the date for the transfer of office. Since the constitution specified that terms would last for 2, 4, or 6 years, all subsequent term expiration dates depended on the arbitrary initial date. In the early years, a new Congress would be elected in November, but the old ("lame duck") Congress could meet until its term expired the next March 4th, and the new Congress would not meet until the following December—13 months after being elected. In 1801 there was an extreme example of a crisis related to the actions of a lame duck administration and Congress, including the final decision on the 1800 Presidential election.[10]

One complication at the end of the Civil War came from the fact that the decision on the 13th amendment abolishing slavery rested with the lame-duck House of Representatives in January 1865, since newly elected Republican members supportive of the amendment did not take office until March. The amendment had to be ratified before slave states returned to the union and would be able to block it.[11]

The 20th amendment (ratified in 1933) greatly improved the situation by advancing the presidential inauguration to January 20, and the start of the congressional term to January 3, but that still provides roughly two months for lame ducks to make decisions. For example, in late 2010 a lame duck Congress attempted to pass a budget (which should have been passed before the start of the fiscal year on September 1). Voters who disagree with actions of Congress can console themselves that they can vote members out of office—except in the case of the lame duck Congress many members had *already* been voted out of office, but they still held on to the power to make decisions.

With today's technology there is no reason a new Congress should not take office within a couple weeks of election.

The problem of shortening the Presidential transition time is that it is hard for an incoming president to put together an administration from scratch.[12] What's needed is a group of officials who would be prepared to take over right away. This means an opposition party needs to have a shadow cabinet (as in parliamentary systems). A new president could appoint new cabinet members later in the term, but the shadow cabinet officials would be ready to take over after a very brief post-election transition (see page 207).

The Vote-Counting Authority Problem

One weird flaw in the constitution is the statement that the president of the Senate presides over the joint session of Congress to count electoral votes.[13]

The president of the Senate is the U.S. vice president, who is often a candidate for president. Even worse, at the time of counting the electoral vote the president of the Senate is the lame duck vice president. Sometimes this flaw just provides for needless public humiliation, as the loser has to preside over the certification of his own defeat (Al Gore in 2001, Hubert Humphrey in 1969, Richard Nixon in 1961); other times the result is extremely unseemly, as the winner counts his own votes (George H.W. Bush in 1989). On occasion, counting the vote becomes a national crisis, as in 1800, 1876, and 2000.

There needs to be an independent authority in charge of counting votes. The best way to achieve independence would be to create a commission with four members appointed by congressional leadership (two from each party) and three appointed by the president, with each of these requiring a three-fourths vote of both chambers to confirm their appointment. The extreme supermajority is needed to make sure there is no chance of trying to slip partisan choices into the deciding votes on the commission. Provide the seven commissioners with six-year terms, then guaranteed lifetime employment with the commission (as assistants once they're no longer commissioners) and prohibit them from taking other jobs in the future.

Congressional Vacancy Problem

There needs to be a uniform constitutional procedure for filling congressional vacancies. In the most egregious case, the rules-in-advance principle[14] was violated by changing the rules for partisan advantage. For example, before the 2004 election the Massachusetts legislature took the power of filling a Senate vacancy away from the governor (when they were worried that an imminent vacancy might be filled by an opposite-party governor) but in 2009 they returned this power to the governor (when they were expecting an imminent vacancy that could be filled by a same-party governor).[15]

One can make a strong case either for allowing governors to fill Senate vacancies until a special election takes place, or for leaving the seat vacant until an election can take place, but in either case it is essential that the rules be established constitutionally for all states for all time.

Filibuster Problem

The Constitution provides that each chamber of Congress sets its own rules. One flaw is that a chamber might adopt dysfunctional rules. The Senate rule providing for almost unlimited debate means that the minority can block action. Since a vote can't be taken until debate is finished, this means that one way to block legislation is to keep talking and talking (a filibuster).

The leadership does have a way of forcing a vote, but it requires a supermajority of 60 Senators to agree to close debate.

This means that a determined minority of 41 Senators can block action.[16]

The filibuster threat is not all bad. It does provide the majority with a strong incentive to try to persuade some minority members to support them. The next chapter (page 204) suggests a better way to accomplish this goal without giving the minority the power to block action.

Each individual Senator finds their personal power magnified by the filibuster rule, and enough senators have been willing to put up with the risk of filibusters derailing their dream legislation. Also, control of the Senate has turned over often enough in recent decades that the current majority can imagine itself in the minority at some point in the near future where it might deeply appreciate having the option to filibuster to death proposals from the other party.

Hypocrisy over filibusters is thoroughly bipartisan. Senators who curse filibusters while in the majority suddenly discover their virtue while in the minority. Partisan control of the Senate changed in 1980, 1986, 1994, 2001, 2002, 2006, and 2014, so the Senate has seen more turnover in control than has the House.

However, there is one important exception where the current rules accidentally get it right. Supreme Court justices should require 60 percent of the Senate vote to be confirmed. This is sort of the same as the current requirement—if the president's party has less than 60 Senators, then the president has to nominate someone to the Supreme Court who will not trigger a filibuster by the other side. There may still be 49 Senators from the other party who vote against the nominee, but the threat of filibuster at least prevents the president from nominating someone who might be perceived as too extreme by the other side. (It is a very different situation if the non-presidential party has a majority in the Senate. In that case they have the power, as they should, to block any presidential nominee by a majority vote if they so desire. However, for the sake of democratic accountability, it is essential that they defeat such a nominee in a roll-call vote, rather than by simply refusing to take a vote.)

The Vague Law Problem

The Supreme Court should be more active at striking down vague laws. Such a decision would not deny Congress the power to make a law in that area, but it would require Congress to pass clear laws that can be clearly enforced—so people know what behavior the law makes illegal.

Problem with Reaching Compromises

If a politician of party *A* adopts a position that is a compromise with adherents of party *B*, then that politician will likely anger fellow party *A* people, while not picking up any support from party *B* people. Although the *B* people will support the politician on this issue, on other issues they still see a party *A* politician and will vote for someone else.

The result is that the polarization tends to push policy makers away from working with each other. In cases where the best policy for society would be a compromise between extremes, the result is worse policy. The problem is exacerbated by the primary nominating process, where candidates first have to win a race among one wing of the electorate before they face the entire electorate.[17]

Presidential Nomination Problem

The Constitution framers, knowing that George Washington would be the first head of the government, apparently imagined an idealized system where the leader would be chosen from among a few self-sacrificing leaders who were unambitious but of obvious merit. As we now know the reality, the presidential selection system must make a choice between ambitious candidates while under the influence of a variety of interests. The framers apparently thought of the electoral college as a kind of nominating system for determining which candidates would take part in the final selection process in the House, but they did not provide a nomination system for determining what candidates the electoral college would consider. The nominating process that has developed over time has four main flaws (1) the timing problem; (2) the centrifugal force problem; (3) the candidate evaluation problem; and (4) the state variation problem.

The timing problem has become ludicrous. If voters all across the country voted in a presidential nominating primary on a single day, it could be argued that lesser-known candidates would have trouble achieving the name recognition needed to have a chance, and we might lose out on some good candidates that way. Also, it might help if the presidential nomination process would last for a long enough time so that people will have a chance to evaluate how the candidates deal with a variety of situations.

However, having presidential primaries on different days creates an obvious problem. Suppose your state is the last state scheduled to have a primary. If the nomination race is very close, so that it comes down to the final state, your state becomes the center of attention, and the candidates will do whatever it takes to win over the voters in your state. However, based on the actual experience of recent decades, the nomination contests will be decided long before the last state holds its primary. As a result, the last state primary will be meaningless and mostly ignored as the candidates prepare for the final election. Lesson learned: if your state is the last primary, the chance that your primary will matter becomes very small. Even if your primary is early enough that the vote will matter, it is possible that your favorite candidate might have dropped out after the results of earlier primaries, so the arbitrary order of state voting will limit the candidate choices available to later states.

However, if you are the first state, or an early state, to hold the primary, there is a 100 percent chance that the candidates will campaign extensively in your state, and that candidates will mostly have to find some campaign themes that are popular in your state. The voters in later primary states can only look on with envy at the influence of the early states. That could lead to an unfair situation, except for one thing: states mostly get to choose when their nomination contest will be. As more states have learned this basic lesson in recent elections, more states have moved their primary earlier. However, if other states move their primary earlier, then it cancels out your ability to be earlier than the others. The result is a day like "super Tuesday" when a dozen or so states hold their primary on the same day. If the purpose of holding primaries on different dates is to make it easier for candidates to get to know voters in one state at a time, then obviously this purpose falls apart when a bunch of states have their primary on the same day anyway. National parties may create rules that limit how early a primary can be held, but then will they really want to disenfranchise the primary voters in a state that violates the rule and holds its primary too early (as in Michigan 2008)?

Another problem with the nomination process is the centrifugal force problem. An object on a spinning platform feels as if a force is pulling it away from the center (known as the centrifugal force). Candidates running in a partisan primary face a centrifugal force that pulls them away from the center of voter opinion.

Some states provide for voters to register as a member of a political party, which violates the principle that voter's preferences should remain confidential (to be sure the voters are free from undue influence). If a state with party registration limits participation in a primary to voters that are registered as members of that party, then voters who prefer to be independent are completely excluded from the nomination process. However, a partisan nomination system that allows non-party members to vote in the primary runs the risk of mischievous voters from another party hoping to nominate a weaker opponent for their party's candidate (particularly if their party's candidate is an incumbent facing no opposition for re-nomination).

It would help to have a Presidential nominating process that favors candidates that seek to appeal to a majority of the electorate, not a narrow group. This is best done by designing a nomination system not based upon political parties, as described in the next chapter. Presidential candidates would still be members of political parties, but the nomination system would be structured so as to create two final election candidates, not to create two (or more) party nominees.

Next, there is the "getting to know you" problem, or the candidate evaluation problem. Voters can probably arrange at some point to meet their representative in the U.S. House, or they might at least be able to find someone that knows their representative. It would be harder to do this for a U.S. Senator, or a state governor, but it becomes impossible for the vast majority of voters to ever meet presidential candidates, or have much contact with those that know the candidates well. If it is harder to evaluate the personal character of a candidate, then voters' decisions inevitably become more superficial, and campaigns become more superficial. We need a way for insiders with personal knowledge of a candidate's character to have more influence in the nomination process, without turning too much influence over to insiders who may lack accountability to the public.

The advantages of a federal system, where different states can be different, were noted earlier. States are free to design their election systems for state and local offices in their own way. However, when it comes to electing a national office-holder (the president) the system becomes weirdly arbitrary and capricious when different states have different rules about how the nomination process works.

Electoral College Problem

A major problem is that the result of the electoral college may differ from the popular vote, as in 1876, 1888, and 2000. However, that is not an unintended design problem: that is a deliberate feature of a system where the popular vote winner does not automatically become the winner.

The Framers apparently intended the electoral college to work like this. The electors are appointed either by the state legislatures or the voters—the constitution lets the legislatures decide. The electors vote for some good candidates, and with it being unlikely that one of these received a majority, the electors essentially become the nominators with the final decision being made by state delegations in the House of Representatives, choosing among the top candidates in the electoral college vote. (One problem in the original design was quickly fixed: after the 1800 election it became clear that it did not work for each elector to cast two votes and then have the second place finisher from the electoral college become the vice president. The 12th amendment provided for separate presidential and vice presidential votes by the electors.)

Here's the basic flaw with the electoral college concept. Suppose you are trying to decide who you should vote for in the race for membership in the electoral college. The only thing an elector does is vote for president, so it comes down to only one thing: you are going to evaluate the electoral college candidate according to whom they will vote for as president. Suppose you support candidate Rosencrantz for president. You're not going to vote for elector candidate Horatio, who has exemplary character but intends to vote for candidate Fortinbras for president. Instead, you'll vote for elector candidate Guildenstern, who may not be the brightest bulb in the chandelier but does promise to vote for your candidate (Rosencrantz) for president. The inherent problem is that it doesn't make sense to elect an independent body whose only purpose is to decide who will hold another office. The elector candidates inevitably become empty suits who are judged only according to whom they promise to vote for in the presidential contest.

This inherent problem in the system occurs even if you don't have to worry about the true nightmare scenario: what if an elector deceives the public, and votes for someone other than whom they have promised? On occasion, electors have become faithless (voting for someone other than who they are committed to) but never in a way that affects the outcome (so far). If an elector's name had been on the public ballot and won the election because the public trusted the elector to vote for a good candidate, then the elector could make the case that they can vote for whomever they want. However, since the elector's name never appears on the ballot, and the voters assume that they are voting for an elector who will faithfully express the presidential preferences of the voters, it would be outrageous if some day a presidential election gets hijacked by electors that change their mind for any reason.[18]

Another disadvantage of the electoral college is the outsize influence of swing states. Candidates have little incentive to campaign in states where they are very likely to win, or in states where they are very likely to lose. Therefore, whichever states end up with a close 50–50 split of voters will find the candidates designing their campaign around the local interests of these swing-state voters, and the arbitrary randomness of geography and demographics determines national policy.

Another problem is that each state can decide on its own system for allocating electoral votes. Most, but not all, allocate all their electoral votes to the statewide popular vote winner, and there is a serious risk if one year that difference in these systems affects the result.

One proposal would provide an electoral vote for the winner for each House district. Another proposal would provide for proportional allocation of electoral votes in each state. Although either proposal would greatly reduce the already small chance of the electoral vote winner differing from the popular vote winner, it would not eliminate the possibility because of rounding errors.[19]

Vice President Problem

The vice president problem became apparent to John Adams, the first person to hold the office. "My country in its wisdom contrived for me the most insignificant office that ever the invention of man contrived or his imagination conceived," he wrote.[20]

The nation needs a vice president, just as a car needs a spare tire for emergencies. However, because of the tendency for V.P.s to become future presidential candidates, they need to be more than spare tires. In every U.S. presidential election between 1956 and 2004, either the incumbent president or the incumbent vice president was one of the final election candidates.

Lacking any serious responsibilities, there is the huge question of what the vice president is supposed to do all day. If the vice president had actual responsibility, then voters could judge the V.P.'s performance when they decide whether that person should become president. However, there isn't any way of judging the V.P. because there is nothing for them to do. In practice, vice presidents have become an advisor to the president, but this doesn't provide a basis for evaluation—you can't evaluate the quality of the V.P.'s confidential advice, and you don't know which advice was taken and which advice was ignored.

The constitution does give the vice president one job: presiding over the Senate. However, a presiding officer who lacks a vote has nothing to do other than make sure that both sides of the argument have a fair chance to be heard—a crucial responsibility, but not one that tests one's ability to make big decisions. The vice president can vote if the Senate is tied, but this doesn't really help because it means that the V.P. can vote only on random unpredictable occasions. In practice, most of the time the Senate is presided over by one of the Senators while the V.P. is off doing something else.

There have been some atrocious vice presidential candidates in recent decades, and some that have been just plain not very good. One later became the only president forced to resign for abuse of power; one had to resign as vice president because of taking bribes in his previous office; one became president and then led the nation into an unpopular war and catastrophically split his party. One was subsequently elected president but received only 38 percent of the vote while attempting re-election. One had to leave the ticket within a couple weeks because of questions about his medical history, and another faced difficult questions about a spouse's business dealings. One was indicted for misappropriating campaign donations to provide hush money to cover-up his cheating on his cancer-stricken wife. Two have been derided as mental lightweights; another mocked for callous indifference of public opinion (when he wasn't shooting his hunting companion).[21]

There is a big difference between a V.P. succeeding to the presidency due to death or resignation, compared to a V.P. being elected president in a subsequent election. In case of succession by death, it would be best to have a V.P. that has been chosen by the president and will have continuity with the policies that the people voted for. However, when a V.P. later becomes a presidential candidate, it would be better to have a V.P. that had acted independently, so people would have a chance to evaluate the candidate's leadership decisions.

WHAT ABOUT A PARLIAMENTARY SYSTEM?

Other democracies commonly use a form of parliamentary system, where the leader of the parliamentary majority serves as prime minister. There are advantages and disadvantages of such a system compared to the congressional/presidential system of the U.S.

1. A parliamentary majority does not face a system of checks and balances as in the U.S. Even when one party controls both the presidency and the Congress, the different branches provide a check on each other. A parliamentary system might have a coalition government if no party obtains a majority, which is approximately analogous to divided partisan control of the government in the U.S. In both such cases, there is an advantage of promoting compromise, but the disadvantage of unclear accountability.
2. A parliamentary system that elects representatives by plurality in single-member districts (called "first-past-the-post" in Britain) faces the same geographic representation issues discussed on page 182. Other parliamentary systems use some version of national proportional representation, such as a list system where parties nominate candidates and the percent of the vote they receive determines how many of their candidates from the top of the list will be elected.[22] The list system provides a closer match of vote percentage to representation percentage, but lessens accountability of individual members to local voters, and voters lose their ability to nominate candidates. Although we have seen the problem when national decisions are made by representatives accountable only to local constituencies, there still is a big advantage in having representatives be closer to the people because they come from local districts. We shouldn't eliminate elections from local districts.
3. Some parliamentary systems encourage multiple parties, which have the advantage of encouraging different voices to be heard. There is a serious disadvantage if a small, narrow-interest party is able to win enough votes to deprive any other party of a majority, and is able to join a coalition government where it might be able to exert influence far out of proportion to the number of votes it actually won.

   There is an advantage in a stable two-party system, as in the U.S., where each party knows it needs to appeal to the broad electorate—as opposed to a multiparty system where niche parties abandon any pretense of trying to obtain a majority of the votes.

4. An advantage of a parliamentary system is the presence of a "loyal opposition" with a shadow cabinet, encouraging the opposition party to discuss serious policy proposals, and facilitating the transition of government from one party to another. The U.S. should adopt this feature (see page 207).

5. A disadvantage of a parliamentary system is the ability of the party in power to manipulate the timing of elections for their own advantage. The U.S. has an advantage with a fixed schedule for periodic elections.

No governmental system is perfect, but heed Churchill's words about democracy being the worst governmental system except for all the others.[23] Adjusting the structure of government can't be expected to bridge chasms of divisions in public opinion. However, the next chapter suggests some possible changes that might improve the U.S. government.

NOTES

1. Gregg (p128) notes Edmund Burke was defeated in a 1780 election when he said he would work for the nation's best interests, rather than necessarily voting for what his constituents wanted.

2. Lazare, p146.

3. Bowen, *Miracle in Philadelphia*, see p112, p268.

4. Lewis provides a detailed survey of narrow interest influence on Congress.

5. O'Neill.

6. Woll, *Debating U.S. Govt*, 1988.

7. Steven Hill (p xii, p15) discusses examples where the number of total votes for a party differs significantly from the number of seats won by that party.

8. A party should not be allowed to dump a sure-to-lose candidate just before an election, as happened in one case in 2002. *New York Times* online, October 3, 2002.

9. Ackerman, p117–18.

10. Ackerman, p36.

11. Goodwin, p688.

12. Hess.

13. Ackerman, p58.

14. Page 8.

15. *Boston Globe* online, December 4, 2012.

16. In 2013 the Senate changed the rules to prevent filibusters on presidential appointments, except for Supreme Court appointments.

17. See the centrifugal force problem, page 190.

18. Michener 1969.

19. See online appendix myhome.spu.edu/ddowning/fos.html.

20. McCullough, p447.

21. The VP references are to Nixon, Agnew, Johnson, G. H. W. Bush, Eagleton, Ferraro, Edwards, Quayle, Palin, Cheney.

22. Lijphart (1994) describes electoral systems in different countries.

23. Enright, p19.

Chapter 14

Government Structure

Improvements

Can we change the structure of the U.S. government so the result will be better policies? We have to proceed cautiously because there is so much that is right about the way the U.S. government works.

GOALS

The specific goals that the modifications proposed here will attempt to achieve:

1. Most all voices are heard, and represented in the House.
2. The legislative majority has the power to act, without worrying about being blocked by the minority, but they have an incentive to try to persuade the minority to support their policies (at least some of them). Robert Dahl writes,

   "The ideal solution, it seems to me, would be a political system that provides strong incentives for political leaders to search for the broadest feasible agreement before adopting a law or policy and yet allows the decision to be made, if need be, by majority vote, always, of course, within the limits set by the need to preserve fundamental democratic rights."[1]
3. Legislative decisions for the nation should be made with some influence from officials who are accountable to the nation, not just local constituencies.
4. It should be harder for narrow interests to buy influence with legislators.
5. Presidential candidates should be evaluated by insiders—those who have first-hand experience of their leadership qualities.

197

6. Insiders should not have a lock on the presidential nomination process. There needs to be a way for outsiders to choose nominees if the insiders don't provide enough choices.

7. There needs to be a multi-stage evaluation of presidential candidates, with more intense scrutiny of a smaller number of candidates at each stage. (By way of contrast, some voting systems require voters to rank their choices by indicating a first choice, a second choice, etc. There is a problem because voters are required to make detailed decisions about rankings that may not turn out to be relevant. A multistage voting system is better, because then voters only need to decide on their first place choice in each stage. They only need to decide on their second choice if their first choice candidate is eliminated in an earlier stage.)

8. Solve the vice president problem: give the V.P. a serious job so it would be possible to evaluate whether a V.P. would be a good presidential candidate.

9. The opposition party should have a strong incentive to try to win, but also have an incentive to be loyal.

10. The transfer of office needs to occur very soon following elections, so that no decisions are made by lame-duck office holders.

11. An opposition party should be encouraged to develop serious alternative policy proposals (rather than simply demagogically attack the incumbent) and they should have officials prepared to take cabinet offices if their party wins election.

12. U.S. voters have chosen divided government often enough that it should remain an option.

13. There needs to be a career ladder for elective office with enough openings on the first step.

14. The political structure should promote a stable, two party system with two broad-based parties, while avoiding entrenching the dominant parties so they don't feel the need to be accountable.

15. Changes to the political system should not be so significant to disrupt continuity.

16. End gerrymandering (manipulating electoral district boundaries to benefit the party in power or to entrench incumbents).

PROPOSAL: MORE REPRESENTATIVES

The current number of representatives (435) is not written in the constitution; it was established by Congress. After Congress fixed the number at 435 and the population continued to grow, the number of voters per representative

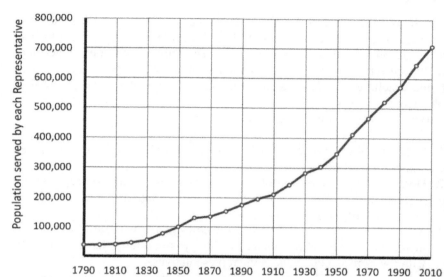

Figure 14.1 Trend in Population Per Representative. *Source*: Figure based on data obtained from the U.S. decennial census and the website for History, Art, & Archives: US House of Representatives

has increased far beyond the level originally intended to provide reasonable representation[2] (see Figure 14.1).

Congress should not be able to set its own size. Current House members would be reluctant to reduce its size and knock some of them out of a job, and they also could be reluctant to increase the size and dilute their influence. In either case they would be acting in their own interests rather than the good of the country.

The constitution (article 1, section 2) states that the number of representatives is not to be more than one per 30,000 citizens. This means that the House could be enlarged to about 300,000,000/30,000 = 10,000 members.

A House with 10,000 members won't function as a deliberative body. However, it doesn't need to. It needs to function as a voting body, and much of the time it can do this with virtual meetings: members remaining in their home districts but remaining connected electronically. They should all meet in person perhaps three months per year.

Some of the members will be full-time members of an Executive Committee, and members of the standing committees will be chosen from this. The Executive committee should have about the same number of members as the current House. To be chosen for the Executive committee a member would need the support of other members with a total of 20 votes, providing for about 500 members of the Executive committee. These members would stay in Washington full-time to perform the necessary committee work of investigating proposed legislation. The Executive Committee would hold a debate on bills passed by the committee. This debate could take place in the current House chamber, with the other members remaining back home watching, and then an electronic on-line vote would determine final passage.

Here are reasons for enlarging the House:

1. Each representative will be closer to the people, with a much smaller number of constituents.
2. Diverse viewpoints and minority groups will find it easier to be represented.
3. A larger House will make it harder for narrow interests to buy influence over a majority of members.
4. A large part-time House will have a wide variety of occupations among its members, so there is less chance of idiosyncratic laws that benefit those with the same occupations as the representatives.
5. A larger House will open up the first stage of the career ladder for national elective office to wider participation. There undoubtedly are talented people now who live in congressional districts with entrenched incumbents that never have a chance to become a viable candidate.

There could be a concern about the cost of paying this many representatives, but this concern disappears because each member would not have as many staff members as do current members.

TWO HOUSE MEMBERS PER DISTRICT
WITH FRACTIONAL VOTES

Here is a proposed revision to the method of election for House members. Elect 10,000 members from 5,000 districts, with two members per district.[3] Each district will have roughly 300,000,000/5,000 = 60,000 people. (about one-tenth the current size). In each district, nominate final election candidates for both major parties as is done now. Both final election candidates become representatives, but with fractional votes. Each representative's vote fraction equals the fraction of the vote that candidate received. For example, if Rosencrantz receives 30,492 votes, and Guildenstern receives 29,508 votes, then Rosencrantz becomes a representative with 30,492/60,000 = 0.5082 votes, and Guildenstern becomes a representative with 29,508/60,000 = 0.4918 votes. Fractional voting would have presented a serious arithmetic challenge in 1789, but modern technology can add fractions easily. The voting fractions need to be rounded. Rounding the fraction to four decimal places should make sure that rounding does not become an issue without containing so many decimal places as to be cumbersome.

With proportional representation in each district there is no ability to gerrymander, so that problem will disappear.

How will this proposal be different from current practice? Consider a district naturally inclined to party *A* under the current system. Party *A*'s candidate Rosencrantz wins two or three elections with 60 percent of the vote. It then becomes harder for a candidate from party *B* to raise funds to run in this district. There could be some donors that don't really agree with party *A*, and would not choose to donate to Rosencrantz in a competitive election, but once it is clear that Rosencrantz will win the donors will get on board. With little chance of winning, and little chance of raising funds for even a semi-competitive campaign, there becomes a dearth of quality candidates from party *B* willing to run in this district. As the quality of party *B* candidates decline, a vicious circle develops and Rosencrantz's victory margins continue to grow. Perhaps he wins the next couple elections by 70 or 80 percent. As an incumbent, he can also provide valuable case-assistance services for his constituents.[4]

Being able to turn to your representative for case assistance services is important—distant federal bureaucrats who may be disinclined to heed the complaints of a lone citizen will snap to attention when they receive a call from congressional members that hold the strings to their purse. However, it's not the best system if House elections are often decided on the basis of who can provide the best case-assistance services. The House takes crucial votes on national policy issues, and at some point the election process for House members should focus on that—not on who can best troubleshoot missing government checks. This would be true even if there was a way to fairly judge House candidates on case-assistance ability; but that's not possible. The incumbent's case assistance ability can be evaluated but the challenger doesn't even get the chance to try. In this proposal, each party will field an incumbent with the ability to perform constituent service, so such service will not provide a basis for deciding which candidate to vote for.

Under the current system there is little reason for a party to contest the race in a district where their percentage of votes is significantly less than half, because there is little chance that any effort they undertake could raise the vote to the winning level. But with this proposal raising their share of vote from 30 percent to 35 percent would increase their representation. All districts become competitive because the vote percentage in every district will matter. With this proposal, both parties will have an incentive to field qualified candidates—and since two candidates will become representatives, they will have incentive to run.

Allowing for independent and third-party candidates is important to prevent the two major parties from feeling permanently entitled to their positions. However, niche parties should not be encouraged. Political parties should feel the need to try to appeal to a broad array of voters rather than to a narrow group who might support a single-purpose party. In the proposed election system, there would need to be a cutoff percentage for minor candidates. If the cutoff percentage is set at 20 percent, then it means that any third-place candidate getting less than 20 percent of the vote does not become a representative, and the top two candidates have their vote fraction determined by their share of the top-two candidate vote. If a third-place candidate does receive at least 20 percent of the vote, then the district sends three representatives to Congress, each with a fractional vote equal to the percentage of the top-three vote that the candidate received. If a third party is able to win 20 percent of the votes in the House, then it will be able to elect members to the executive committee and participate in debates; otherwise its members can vote but not participate in debates or committees.

NATIONAL ACCOUNTABILITY OF CONGRESSIONAL LEADERSHIP

The Speaker of the House should focus on national policy, but currently the Speaker must also focus on being reelected in a local district. The solution is to provide for the Speaker to be elected nationally, and for the Vice President to become the true President of the Senate.

Here is the proposal. At the final election every presidential year, each voter makes three choices on the national ballot:

1. President
2. Vice President
3. Speaker

The two final candidates for president will name their vice presidential choices, and the members of the two largest parties in the House nominate their candidate for Speaker. Commonly, voters will vote for all three offices from the same party, and the three would be elected as a team. However, they're not voting for a single ticket, as in the current V.P. / President race. This raises the stakes for choosing a qualified candidate for V.P. Instead of choosing V.P. candidates for ticket balancing, presidential candidates will need to choose V.P. candidates who will be strong enough to be elected on their own. Voters might split their tickets, and elect a V.P. and/or Speaker of a different party than the President. If that happens, it means the voters have indicated a preference for divided government, as they can do now. The difference is that with this proposal the divided government will have come about because of an explicit choice of the national electorate, not because of the idiosyncrasies of local/state election of Congress. Each party has a strong incentive to avoid divided government by presenting a program to the electorate that is so appealing that it will win the election.

The Vice President and Speaker as Leaders of Congress

The constitution provides for the V.P. being president of senate, without specifying what those duties are. There should be such a list to include:

1. Have a regular vote (instead of having a vote only in case of a Senate tie).
2. Set the agenda for the Senate; determine when votes will take place (with a provision that a petition signed by 55 percent of senators could force a bill to be discharged from committee and voted on).
3. Assign bills to committee.
4. Appoint committee chairs (the important feature is that committee chairs are appointed by someone accountable to national voters).
5. When a bill is presented to the floor, the V.P. appoints the floor manager for that bill, who will be first and last to speak in debate, and will answer questions posed by members. (If there is opposition to the bill, the minority leader or some other opponent appoints the opposition floor manager, who speaks second and second to last in debate, and also answers questions.)

These responsibilities are similar to those that the Senate Majority Leader holds now. The nationally elected Speaker will have a similar list of powers (much as the Speaker does now). The Speaker will appoint committee chairs who resign their regular House seats (so they do not have to be reelected by local constituencies), but the committee chairs and the Speaker each have one full vote in the House. Committee chairs have power over the bills under their jurisdiction, as in the old pre-1975 days, except now the committee chairs are accountable to the Speaker (who can remove committee chairs) and the Speaker is accountable to national voters.

National election for the speaker would help because individual contributors would have less influence in a larger election (just as pouring water into a large lake will have less effect than pouring it into a small pond). Voters all over the country will have a chance to vote against a Speaker or V.P. who appointed committee chairs that focused on advancing narrow interests.

Also, national candidates would find it much harder to be reelected on the basis of local pork barrel projects.

This proposal does create the possibility that the presiding officer of a house may be of the opposite party of the majority of members of that house. In that case the parties will have to work together, because the voters made their choice to split the power.

INCENTIVE TO WORK WITH MINORITY

It would be good if the majority in Congress tries to win over the minority. People would feel less alienated from the political process if there's less worry about the other side jamming through controversial legislation by narrow majorities.

The U.S. Congress meets this goal in an odd way. Although leaders of the House control the agenda in their chamber, the Senate has a longstanding tradition of nearly unlimited debate, providing for the opportunity to kill a bill by filibuster (see page 187).

How can we encourage the majority to seek the support of the minority without empowering minority party obstructionism?

A narrow majority in Congress should be able to pass whatever legislation it wishes, but it should not be able to enact binding changes with long-term consequences. So, if a piece of legislation passes by an extremely narrow majority, there should be a provision for it to be automatically repealed in two years. If the same party has the majority in the next Congress, they can reenact this law, but it still says subject to automatic repeal in two years unless they can either increase their majority or else persuade some members of the minority party to come along.[5]

Here's the specific proposal, which gives an incentive to the congressional majority to increase their share of the vote in order to provide for the legislation to stay in place for a longer period of time before autorepeal.

Calculate the percentage of the vote in Congress the bill receives (average both houses, and round to a whole number not less than 51).

if the vote in favor was:	then
51 percent:	autorepeal in 2 years (one Congress)
52 percent:	autorepeal in 4 years (two Congresses)
53 percent:	autorepeal in 6 years (three Congresses)
54 percent:	autorepeal in 8 years (four Congresses)
55 percent:	autorepeal in 10 years (five Congresses)
56 percent:	no autorepeal

MEDIAN VOTING FOR AMOUNTS

Some decisions are yes–no questions, and majority vote works well as a decision making process in this case. Other decisions require determining the amount of something. In this case the decision is not "yes or no" but rather "more or less." The voting decision process should be different in this case.

Suppose n members of a legislative body have an opinion on how much should be spent on program X. One possible rule that might give the best results would be to let the median member determine the amount. If there are an odd number of members, and their desired amounts are arranged in order, then one of them will be exactly in the middle. Although there is no way to make everyone happy, choosing the median amount will likely reduce the amount of unhappiness that the decision causes.

The median voting process works like this.

The chamber votes on a proposal to spend X dollars for project A. Instead of a yes or no vote, there are three choices:

1. Approve this amount.
2. Spend more.
3. Spend less.

If the proposal to approve this amount wins a majority, then the decision is finished, and that amount is approved. Otherwise, follow this rule:

- If the "spend more" choice has more votes than "spend less," then amount X now becomes a minimum amount as the process continues. The next proposed amount will be greater than X.
- If the "spend less" choice has more votes than "spend more," then amount X now becomes a maximum amount as the process continues. The next proposed amount will be less than X.

At some point the process will result in two amounts: a minimum amount X_{min} and a maximum amount X_{max}. Now continue the process with the next proposed amount being the midpoint between these two extremes:

$$\frac{X_{min} + X_{max}}{2}$$

Continue following this binary search method, with the difference between the amounts getting smaller and smaller until a predetermined minimum distance is reached.

This is better than averaging out different desired amounts, because then each side has incentive to propose an extreme amount to pull the average in their direction.

If there are an even number of members in the chamber, then the median becomes the halfway point between the two middle members. If there is an evenly split chamber with two highly polarized sides there is a problem (for example, 50 members favoring 0, and 50 members favoring 1,000,000). However, a legislative chamber generally should not have an even number of members (for obvious reasons). (The U.S. Senate does, but the V.P. can break ties).

Here is an example of how median voting could work in a chamber with 101 members. The first member favors the amount $1, the second member favors the amount $2, and so on, up to the 101st member who favors the amount $101. The predetermined stopping difference is $2.

The initial proposal is for an amount of $40. Take a yes or no vote on $40. If it fails to receive a majority, then use the median voting procedure, with a more/less vote on $40 (in which "more" will win). Other members will submit a proposal with an amount more than 40. In this example, the second proposal will be for an amount of $60. When the vote is taken on $60, "less" will win. Here are the steps for how this will work (see also Figure 14.2).

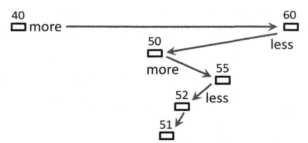

Figure 14.2 Example of Median Voting Procedure, with the Two Initial Proposals being $40 and $60. The process stops when the difference between the lower limit and upper limit becomes $2, in which case the midpoint of those two values becomes the final amount. In this case, $51 is the midpoint between $50 and $52.

proposal: $40: vote: 1 OK, 39 less, 61* more [set the minimum at $40]
proposal: $60: vote: 1 OK, 59* less, 41 more [min. at $40, max. at $60]
proposal: $50: vote: 1 OK, 49 less, 51* more [min. at $50, max. at $60]
proposal: $55: vote: 1 OK, 54* less, 46 more [min. at $50, max. at $55]
proposal: $52: vote: 1 OK, 51* less, 49 more [min. at $50, max. at $52]

difference between max and min is now $2, so split the difference between $50 and $52, and result is $51 (which is the median among the 101 members)

Median voting will be helpful when some members have promised their constituents they will never vote for a large amount, and other members have promised their constituents they will never vote for a small amount. Under the current system, the amount cannot be finally agreed upon until there is some value that can attract a majority of "yes" votes. Suppose 26 percent of the members are small-value-promisers and another 26 percent of the members are large-value-promisers (and the other 48 percent of the members would be willing to compromise somewhere in between). There is no way that any amount can achieve a majority unless some of the small-value-promisers or large-value-promisers will be willing to break their promise and compromise.

With median voting, the small-value-promisers can always vote for "less," and the large-value-promisers can always vote for "more," but a final decision will be reached for some value in the middle.

For this to work, the votes need to be taken quickly—which means no further debate once the process gets started, and each vote needs to be taken with a fast pushbutton electronic system.

THE SHADOW CABINET

One advantage of the British system that should be adopted in the U.S. is the shadow cabinet.[6] The non-presidential party in the House would elect a shadow cabinet, who would not be House members but would be paid a public salary. The shadow cabinet would have the responsibility to come up with an alternative budget and other policy proposals.

The losing presidential candidate becomes leader of the shadow cabinet. Also joining the shadow cabinet will be the losing V.P. and Speaker candidate, if they are of the same party as the losing presidential candidate. The shadow cabinet members would take part in committee and floor debates in the Senate and House, but they would not have votes.

When the White House changes parties, then the shadow cabinet members become the new cabinet members. (A new president could later appoint new cabinet members, but at least the administration would be off to an immediate start). Then the lame-duck period between the election and the inauguration could be shortened.

CAMPAIGN FUNDING

The problem of narrow-interest legislation cannot be solved merely by hoping to elect more virtuous legislators. How can the voters know which candidates are more virtuous? The candidates need to get their message across to voters, and for that they need money. Virtuous candidates who don't take campaign contributions likely will not be elected because voters won't ever hear their messages. A legislator who does take campaign contributions will find it hard to avoid paying special attention to the contributors. Something needs to be done to reduce the influence of those with money.[7]

Recently, presidents of both parties have spent literally hundreds of days during their terms speaking at partisan fundraisers for rich donors, which is both unseemly and distracting from the actual responsibilities of the office. Although there is no way to prohibit presidential fundraising, it would help to establish a behavioral expectation that presidents should refrain from selling access to their office. Because the U.S. president also serves as the head of state, it is better for the country for the president not to be perceived as excessively partisan. There is nothing inherently wrong with fundraising, but the vice president and other officials can handle the fundraising for their party, instead of the head of state.

Why Limiting Campaign Spending doesn't Work

One thing that doesn't work is limitations on campaign contributions or spending. Here's the basic reason why not. Suppose you are having lunch with a friend and you explain why candidate Rosencrantz is the best choice. We'll assume (or hope?) that nobody in their wildest fantasies would imagine that the first amendment would permit Congress to pass any law that would make lunchtime advocacy illegal.[8]

Now suppose you call, email, or text message a few friends to advocate for your candidate. Again, these are actions that are unquestionably protected by the first amendment. Now suppose you put up a few campaign signs or posters that were printed at your own expense. There still should be no doubt that first amendment protection applies to this activity. What if you print up a few thousand signs, or create a web page, or write a newspaper editorial, or write a book? If you do this independently of the candidate's campaign, it still has to have first amendment protection. Advocates of campaign spending limits are forced to argue that your independent advocacy is constitutionally protected, but the same signs printed by a candidate's campaign lack such protection and can be legislatively restricted. The problems with this legal view become clear when you try to draw the line between independent expenditures and official campaign expenditures. Are the independent advocates allowed to socialize with campaign workers? Can they phone, mail, or text the campaign? Is it legal for a third party to have contact with both of them? Can a campaign worker wink at an independent advocate ("that's nice of you to independently support our message?")

It would be hard to see how independence could be legally maintained, but even if the distinction were legally sensible it misses the point. Although they should be allowed, independent expenditures on behalf of candidates should not be encouraged. It would be better for voters to hear the messages that the candidates present themselves, so they can better judge what they think of the candidate's message. It can become extremely awkward for a candidate if independent supporters present a slightly muddled version of the candidate's message (as in a *Doonesbury* cartoon where an over-exuberant campaigner promised voters that his candidate's platform included free cheeseburgers for the elderly.[9])

Furthermore, there clearly cannot be any government-imposed limits on what news organizations may report about a campaign, but there is no constitutional justification for privileging certain people as "news" people with unlimited press rights, while denying those rights to "non-news" people such as novelists, playwrights, screenwriters, academics, bloggers, and anybody else that wants to write or say something. It is the act of reporting the news and expressing opinions that is protected, not any privileged class that has a special right to be the reporters and commentators.[10]

The implication of this analysis is that all limits on campaign contributions and campaign spending should be struck down as unconstitutional first-amendment violations. People and organizations should be free to contribute to campaigns (as long as nobody is coerced into donating to campaigns they don't support).

Public Funding

Instead of limits, there needs to be both disclosure of major donors, and public funding for candidates. There already are laws for disclosing donors, and there already is some public funding for presidential campaigns. Public funding needs to be extended to congressional campaigns, so a candidate has the option of turning down narrow-interest campaign donors.

There is an obvious problem with handing out money to anyone who says they are a congressional candidate. To deter frivolous candidates, there would need to be a deposit requirement. The candidate pays the initial deposit, which can be raised from campaign donations. The deposit is refunded if the candidate gets one percent of the votes in the primary (see page 212 for a similar example in a different context). The deposit requirement should be lower for candidates that have some public office experience (such as a state legislator, mayor or city council member, or local administrative office). There should not be a requirement that candidates for Congress have previous public office experience, but it would be a good idea to encourage that.

A candidate may need to borrow to conduct the campaign. The deposit can be used as collateral for any candidate who is expected to get more than one percent of the vote, since then the deposit will be refunded and can repay the campaign loans. Only truly frivolous candidates would have trouble borrowing to conduct their campaign because lenders would not expect that they would get one percent of the vote and so they would lose their deposit.

For example, a candidate may need to borrow 5 million dollars. 2 million dollars are paid as the deposit. The other three million are available to use for the campaign. If the candidate does get one percent of the vote, then the government pays the candidate 5 million dollars (2 million to refund the deposit and 3 million for the campaign expenses). The candidate can use the money to repay the 5 million dollar loan. Since the only risk to the lender happens if the candidate gets less than one percent of the vote, it should be the case that any serious candidate could borrow the money they need, whereas frivolous candidates will be unable to borrow the money.

In the final election, the two candidates have already won primaries, so they have established themselves as legitimate candidates and are therefore eligible for the campaign funding.

Supreme Court Justice Steve Breyer writes about the importance of preserving the democratic objective of the constitution and the integrity of the electoral system, and that campaign limits that achieve this may pass constitutional scrutiny. This goal is important, but it should not be achieved by establishing any limits. Instead, making sure that all candidates have access to adequate public funding will prevent moneyed interests from obtaining near-exclusive access to the information conduits to the public. If there is a problem with too much of one kind of speech, it is far better to solve the problem by enabling more speech rather than trying to restrict excessive speech.

Under this system, congressional candidates should feel free to decline campaign contributions from those who might exert undue influence. They can still get their message out with the public funding. The revised election process for House candidates will also make it easier to decline donations because the stakes in the election are different. Under the current system, a House candidate in a close race who is considering declining a donation runs the risk that a slight reduction in the candidate's ability to reach voters might result in the difference between victory (becoming a representative with one vote) and defeat (becoming a former candidate with zero votes). Under the proposed system, a slight change in the vote percentage might make a difference between being a representative with a .51 vote fraction, or a representative with a .49 vote fraction.

Public funding of campaigns is sometimes opposed by those favoring smaller government. Although it may seem paradoxical, the *lack* of public funding of campaigns leads to *needlessly large* government. Congressional candidates who have no way for their message to reach voters without donations then become subject to influence from those donors.

This proposal will cost some money. If a total of 1 million dollars was provided for the campaign in each House district (which would be generous considering that these districts are smaller than current House districts), the total cost would be 5 billion dollars. Although a large amount of money by ordinary standards, this is a small amount by Federal government standards, and we might save more than this in reduced pork barrel spending when candidates are not dependent on donations. Also, since elections are every two years, the annual average amount will be half of this. If 20 million dollars was provided for each of 33 Senate races, the total cost would be 660 million dollars (again the annual average would be half of that).

THREE-STAGE PRESIDENTIAL ELECTION

The constitution framers despised factions and had no knowledge of how political parties would develop. It was fairly clear to the Philadelphia convention attendees that George Washington would be the nation's first president, so there was a tendency to think of the presidential selection process as a way to identify who would be a highly qualified selfless leader who would (reluctantly) take on the burden of leadership when called upon by the nation.[11] Not surprisingly, in subsequent elections there usually was not such an obvious candidate. Inevitably, a nominating process developed. In the early years, congressional party members nominated candidates. Then party conventions developed, putting the nominating decisions in the hands of delegates chosen by a variety of different processes. Gradually the nomination decision shifted to primary elections. In 1968 the nomination process was still dominated by convention delegates, but there were 15 states with primaries, creating a kind of hybrid system. In the next couple elections more states introduced primaries. The final end to the convention system came in 1980, with a vote against a rule to free delegates from voting for the candidate for whom they were bound by the result of the primaries. Now that delegates are bound to vote for certain candidates they no longer act as decision makers. National party conventions continue to be held every four years, but they don't determine who will be the nominee.

Here are goals for the proposed election system described here:

1. Elected officials who know the candidates personally should have a voice.
2. Outsiders need to have an opportunity to vote out insiders if necessary.
3. The process should last over a period of time long enough for voters to assess candidate performance.

4. Frivolous candidates should be screened out before being on the ballot.
5. Candidates should have served at least two years in one of these elective offices: Vice President, Congress, governor, state legislature, or mayor of one of the 100 largest cities; or else have national cabinet-level experience, or experience as general or admiral. All U.S. presidents have met this requirement, but some candidates have not. The experience requirement is essential because being president is not an entry-level job. The voters need to be able to assess the performance of the candidate in previous offices.
6. The initial selection process should be open to a variety of candidates. In a large field of candidates it will be harder for voters to get to know all the candidates. The system should be designed so that it is not too hard to make it to the next stage, so most truly qualified candidates should make it.
7. The final election should only have two candidates, so voters can focus on making judgments about those two, and the winner will have a majority of votes.

The last two goals suggest the need for a middle stage of the selection process. Too many stages could be too confusing, so the proposal here is for a three-stage (or possibly four-stage) election. Here's the basic idea: the top four candidates in the first stage advance to the semi-final stage, and then the top two candidates in that stage advance to the final election. However, if the combined vote total of the top four candidates in the first stage does not add up to a majority of the votes, then there will be four stages: the top 8 candidates in the first stage advance to the quarter-finals; then the top four candidates advance to the semi-finals; and the top two advance to the finals.

Here are the details.

1. Qualifying for the first stage ballot: the combined congressional caucus for each party, along with the governors of that party, meet to nominate candidates. Anyone getting at least 10 percent of the vote among members makes the first stage ballot.

   Other candidates can join the race (provided they meet the experience requirement on page above), but they must pay a substantial deposit. There will be no refund on the deposit if the candidate gets less than 0.5 percent of the vote in the first election. There will be a complete refund of the deposit if the candidate gets at least 1 percent of the vote. There will be a partial refund if the vote is between 0.5 and 1 percent; for example, half of the deposit is refunded if a candidate gets 0.75 percent of the vote. The purpose of the deposit requirement is to deter frivolous candidates. Any serious candidate would be able to get at least 1 percent of the vote.

   Although the Presidency and Congress are distinct branches of government, the system could work better if they felt more connected to each other. Members of Congress should have a say in determining the nominee of their party, as long as they do not have exclusive control over it. Voters should know what members of Congress think of a presidential candidate. That doesn't mean they should automatically agree with these assessments. The proposal here provides for a way for a presidential candidate to make the ballot without the support of any member of Congress. However, many serious presidential candidates should be able to win the support of 10 percent of the votes of Congress, and a candidate starting with that support may well have a better chance of dealing with Congress if elected.

2. First stage election: As in the current system, a lesser-known candidate does not have to compete in all 50 states in the first-stage election. In an improvement over the current system, a lesser-known candidate can choose which states to focus on. (In the current system you have to focus on the states arbitrarily chosen to have early primaries.) A candidate receiving more than 20 percent of the vote in the first stage election is guaranteed to finish in the top four and thus advance to the next stage (and it might take a smaller percentage than 20 to advance, depending on how the other votes are distributed).

The centrifugal-force problem will be lessened because the candidates are not competing only in partisan primaries. Independent voters can help a candidate advance.

The candidates' goal is not to convince partisans—it is to convince enough voters to advance to the next stage, and then win the election. The focus is on how to obtain enough voters to win. The first stage election will not be a place for partisans to try to purify their party, as happens sometimes with the current nomination process.

No more than 10 candidates could make the first-stage ballot by congressional caucus nomination. There is not a limit on the number of candidates making the ballot by paying the deposit.

If one candidate gets 60 percent of the vote in the first stage, that candidate is elected with no more voting; otherwise, advance to the next stage.

3. Quarter-final stage (if needed): If the total combined vote for the top four candidates in the first stage is less than 50 percent of the vote, then the top 8 candidates advance to the quarter-final stage. Otherwise, the top four first-stage candidates advance to the semi-final stage. Note: In the quarter-final election with 8 candidates, it is guaranteed that the top four finishers will have gained at least half of the total votes.

4. Semi-final stage: The top four candidates from the previous stage appear on the ballot for the semi-final stage.

If one candidate gets 55 percent of the vote in the semifinal election, that candidate is elected with no more voting; otherwise, advance to the final stage.

In the unlikely event there are only four candidates on the initial ballot, then the first election will be the semifinal. Also, impose the requirement that any candidate needs at least 3 percent of the vote to advance to the next stage, so there might only be three candidates in the semifinal election if there are only three realistic candidates in the first stage.

5. Final election:
   The top two vote-getters in the semi-final election advance to the final election.

There likely will be two candidates of each party among the four candidates in the semifinal stage. Most likely one candidate from each party will advance to the final. If two candidates from the same party advance to the final, then that party deserves to have the two final election candidates, because both of its candidates beat the two candidates of the other party.

Another possibility is that one of the four semifinal candidates will be from one party and three from the other party. This situation is likely to arise when an incumbent is running for reelection (and the incumbent is popular enough so as to not draw an intraparty challenge). The result in this case will most likely be that the incumbent and one of the other party's challengers will advance to the final election. If it actually works out that two of the challenger party candidates beat the incumbent in the semifinal, then that party deserves to have both candidates in the final election.

It seems extremely unlikely that all four semifinal candidates are from the same party. This situation could only happen if four candidates from that party beat all other candidates in the first stage, and those four win a combined total of more than fifty percent of the vote. If that situation does arise, then this party will deserve to have all four of the semifinal candidates. For example, suppose party 1 has 4 candidates, each with 13 percent of the vote; and party 2 has 8 candidates, each with 6 percent of the vote. In this case the combined vote of party 1 candidates is more than half of the vote, so it is reasonable that the future stages are limited to members of that party.

However, what if party 1 has 4 candidates each with 12 percent of the vote, and party 2 has 8 candidates each with 6.5 percent of the vote. In this case party 2 has a majority of the votes, so it would clearly be bad for party 1 to claim all 4 spots in the semi-final election because the party 2 vote is divided among 8 candidates. However, that would not happen under this proposal, because the party 1 candidates have gained a total of only $4 \times 12 = 48$ percent of the vote, so there would have to be a quarter-final election. The four candidates from party 1 would advance, as well as the top 4 candidates from party 2.[12] In the quarter-final election there would be four candidates from each party, so the party 2 candidates do not need to worry about the possibility that none of them advance to the semifinal because of their vote being split too many different ways.

In this system, the Democrats and Republicans have no privileged position on the ballot. Independent or third-party candidates have just as much right to appear on the ballot, as they should be able to so as to provide a measure of accountability for the major parties. The only limitation is that frivolous candidates will lose the substantial deposit if they insist on appearing on the first stage ballot. Any candidate that can get at least one percent of the vote in the first stage is not regarded as frivolous and will get the entire deposit back. Serious third-party candidates have a reasonable chance to make the semifinal ballot.[13]

The final election ballot will only have two candidates, which is a good thing. In a three-candidate election there is always the risk that the plurality winner may be ranked low by the majority. Suppose the three candidates are Rosencrantz, Guildenstern, and Polonius, and they all have support from roughly one-third of the voters. However, Rosencrantz and Guildenstern have very similar views, and any voter for one of them would actually be very happy if the other were to win. Polonius, by contrast, has very different views that are despised by almost two-thirds of the voters. In a three-way race in this example, Polonius has just as much of a chance of winning as do the other two.[14] In the proposal described here, if there are only three candidates in the semi-final election (instead of the usual four), then either Rosencrantz or Guildenstern (or possibly both) would advance to the final election, and either one would beat Polonius if he made it to the final.

Several possible voting systems require voters to judge multiple candidates and record their preferences on one ballot. (Poundstone describes examples: rank voting, single transferable vote, approval voting, Condorcet voting, Borda counting). The problem with these methods is that a careful evaluation of multiple candidates is a hard task for voters. In the proposal here, each voter only votes for one candidate at each stage. A voter doesn't have to decide who is second choice or third choice, etc. If your favored candidate advances to the final election, you never have to worry about deciding on a second choice. If your first choice candidate is eliminated at an earlier stage, then you do need to decide who is your next choice—but you only have to make this choice if it is actually necessary.

The proposal here functions more like a typical job search process where you provide increasingly detailed scrutiny to the candidates as the field is narrowed down. Consider how a job-selection process would work for a high-responsibility position. There may be multiple applicants. You won't hire someone without conducting a detailed interview, but you don't have time to conduct detailed interviews with all of the candidates. What you need to do is conduct a multi-stage evaluation process. Initial screening of the applicants will help select more promising candidates that are worth further review, such as a phone interview. You can devote more time to the evaluation of a smaller number of candidates, allowing you to narrow the field down to two candidates with whom you will conduct extensive in-person interviews.

The same basic idea applies to the multi-stage election. Voters' time is limited, so they shouldn't be expected to put a lot of time into detailed evaluation of all 8 candidates when most of them will not be supported by enough voters to advance to the next round. It's worth putting more effort into evaluating the four candidates that advance to the semifinal round, and it's worth detailed investigation into the two candidates in the final round.

It is impossible to devise a perfect voting system. That fact has been proven mathematically—in a result known as the Arrow impossibility theorem. If society needs to choose between more than two options, there is no way to design a reasonable voting system that is guaranteed to work.[15] For any voting system, it would be possible to imagine a possible set of preference orderings for the voters in the society so that the voting system does not have a reasonable result.

However, if we can find a voting system that will be reasonable most of the time, we've done the best we can. (See the online appendix myhome.spu.edu/ddowning/fos.html for some examples.)

CONCLUSION

The grip of narrow interests on the policy-making process is not inevitable. As we've seen there are changes we can make to preserve the best features of American government while also improving the ability to create economic policy that promotes freedom, opportunity, and security.

Here's a review of the list from chapter 1 of what we are trying to accomplish:

1. Reduce narrow interest influence.
2. Make benefit programs secure and sustainable.
3. Make macroeconomic policy predictable.
4. Make sure everyone is responsible for bearing the costs of their actions.
5. Increase average productivity (the only way to increase average real wages).
6. Provide an environment where innovators and entrepreneurs can flourish (their dreams, visions, and labor will determine our destiny).

NOTES

1. Dahl, *How Democratic is the American Constitution?* p148.
2. See Steven Hill, p296. Also, Taagepera and Shugart (chapter 15) describe a model to optimize the number of representatives by minimizing the number of communication channels to constituents and other members. The optimum in this model

happens when the number of representatives is proportional to the cube root of the population. For the U.S., this would lead to approximately 680 representatives. However, in order for the representatives do a good job of representing their constituents, it is more important to attach more weight to minimizing the number of communication paths to constituents than it is to minimizing the number of communication paths to other representatives. In the proposal in this book, it is not necessary for each representative to maintain communication paths to each other representative, because much of the communication between representatives will take place in the executive committee or other committees. Therefore, this proposal calls for more representatives than would be obtained by using the cube-root rule.

3. There could be three members in a district in a few cases (see page 202).

4. Fiorina.

5. A budget can be passed with a narrow majority; autorepeal becomes irrelevant since a budget only applies for one year anyway and a new Congress needs to pass a new budget.

6. Brazier, chapter 8.

7. Breyer.

8. However, the staggeringly unbelievable reality is that in 2014 Congress did hold hearings on a proposal to repeal the first amendment (Senate Joint Resolution 19). Instead of clear language saying Congress shall pass no law abridging freedom of speech or the press, the proposed amendment *would* allow Congress to restrict speech and the press. Saying that "the press" has an exemption doesn't protect freedom if Congress can pass laws that decide who deserves press freedom and who doesn't.

9. Trudeau, p89.

10. In 2010 the Supreme Court ruled that other organizations have the same rights as newspapers to communicate with the public during a campaign (*Citizens United v. Federal Election Commission*).

11. Ackerman, p18.

12. If all the party 2 candidates have *exactly* 6.5 percent of the vote there is a problem because of the 8-way tie, but in reality this would be extremely unlikely.

13. Washington state provides an example of a jurisdiction that adopted a top-two primary system, so that the top two candidates in the primary advance to the final election. This means that the final election will not necessarily include one Democrat and one Republican. This system will work well in most cases, but here is an example where there will be a problem. If party 1 has two candidates each with 21 percent of the vote, and party 2 has three candidates each with 16 percent of the vote, then both final election candidates would be from party 1 even though party 1 candidates earned only 42 percent of the vote in the primary. Party 2 candidates are hurt because their vote is split three ways. This example shows that a top-two primary system with five candidates could be a potential problem. In the proposal described in this book, this problem cannot happen because the semi-final election has only four candidates.

14. The history of elections where the result was affected because there were more than two candidates is reviewed by Poundstone (chapter 3).

15. See Sen for technical details of what the reasonable conditions are.

Appendix

Note on Terminology

"What's in a name—that which we call a rose by any other name would smell as sweet"

Although not affecting the sweetness of smell, names do affect the clarity of thought. Public understanding of economics is ill-served by technical terms whose meaning is perfectly clear to economists, but when taken at face value mean something different.

POLYPOLY/PERFECT COMPETITION

If a market has many sellers, so no one seller has the ability to decide what price to charge, economists use the term *perfect competition*. The word "perfect" has unfortunate normative connotations, but the real problem is the word "competition." In normal usage, people think of a competition as an event where you try to beat an opponent. The economist's sense of perfect competition is very different. A wheat farmer is a "competitor" with every other wheat farmer in the world (according to economists), but they are not at all "competitors" in the everyday sense of the word. No wheat farmer is trying to "beat" any other wheat farmer. One individual wheat farmer won't even know most of the other wheat farmers in the world. The terminology becomes even more pernicious when people think that economists value "competition" instead of "cooperation."

In reality people cooperate with other people in the organization they work for. Any person who tries to do a good job (be they a doctor, teacher, artist, musician, farmer, carpenter, plumber, baker, or inventor) is a competitor in the economic sense, even if they don't think of themselves as being in a competition. Telling people not to be economic competitors means telling them to stop trying to serve their patients, students, viewers, listeners, or customers. It becomes even more confusing. In cases where firms really do directly compete with each other (such as Ford and General Motors) the term applied by economists is *oligopoly* (meaning "few sellers") rather than "perfect competition." A better term for what economists call *perfect competition* would be *polypoly*, indicating "many suppliers." "Polypoly" is derived from two different Greek words (even if they have both come across as "poly.") The two Greek words are "poly" meaning "many," and "poleia" meaning "supplier." This term was suggested by linguist Michael Covington of the University of Georgia. It has the advantage of being consistent with the terms "monopoly" and "monopsony" that are already used by economists. Here are the four related terms:

- *Monopoly* is from Greek *mono-* (μονο-) "single" and $p\bar{}ol\,'e\bar{}o$ (πωλε'ω) "sell."
- *Polypoly* (suggested new term; pronounced *pol-IP-o-lee*) is from Greek-*poly-* (πολυ-) "many" and $p\bar{}ol\,'e\bar{}o$ (πωλε'ω) "sell."
- *Monopsony* (pronounced *mon-OP-so-nee*) is from Greek *mono-* (μονο-) "single" and $ops\bar{}on\,'e\bar{}o$ (οψωνε'ω) "purchase."
- *Polyopsony* (also a suggested new term; pronounced *poly-OP-so-nee*) is from Greek *poly-* (πολυ-) "many" and $ops\bar{}on\,'e\bar{}o$ (οψωνε'ω) "purchase."

DEMAND/BUYERS

Economists use the term *demand* when they mean "buyers." This term is unfortunate, because "demand" carries the connotation of someone ordering you to do something, at gunpoint or under some other means of coercion. "Demand" in the economist's sense means something completely different: the demand for a product is the amount of a product that potential buyers are willing to buy. The sellers will hand the product over only if they are willing to sell it at that price.

The "demand curve" indicates how the amount of "demand" varies with changes in the price of the product. A better term would be *buyer's curve* for what is now called the "demand curve." There is no similar problem with the term *supply curve*, but it might be convenient to call it the *seller's curve* to go along with the buyer's curve.

FREE GOOD/SCARCE GOOD/DECISION GOOD

Economists use the term *free good* for a good that is so exceedingly abundant that anyone can use as much as they want without depriving anyone else from being able to use as much as they want. Air is the most notable example, and the only one for which this is globally true: you can breathe as much as you want without taking away air from anyone else. Economists use the term *scarce good* for any good that is not a free good. However, both of these terms are problematic. The term *free good* brings to mind the common meaning of a free product (something that is given away at no charge). Although a free good is available at no charge, the converse is not true: just because something is available at no charge does not make it a *free good* in the economic sense. Furthermore, the term *free good* could be interpreted to mean that the good is freely available to be abused as well as used—for example, if air polluters feel they can freely pour pollution into the air without having to pay for the externality damage they cause. The term *scarce good* makes one think of the common meaning of the word scarce that is, something that is in limited supply. Confusingly, a *scarce good* (by the economist's definition) can be in abundant supply.

Instead of *scarce good*, it would be better to use the term *decision good* for any resource that society must make a decision about how to use. Economics does not assume "scarcity" (in the normal meaning of the word, where scarcity is the opposite of abundance). Rather, any society (whether or not it relies on markets) must make decisions about how *decision goods* will be used.

CONSERVATIVE/LIBERAL

The common political labels "conservative" and "liberal" are problematic. Too often labels can be used as a substitute for thought, as in "Candidate X is too conservative" or "Candidate Y is too liberal."

Attempting to untangle the meaning of these labels reveals their multi-dimensional character. "Liberal" comes from a root meaning "liberty," so one dimension of political philosophy would be the more-liberty / more-government-action dimension. In this case the meanings have been reversed in that the modern label "liberal" applies to the direction away from liberty (opposite the meaning of the word "libertarian.") "Conservative" in the sense of "support of the status quo" can't be a political philosophy by itself because it depends on the nature of the status quo to determine whether or not you support it (and, in fact, any thoughtful person should support some parts of the status quo while also supporting changes to other parts). When the hardline Russian communists that staged the unsuccessful 1991 coup against Mikhail Gorbachev were labeled "conservatives," it became clear that the word had been twisted around to mean exactly the opposite of what it meant when applied to "conservatives" in other countries.

Along the "spending money" dimension, "liberal" would mean "spend more" and "conservative" would mean "spend less." Along the social dimension, conservative generally means supporting certain traditional values which liberals might not support, but there is no logical reason that the terms used along this dimension should relate to their use along other dimensions.

Specific labels can provide clarity. For example, saying "Candidate *A* is pro-*X*", or "Candidate *A* is anti-*X*" is helpful, where *X* is a specific issue.

OTHER

1. Avoid "heartless," "socialist," "fascist," "nazi", or "Hitler," in policy arguments, unless they truly apply, as in these situations:
   - *Socialist* applies to someone who advocates having the government own *all* the means of production in society (farms, factories, publishers, broadcasters, churches, etc.).
   - *Fascist*, *nazi* or *Hitler* apply to someone who literally controls an army that violently kills millions of people
   - *Generous* applies to someone who willingly gives away some of their own riches to benefit those in need (it does not apply to someone who advocates taking money away from someone *else* to benefit those in need)
   - *Heartless* the same as "generous" above, except change "willingly gives" to "does not give," and change "advocates" to "opposes."
2. It's best to use neutral terms, rather than terms that implicitly bias the argument one way or another. A "progressive" policy may or may not really be progress; whether it is or not needs to be established by careful argument, not just assumed by the choice of label. It is better for a law to have a neutral title (such as "the farm act of 2014" or the "Health Care act of 2010") rather than a title that assumes the law provides a benefit (such as "the Affordable Care act").
3. The term "capital" in these discussions is best left to refer to a durable good used to produce other goods. In common use, the word capital has different meanings; for example, it often applies to the money that a business raises to get started or to expand. The important thing about "capital" as it is used here is that the stock of capital for a society needs to be *produced*, and the only way it can be produced is by using *savings*—that is, somebody has to refrain from current consumption to provide benefits for the future. This means that capital is very different from land. A factory owner who earns a profit from the factory is not the same as a landlord collecting rent from tenant farmers. A high tax on landowners will not affect the amount of land in the world, but a high tax

on capital owners might affect the amount of capital that will be available in the future. Confusingly, economists sometimes use the term "land" as a generic term that includes both land itself and resources that come from the land. It would be clearer if economists divided the factors of production into four categories: labor, capital, land, and natural resources (rather than just labor, capital, and land, as is often done).

4. The term "capitalist" refers to a system with private ownership of the means of production. However, the term could apply to a system where most economic power is concentrated by a relatively small group that owns most of the wealth, or it could apply to a system where many people in the society own some wealth.

5. Avoid the label "neoliberal," which has weirdly morphed into meaning something like what "conservative" means (which is also a label it would help to avoid).

6. The label "extreme" may or may not apply to a particular policy proposal, but even if the label is accurate calling a proposal "extreme" does not count as an argument—you still need to carefully analyze the proposal and discuss costs and benefits.

7. It would be better to avoid personalized terms such as "Reaganomics" or "Obamacare" because these terms tend to mix up the merits of the person with the merits of the policy.

8. The term "deregulation" should be avoided as too vague unless you are also specifying which specific deregulations you are referring to. Some actions have been deregulated and other actions remain regulated; it is crucially important to distinguish which is which. Therefore, avoid a statement such as "Deregulation caused the 2008 market meltdown." In fact, you should avoid any sentence of the form "*X* caused the 2008 market meltdown" unless *X* is a long list. Banks lose money on loans that aren't paid back, so deregulation wasn't the reason why banks would make those loans (see chapter 8).

   "Airlines were deregulated in 1978" is partly true, but that statement is too vague. Prior to 1978, an agency called the Civil Aeronautics Board (CAB) regulated airlines by making sure that they kept their ticket prices *high*. Airline fares were deregulated and the CAB was abolished, and many airline fares went down. However, airlines are still subject to safety regulation by the Federal Aviation Administration (FAA). Trucks were regulated by the ICC (Interstate Commerce Commission) before 1978–with the purpose of keeping prices high.

9. A "bank" is used here to mean a business that takes deposits and makes loans, which includes commercial banks, savings and loan associations, and credit unions (but does not include companies that underwrite and sell securities, which are [confusingly] called "investment banks.")

10. A "consumer" is someone who consumes something. This means we are all consumers in the same sense that we are all "eaters" or we are all "breathers" or we are all "sleepers." Calling someone a consumer does not mean to imply that we think that consumption is the only purpose of their life, or that they only have value as a consumer (and not as a person).

11. The term "narrow interest" more accurately describes the nature of the Congressional-influence problem than the common term "special interest," so that term is used in this book.

12. The term "lame duck" should be used only for its technical meaning. A "lame duck" office holder is one who is still in office, but whose successor has been elected or chosen. It should not be used as a general term for an office holder who seems to be less influential late in a term.

13. Accusing an elected official or candidate of acting "politically" is not an argument. Elected officials and candidates are politicians. *Everything* they do is political. When a politician accuses another politician of acting politically we can assume that the accuser is trying to dodge the substance of the issue and avoid having to make a serious argument.

Bibliography

Ackerman, Bruce, *The Failure of the Founding Fathers*, Cambridge, MA: Harvard Univ. Press, 2005.

Akerlof, George, and Robert Shiller, *Animal Spirits: How Human Psychology Drives the Economy and Why it Matters for Global Capitalism*, Princeton: Princeton Univ. Press, 2009.

Barro, Robert, "Are Government Bonds Net Wealth?" *Journal of Political Economy*, November/December, 1974.

Bartlett, Bruce, *The Benefit and the Burden: Tax Reform, Why we need it, and What it Will Take*, New York: Simon and Schuster, 2012.

Bastiat, Frederic, *Economic Sophisms*, Foundation for Economic Education, 1964 edition.

Bastiat, Frederic, *Selected Essays on Political Economy*, Foundation for Economic Education, 1964 edition.

Baumol, William, *The Cost Disease: Why Computers Get Cheaper and Health Care Doesn't*, New Haven: Yale Univ. Press, 2012.

Bhagwati, Jagdish, and Arvind Panagariya, *Why Growth Matters*, New York: Public Affairs, 2013.

Biello, David, "The False Promise of Biofuels," *Scientific American*, August 2011.

Blinder, Alan, *Hard Heads, Soft Hearts*, Reading, Mass: AddisonWesley, 1987.

Booth, James, "The Securitization of Lending Markets," FRBSF (Federal Reserve Bank of San Francisco) Weekly Letter, September 29, 1989.

Bovard, James, *The Farm Fiasco*, ICS Press, 1989.

Bowen, Catherine Drinker, *Miracle at Philadelphia*, Boston: Little, Brown, and Co., 1966.

Braudel, Fernand, *Afterthoughts on Material Civilization and Capitalism*, Baltimore: The Johns Hopkins Univ. Press, 1977.

Brazier, Rodney, *Constitutional Practice*, Oxford Univ. Press, 1999.

Breyer, Stephen, *Active Liberty*, New York: Vintage Books, 2005.

Brooks, Arthur, *The Battle*, New York: Basic Books, 2010.

Buchanan, James, and Gordon Tullock, *The Calculus of Consent*, Ann Arbor: The Univ. of Michigan Press, 1962.

Burtless, Gary, Robert Lawrence, Robert Litan, Robert Shapiro, *Globaphobia: Confronting Fears About Open Trade*, Washington D.C.: The Brookings Institution, 1998.

Carter, Stephen, *Civility*, New York: Harper Collins, 1998.

Chang, Leslie, *Factory Girls: From Village to City in a Changing China*, New York: Speigel and Grau, 2008.

Claar, Victor, and Robin Klay, *Economics in Christian Perspective*, Downers Grove, Illinois: IVP Academic, 2007.

Collier, Paul, *The Bottom Billion: Why the Poorest Countries are Failing and What Can be Done about It*, Oxford: Oxford Univ. Press, 2007.

Collier, Peter, and David Horowitz, *The Anti-Chomsky Reader*, San Francisco: Encounter Books, 2004.

Colvin, Geoffrey, "Will CEOs Fnd Their Inner Choirboy?" *Fortune*, April 28, 2003. p45.

Council of Economic Advisors (CEA), *Economic Report of the President*, 2003.

Cox, W. Michael, and Richard Alm, *Myths of Rich and Poor*, New York: Basic Books, 1999.

Dahl, Robert, *How Democratic is the American Constitution?* New Haven: Yale Univ. Press, 2001.

de Soto, Hernando, *The Other Path*, New York: Basic Books, 1989.

de Tocqueville, Alexis, *Democracy in America*, New York: Vintage Books, 1945, originally published 1835, 1840.

DeFoe, Daniel, *Robinson Crusoe*, 1719.

Diamond, Jared, *Collapse*, Viking Press, 2005.

Dornbusch, Rudiger, and Stanley Fischer, *Macroeconomics*, 3rd ed., New York: McGraw Hill, 1984.

Douglass, Frederick, *My Bondage and My Freedom*, New York: Dover Publications, 1969 edition (originally published in 1855).

Downing, Douglas, *Teenage Employment: Personal Characteristics, Job Duration, and the Racial Unemployment Differential*, Yale Univ. Ph.D. dissertation, 1987.

Dueker, Michael, "Can Nominal GDP Targeting Rules Stabilize the Economy?", *Federal Reserve Bank of St. Louis Review*, vol. 75, no. 3, May/June 1993.

Eagle, David, *The Macro-Share Economy and Nominal GDP Targeting*, Western Economic Association International, July 2013

Eaton, Philip, *Engaging the Culture, Changing the World*, Downers Grove, Ill: IVP Academic, 2011.

Enright, Dominique, *The Wicked Wit of Winston Churchill*, London: Michael O'Mara Books Limited, 2001.

Feldstein, Martin, "Social Security, Induced Retirement and Aggregate Capital Accumulation," *Journal of Politcal Economy*, vol. 82, no. 5, September-October 1974.

Feldstein, Martin, "Did Wages Reflect Growth in Productivity?" NBER Working paper 13953, April 2008.

Fellner, William, *Towards a Reconstruction of Macroeconomics*, Washington D.C.: American Enterprise Institute, 1976.

Ferris, Timothy, *The Science of Liberty*, New York: Harper, 2010.

Fiorina, Morris, *Congress: Keystone of the Washington Establishment*, 2nd ed., New Haven: Yale Univ. Press, 1989.

Fontova, Humberto, *Exposing the Real Che Guevara and the Useful Idiots Who Idolize Him*, New York: Sentinel, 2007.

Frame, W. Scott, and Lawrence White, "Fussing and Fuming over Fannie and Freddie: How Much Smoke, How Much Fire?", *Journal of Economic Perspectives*, vol. 19, no. 2, Spring 2005.

Friedman, Milton and Rose, *Free to Choose*, New York: Harcourt Brace Jovanovich, 1980.

Galbraith, John Kenneth, *Money: Whence it Came, Where it Went*, London: Penguin, 1975.

Galbraith, John Kenneth, *The New Industrial State*, Princeton Univ. Press, 1967.

Gasparino, Charles, *The Sellout*, Harper Collins, 2009.

Geanakoplos, John, and A. Fostel, "Leverage Cycles and the Anxious Economy," *American Economic Review*, 98(4), 2008.

Goff, Brian, and Arthur, Fleisher, *Spoiled Rotten*, Boulder, Colorado: Westview Press, 1999.

Goldin, Claudia, and Cecilia Rouse, "Orchestrating Impartiality: The Impact of 'Blind' Auditions on Female Musicians," *American Economic Review*, 90(4): 715–741, 2000.

Goldsworthy, Adrian, *Caesar*, New Haven: Yale Univ. Press, 2006.

Goodwin, Doris Kearns, *Team of Rivals*, New York: Simon and Schuster, 2005.

Gratzer, David, *The Cure*, New York: Encounter Books, 2006, 2008.

Gregg, Samuel, *The Commercial Society*, Lanham: Lexington Books, 2007.

Grind, Kirsten, *The Lost Bank*, New York: Simon and Schuster, 2012.

Halteman, James, *The Clashing Worlds of Economics and Faith*, Scottdale, Pennsylvania: Herald Press, 1995.

Harberger, Arnold, "The Incidence of the Corporation Income Tax", *Journal of Political Economy*, June 1962.

Hardin, Garrett, "The Tragedy of the Commons," *Science*, 1968.

Hayek, Friedrich, "The Use of Knowledge in Society," *American Economic Review*, September 1945, p519–30

Hess, Stephen, *What do we do now?*, Washington: Brookings, 2008.

Hill, Alexander, *Just Business*, Downers Grove, Illinois: InterVarsity Press, 1997.

Hill, Steven, *Fixing Elections*, New York: Routledge, 2002.

Howe, John, *The Changing Political Thought of John Adams*, Princeton: Princeton Univ. Press, 1966.

Ingrassia, Paul, *Crash Course*, New York: Random House, 2010.

Johnson, Calvin, "Taking GE and Other Masters of the Universe," *The Univ. of Texas Law and Economics Research Paper No. 226*, 132 Tax Notes 175, July 11, 2011.

Kahn, R. F., "The Relation of Home Investment to Unemployment," *The Economic Journal*, 1931.

Kantor, Elizabeth, *The Politically Incorrect Guide to English and American Literature*, Washington D.C.: Regnery Publishing, 2006.

Karlan, Dean, and Jacob Appel, *More than Good Intentions*, Dutton, 2011.

Kelly, Marjorie, *The Divine Right of Capital*, San Francisco: BerrettKoehler, 2001.

Keynes, John Maynard, *A General Theory of Employment, Interest, and Money*, 1936.

Keynes, John Maynard, *Economic Consequences of the Peace*, 1919.

Kindleberger, Charles, *Manias, Panics, and Crashes*, Basic Books, 1989.

Koenig, Evan, *Like a Good Neighbor: Monetary Policy, Financial Stability, and the Distribution of Risk*, Western Economic Association International, July 2013.

Kotlikoff, Laurence, and Scott Burns, *The Clash of Generations*, Cambridge, MA: The MIT Press, 2012.

Kranz, Gene, *Failure is not an Option*, New York: Simon and Schuster, 2000.

Kristof, Nicholas, and Sheryl WuDunn, "Two Cheers for Sweatshops," *New York Times Magazine*, September 24, 2000.

Krugman, Paul, *The Age of Diminished Expectations*, Cambridge, MA: The MIT Press, 1994.

Krugman, Paul, *End This Depression Now*, New York: W. W. Norton, 2012.

Landes, David, *The Wealth and Poverty of Nations*, New York: Norton, 1999.

Lazare, Daniel, *The Frozen Republic*, New York: Harcourt Brace. and Co., 1996.

Lijphart, Arend, *Electoral Systems and Party Systems*, Oxford: Oxford Univ. Press, 1994.

Lewis, Charles, *The Buying of the Congress*, New York: Avon Books, 1998.

Lindblom, Charles, *The Market System*, New Haven: Yale Univ. Press, 2001.

Madrick Jeff, *Age of Greed*, New York: Alfred Knopf, 2011.

Martin, Deborah, and Randall Pozdena, "Taxpayer Risk in Mortgage Policy," FRBSF (Federal Reserve Bank of San Francisco) Weekly Newsletter, Number 91–44, December 20, 1991.

Marx, Karl, *Communist Manifesto*, 1848.

McCallum, Bennett, "The Case for Rules in the Conduct of Monetary Policy: A Concrete Example," *Federal Reserve Bank of Richmond Economic Review*, September/October 1987.

McLure, Charles, *Must Corporate Income be Taxed Twice?* Washington D.C.: Brookings Institution, 1979.

McCullough, David, *John Adams*, New York: Simon and Schuster, 2001.

Michener, James, *Presidential Lottery: The Reckless Gamble in our Electoral System*, New York: Random House, 1969.

Mill, John Stuart, *On Liberty*, Indianapolis: Hackett Publishing Company, 1978 (original publication 1859).

Mishkin, Frederic, *The Economics of Money, Banking, and Financial Markets*, 9th ed., New York: Addison-Wesley, 2010.

Montesquieu, *The Spirit of the Laws*, 1748.

Morgenson, Gretchen, and Joshua Rosner, *Reckless Endangerment*, New York: Times books, 2011.

Morse, Jennifer Roback, *Love and Economics*, Dallas: Spence Publishing Company, 2001.

Muollo, Paul, and Mathew Padilla, *Chain of Blame*, Hoboken, N.J.: John Wiley and Sons, 2008.

Neuhouser, Kevin, *Modern Brazil*, New York: McGraw Hill, 1999.

Noah, Timothy, *The Great Divergence*, New York: Bloomsbury Press, 2012.

Noell, Edd, Stephen Smith, and Bruce Webb, *Economic Growth*, Washington, D.C.: AEI Press, 2013.

Norberg, Johan, *In Defense of Global Capitalism*, Stockholm: Timbro, 2001. (English translation Cato, 2003).

Novak, Michael, *The Spirit of Democratic Capitalism*, Lanham: Madison books, 1982.

Okun, Arthur, *Prices and Quantities*, Brookings Institution Press, 1981.

O'Neill, Tip, *All Politics is Local*, New York: Random House, 1994.

Orwell, George, (Eric Arthur Blair), *Nineteen Eighty-Four*, 1949.

Perkins, John M., *Beyond Charity: The Call to Christian Community Development*, Grand Rapids, Michigan: Baker Books, 1993.

Piketty, Thomas, *Capital in the Twenty-First Century*, Cambridge, MA: Harvard Univ. Press, 2014.

Poundstone, William, *Gaming the Vote*, New York: Hill and Wang, 2008.

Rawls, John, *Political Liberalism*, New York: Columbia Univ. Press, 2005.

Reynolds, Alan, *Wealth and Income*, Westport, CT: Greenwood Press, 2006.

Richards, Jay, *Infiltrated*, New York: McGraw-Hill, 2013.

Rivoli, Pietra, *The Travels of a T-shirt in the Global Economy*, 2nd ed., Hoboken, N.J.: 2009.

Rose-Ackerman, Susan, *Corruption and Government*, Cambridge Univ. Press, 1999.

Sachs, Jeffrey, *The End of Poverty*, New York: The Penguin Press, 2005.

Samuelson, Paul, *Economics*, 7th edition, New York: McGraw Hill, 1967.

Savitz, Andrew, *The Triple Bottom Line*, Wiley, 2006.

Say, Jean-Baptiste, *Treatise on Political Economy*, 1803.

Schlossberg, Herbert, Vinay Samuel, and Ronald Sider, *Christianity and Economics in the Post-Cold War Era: The Oxford Declaration and Beyond*, Grand Rapids, Michigan: Eerdmans, 1994.

Schnick, Chris, and Paul Petrequin, "Deconstructing the American Dream through Global Learning," *Diversity and Democracy*, vol. 10, no. 3, Fall 2007, p10.

Schor, Juliet, *The Overworked American*, New York: Basic Books, 1992.

Schumacher, E. F., *Small is Beautiful*, London: Blond and Briggs Ltd, 1973.

Schumpeter, Joseph, *Capitalism, Socialism, and Democracy*, New York: Harper and Row, 3rd edition, 1950.

Sen, Amartya, *Collective Choice and Social Welfare*, Amsterdam: North Holland, 1979.

Shiller, Robert, *The Subprime solution*, Princeton: Princeton Univ. Press, 2008.

Shoup, Carl, *Facing the Tax Problem*, New York: The Twentieth Century Fund, 1937.

Sirico, Rev. Robert, *Defending the Free Market*, Washington D.C.: Regnery Publishing, 2012.

Skidelsky, Robert, *Keynes: The Return of The Master*, New York: PublicAffairs, 2010.

Smith, Adam, *An Inquiry into the Nature and Causes of the Wealth of Nations*, 1776.

Smith, Hedrick, *The New Russians*, New York: Random House, 1990.

Stiglitz, Joseph, "The Corporation Tax," *Journal of Public Economics*, (5), 1976.

Stiglitz, Joseph, *Freefall*, New York: W. W. Norton, 2010.

Stiglitz, Joseph, *Making Globalization Work*, New York: W. W. Norton, 2006.

Sumner, Scott, *Nominal GDP Futures Targeting*, Western Economic Association International, July 2013.

Sweeney, John, *America Needs a Raise*, Boston: Houghton-Mifflin, 1996.

Taagepera, Rein, and Matthew Shugart, *Seats and Votes*, New Haven: Yale Univ. Press, 1989.

Tanner, Kathryn, *Economy of Grace*, Minneapolis: Fortress Press, 2005.

Taylor, John, *First Principles*, New York: W. W. Norton & Co., 2012.

Tobin, James, *Asset Accumulation and Economic Activity*, Chicago: The Univ. of Chicago Press, 1980.

Tobin, James, *Money, Credit, and Capital*, New York: McGraw Hill, 1997.

Tobin, James, and William Nordhaus, "Measure of Economic Welfare," *American Economic Review*, 1972.

Trudeau, G. B., *Doonesbury's Greatest Hits*, New York: Holt, Rinehart, and Winston, 1978.

van den Haag, Ernest, ed., *Capitalism: Sources of Hostility*, New Rochelle, N.Y.: Epoch books, 1979.

Van Duzer, Jeff, *Why Business Matters to God*, Downers Grove, Illinois: Inter Varsity Press, 2010.

Weitzman, Martin, *The Share Economy*, Cambridge, MA: Harvard Univ. Press, 1984.

Wilson, James Q., *The Marriage Problem*, New York: Harper Collins, 2002.

Wolf, David, *Foul! The Connie Hawkins Story*, New York: Holt, Rinehart, and Winston, 1972.

Woll, Peter, *Debating American Government*, 2nd. ed., Boston: Scott, Foresman, & Co., 1988.

Woolsey, Bill, *Index Futures Targeting and Monetary Disequilibrium*, Western Economic Association International, July 2013

Index

About the Author

Douglas Downing has taught economics and quantitative methods at the school of Business, Government, and Economics at Seattle Pacific University since 1983. He studied at Yale, earning a B.S. with double majors in economics/political science and astronomy/physics in 1979, and a Ph.D. in economics in 1987. He has written 15 books, many of which have been published in multiple editions. They include a trilogy of math textbooks (Algebra, Trigonometry, Calculus) written as fantasy adventure novels. He is coauthor of *Dictionary of Computer and Internet Terms* and *Business Statistics* and has written other books on math and computer programming. He has been a leader for study abroad trips in China. His mother Peggy wrote children's books and his father was business director at a public school district. Two of his grandparents were immigrants to the U.S., and another grandparent was the child of immigrants.